A FAITH THAT LOVES THE EARTH

The Ecological Theology of Karl Rahner

Michael W. Petty

University Press of America, Inc.
Lanham • New York • London

Copyright © 1996 by
University Press of America,® Inc.
4720 Boston Way
Lanham, Maryland 20706

3 Henrietta Street
London, WC2E 8LU England

Library of Congress Cataloging-in-Publication Data

Petty, Michael W.
A faith that loves the earth : the ecological theology of Karl Rahner /
Michael W. Petty.
p.   cm.
Includes bibliographical references and index.
1. Rahner, Karl, 1904---Contributions in ecological theology. 2.
Human ecology--Religious aspects--Catholic Church--History of
doctrines--20th century. 3. Catholic Church--Doctrines--History--
20th century. I. Title.
BX1795.H82P48   1996   261.8'362'092--dc20   96-1011 CIP

ISBN 0-7618-0277-0 (cloth: alk. ppr.)
ISBN 0-7618-0278-9 (pbk: alk. ppr.)

 # 34151127

Contents

Preface

Charles Taylor begins the preface to his important book *Sources of the Self: The Making of Modern Identity* (Cambridge, MA: Harvard University Press, 1989) with the disarmingly simple sentence "I've had a difficult time writing this book." While I do not want to suggest that the present work is of the same stature as Taylor's, he has expressed by sentiments exactly. The depth, scope, and complexity of Karl Rahner's work is for me both a source of wonder and a reason for being humble. I have had a difficult time writing this book! Despite its depth, scope, and complexity, however, Rahner's theology is characterized by an amazing consistency and even an elegant simplicity. I hope that this consistency and simplicity are conveyed in this study.

There are many fine introductions to and expositions of Rahner's theology but the present work does not aspire to be one of them. The task I have chosen for myself here is to explore a *dimension* of Rahner's theology, a dimension which I call "ecological". Simply stated, I attempt here to argue that Rahner's theology is ecological in that his entire theological project can be seen as an attempt to produce a *unified view of the world* that is *Christian* because it is founded on the Incarnation. More specifically, I am attempting to make the case that in his anthropology, doctrine of God, and eschatology (though not only these), Rahner provides us with a theology that always strives to see all things--God, human being, the world--in their interrelatedness. In this sense, Rahner has developed a theology that is profoundly ecological even though, as far as I know, it was not his intention to construct a theological response to the ecological crisis. In my judgment, Rahner addresses the crucial questions for which an ecological theology must supply answers. These questions are discussed in the first chapter and the bulk of what follows is an attempt to present Rahner's answers.

As will become clear, I have a different understanding of the ecological crisis than many of the theologians discussed here. While many theologians argue that the ecological crisis stems from an inherent flaw in traditional Christianity (such as dualism or a profound disinterest in the world), I argue that most of Christian theology's problems with ecology actually stem from the attempt (until recently almost unquestioned) to "reconstruct" Christianity on Enlightenment presuppositions. While I do not make it here, the argument could be made the ecological dimension of Rahner's theology is due at least in part to the strong patristic influence on his thinking. If this argument is valid, and I think that it is, we must approach attempts to "revision" Christianity in accordance with the latest (ideological) demands of the day with extreme caution and, perhaps, even suspicion. Ecological theology can not be taken seriously if it appears to be an auxiliary enterprise or, worse, a fad. To be taken seriously, ecological theology must be seen as a *dimension of theology itself.* This, I am convinced, is precisely what we find in Rahner.

I want to express my profound thanks to a number of people who have helped me with this work. Professors Eugene TeSelle and Edward Farley of Vanderbilt University both read the manuscript and provided helpful comments and asked important questions, both of which resulted in a stronger manuscript. Professor Sallie McFague, also of Vanderbilt University, did me the great service of first introducing me to Rahner in her classroom. What would we do without good teachers? A final word of thanks is due to the trustees of the Permanent Endowment Fund of Moody Memorial First United Methodist Church for their support of this project and to the people of Moody Memorial First United Methodist Church for providing their pastor with such a fine place to work.

One final note. I have attempted to use sex inclusive language when speaking about both human beings and about God even though, it will be noticed, this does not make for flowing prose. I have, however, left the language of other authors in its original form which means that most of the quoted material in this study is not sex inclusive and I do not attempt to call this fact to the reader's attention in the text.

Michael W. Petty
St. Michael and All Angels, 1995

We know that the whole creation has been groaning in labor pains until now; and not only creation, but we ourselves, who have the first fruits of the Spirit, groan inwardly while we wait for adoption, the redemption of our bodies.[1]

Chapter 1

The Groaning of Creation: Ecological Crisis and Theological Responses

The present chapter has at its goal the accomplishment of some preparatory work; it attempts to articulate the point of departure for this entire study. In the first section an attempt is made to clarify the concept of nature and to advance a certain thesis about the place of this concept in biblical faith. This thesis is that despite arguments to the contrary, there is an "ecological" concern within the biblical tradition, though to so designate this concern is anachronistic. The second section attempts to discuss the several causes of the present ecological crisis in a way appropriate to a *theological* study. This section advances a thesis concerning the inability of post-Enlightenment theology to deal with the natural world and the disappearance of nature (as *creation*) from the agenda of theology. The third section attempts to discuss the ways in which contemporary theologians are responding to the ecological crisis by overcoming (or attempting to overcome) the deficiencies of post-Enlightenment theology. Finally, the fifth section states the thesis which will guide the present study and the procedure which will be followed as it runs its course.

A Theological Crisis
Biblical Vision and the Problem of Nature

"Nature"

Nature has long been the subject of human speculation. One might even say that Western philosophy arose out of the attempt to understand the world and the processes operative within it in a way that diverged from ancient mythology. In other words, Western philosophy and modern science are inconceivable apart from the replacement of cosmogony and theogony by cosmological speculation, particularly that of the Ionians who asked after the *one thing* out of which all things were made. Western philosophy, of course, later embarked on lines of inquiry which took it far beyond Ionian speculation (which was always rudimentary). These lines of inquiry became increasingly sophisticated and comprehensive, as can be seen in the movement from Plato's *Timaeus* and Aristotle's *Metaphysics* to Copernicus's *De reolutionibus orbium coelestium* and Newton's *Principia*, to the modern metaphysical systems of Hegel and Whitehead. All these efforts, whether quasi-mythological, metaphysical, scientific, or a mixture thereof, were aimed at understanding the character and processes of the world which human beings experienced. This important effort began with the Ionians of the seventh and sixth centuries B.C.E. who were so involved with the attempt to understand nature that Aristotle referred to them as the *physiologoi*.[2]

If the Greeks bequeathed to the West their fascination with nature they also passed along to it the ambiguity which envelopes the term itself. The Greek word *physis* (nature) had two principal meanings. On one hand *physis* could mean the aggregate of natural things, what we might call the "world of nature". In this usage *physis* was close in meaning to the Greek word *kosmos*. On the other hand *physis* could also refer to the *principle* of something, that which made it what it was. In this usage *physis* was similar in meaning to the Greek word *arche*. More attention will be given to this ambiguity later. For the time being it may be assumed that "nature" is being used in the former of the two senses even though this does not embrace all the nuances of the word.

While a sketch or, *a fortiori*, a complete account of Western thinking about nature is beyond the scope and competence of the present study, a remark about the general movement of that thinking is necessary. Western thinking about nature (the *kosmos*) underwent an interesting and (viewed retrospectively) ultimately dangerous change. For the Greeks, the Ionians as well as Plato and Aristotle, nature was seen as a kind of living organism. The world of nature, the totality of what human beings experienced, was permeated by both vitality and rationality. Thus, according to R. G. Collingwood, the *Timaeus* held that the "world of nature is a material organism or animal, alive everywhere with spontaneous movement".[3] While Greek thought underwent what we might call an "anthropological turn" in Socrates it never ceased, during the period from the Ionians to Aristotle, to hold this view of nature nor did it abstract human beings from nature and see them as being alien to the natural world.[4] Human beings certainly had souls, but so then did the natural world.

The thinking of the sixteenth and seventeenth centuries abandoned this Greek view. It did so, according to Collingwood, because one of its major features was a "sustained polemic against medieval thought inspired partly by Aristotle and partly by the philosophical view implicit in the Christian religion."[5] Particularly attacked was the idea that there was a teleology in nature. The reasons for this attack were complex but one of them certainly was the fact that nature was no longer understood as a living organism. In the thinking of Copernicus, Galileo, Bacon, and, preeminently, Newton, nature was seen as a *machine* and machines are not alive and do not possess souls. This is the movement in Western thinking about nature that needs to be noted and reflected upon. It was a movement from an organic view of nature to a mechanical one. Nature was understood to be a machine in the proper sense of this term, that is "an arrangement of bodily parts designed and put together and set going for a definite purpose by an intelligent mind *outside itself*."[6] The key idea here is "outside itself". The purpose of nature had to be found outside of it, either in God (who was moved further and further away from the world) or in human beings (whose status increased as God's decreased).

The consequences of this movement were very ambiguous indeed. Phenomenal progress was made in the natural sciences. Bacon, of course, had spoken of science as an instrument of torture the use of which would force nature to divulge her (ironically the personal pronoun was retained) secrets.[7] In the realm of philosophy the result was sheer muddle. Mind (soul) and matter (machine) were seen as two irreconcilable things. On this view one could not really say that human beings were part of nature-- nature was dead, mechanical, and devoid of purpose. Descartes found himself faced with a potential dualism of *res cogitans* ("thinking stuff" or mind) and *res extensa* ("extended stuff" or everything else). This otherwise brilliant man was forced to put forward the manifestly nonsensical view that in the human being, at least, the dualism was resolved by the meeting of these two things in the pineal gland (!).[8] To avoid an ontological dualism, something which his Christian faith would not allow, Descartes had to bring in God--*deus ex machina.* However, God was no longer really involved with the world but could only be brought in as an emergency explanatory principle when human thought came to grief over the contradictions which it itself had created.

The critical philosophy of Kant was to contribute further to the imperilment of nature. To the view that nature was a dead mechanism wholly alien to human beings was added to the view that nature was unknowable. For Kant nature, the physical world in its totality, was a construct of the transcendental ego. This is not to say that the self creates nature in the sense that God created it but that nature, the world, is only a collection of phenomena which exists as knowable only in relation to a (human) subject and that subject's epistemological apparatus. Nature then, for Kant, is a *construct*, a necessary one to be sure but construct nevertheless. The question of what nature *really is* can not be answered. Nature, from this perspective, can only be spoken of in relation to human subjects. This way of thinking led to a certain type of epistemology, one which places the subject at the center of all things and understands knowledge as, to use Richard Rorty's phrase, the "mirror of nature". It also led to the reduction of philosophy (and theology) to epistemology. This "modern" development would later be called into question by "postmodernists" (hypermodernists?).[9]

Bacon's metaphor of science as an instrument of torture turned out to be more than a metaphor. It became a methodology. As something lifeless and mechanical, something without a soul, nature was something to be *dominated* and *used* by human beings. As something radically different from human being, nature was that which existed to be used in the accomplishment of *human* purposes. Jürgen Moltmann notes that within modern science and epistemology there is operative a kind of *divide et impera* logic; the world of nature is to be broken down into component parts and mastered for human use.[10]

A Theological Crisis

The preceding reflection has been presented with a view to introducing the line of inquiry to be undertaken in the present chapter. We find ourselves faced with what has been called an "ecological crisis," a crisis which need not be described in apocalyptic terms in order to merit serious attention. This crisis presents us with a particularly vexing problem because it stems not from a mistake or minor miscalculation but from the very logic, as just discussed, of Western (Enlightenment) thinking or, at least, from the dominant logic of that thinking. Simply stated, we find ourselves in a situation in which the twofold assumption that nature is a lifeless machine to be controlled and that nature exists simply for human use and exploitation has led to the debilitation (hopefully not permanent) of the earth's ability to sustain life. Langdon Gilkey, who divines the meaning of intellectual and cultural trends, describes this situation well when he writes that "we are suddenly aware that technical industrialism--in expanding as the Enlightenment hoped--threatens to destroy the nature system and to use up the natural resources on which we all depend."[11]

If what Gilkey says is true, it is clear that the state of nature, since it is *our* environment, is of immediate practical concern to everyone. Yet, and this brings us to a central theological question, should the state of the environment, the condition of nature, be an object of *theological* interest? Is the "ecological crisis" also a theological crisis? The degree to which the connection between ecology and theology is denied, the degree to which the ecological problem is seen as a problem (if it is seen as a problem at all) simply for science and technology or for environmental activists ("people who like that sort of thing"), is the degree to which testimony is given to the marginalization and constriction of Christian faith. It will be the concern of the next section to reflect upon how the ecological crisis came about and what role theological reflection played in this.

For the moment, however, it is not my intention to prove that the world of nature demands theological attention or that the ecological crisis is also a theological crisis. How one views this issue will largely rest upon one's theological presuppositions. Yet, what I do wish to do is to state in as clear a way as possible why I think that the ecological crisis is also a *theological* crisis. As Moltmann has argued, the ecological crisis is, for Christian theology, ultimately a crisis of the doctrine of creation. If, as he says, seeing the world as *creation* means not seeing it as being completely at the disposal of human beings, the ecological crisis represents a severe attenuation of the doctrine of creation. It is not that the doctrine has been denied outright by skeptical theologians; it is that the doctrine has been allowed to wither and now survives only in an etiolated form. It is as if the first article of the Creed--God as creator of heaven and earth--has become a theological embellishment, something like the furniture in the parlor--decorative but not actually used.[12] To put it simply, the doctrine of creation has been reduced to a matter of personal faith in as much as it means simply that God is "my creator". This is precisely the view which must be resisted and reversed. As Moltmann says, the doctrine of creation cannot be reduced "to the existential self-understanding of the person. It must also mean the whole knowable world. If God is not the Creator of the world, he can not be my Creator either."[13]

The ecological crisis is also a crisis of soteriology. If the dichotomies between mind and matter, soul and body, and the human and the natural, which led to the present crisis, are accepted by Christian faith then the scope of God's saving activity is diminished considerably. To accept the thinking which led to the ecological crisis is to accept the view that the material world is either antithetical or, at least, irrelevant to God's purposes. To accept either one of these views is to accept a radically diminished understanding of God's creatorship and the scope of God's redemptive activity.

The Poisoned Well?

I have put the issue in these terms in order to meet one objection which has been raised against the view that nature should be an object of theological concern. This objection is that biblical faith (or, really, a particular reading of it) is primarily interested in *history* not nature. Does not, it is asked, the Old Testament provide a relentless stream of invective against the depravities of Canaanite nature religion? The God of the Bible, in this view, is the righteous Lord of history for whom nature is but a backdrop to the activity of saving human beings. Thus, *"Christian theology has to do primarily with human history*--with the unfolding providential story of God and humanity, with God and the people of God, or with the believing human soul--not with nature."[14]

This interpretation of the scriptural tradition has found acceptance among at least three different groups. First, it has been accepted by some Christian theologians who affirm that it represents orthodox Christianity and should be defended as such. It is not (necessarily) that this group is disinterested in nature but that it thinks that a theology of nature is inappropriate; nature is best understood as an object of human stewardship.[15] Second, this view has been accepted as an accurate reading of the biblical and Christian tradition by those who are outside it and who see it as the cause of the present ecological crisis. An example of this view is Lynn White, author of the famous essay "The Historical Roots of Our Ecological Crisis" which traces the roots of the ecological crisis to Genesis and the Christian interpretation of it. Not to put too fine a point upon it, the essay takes the position that Genesis (in Christian interpretation) grants human beings a blank check *dominus terrae*.[16] A third group consists of Christian theologians who see this view as an accurate description of the Christian tradition and who argue for its abandonment or, better, "reconstruction". Thus, Gordon Kaufman writes that the

> great words of the Christian vocabulary--sin, salvation, forgiveness, repentance, hope, faith, love, righteousness--have to do primarily with man and with man's relation to God and his fellows...The rest of creation, though always recognized and sometimes acknowledged and even reflected upon, simply was not of central theological interest or importance.[17]

Kaufman argues that the concepts of God and of human being have been developed in such an anthropocentric way that without radical reconstruction of these concepts theology can not deal with nature or the ecological crisis.[18]

Is this view, nuanced in the three ways just mentioned, really true? Must we read the biblical and Christian tradition as not being very (or not at all) interested in nature and, therefore, in need of radical reconstruction if it is to deal with the ecological crisis? My own response to these questions is in the negative and I wish to justify this response as a way of substantiating what was said earlier about the ecological crisis being a crisis of the doctrines of creation and soteriology. I do not mean to suggest that Christian theology has, for various reasons and under various influences, not ignored nature. I do mean to suggest that the view that Christianity at its roots is uninterested in nature and the corollary view that in order to deal with the ecological crisis Christian theology must now adopt a concern which it never really had (a position Paul Santmire had designated the "critical ecological wisdom") is not quite true. It is much more accurate to say with Santmire that the Christian tradition as it has developed manifests an "ambiguous ecological promise" but that this tradition can ignore nature only by divorcing itself from its own roots and central concerns.[19]

The first creation account (Genesis 1:1-2:4a) has long been seen by those who accept the "critical ecological wisdom" as the poisoned well from which the Christian tradition has drunk. Genesis 1:26 and 1:28 (and the parallel text in Psalm 8:5-9), in which human beings are given dominion over animals and the earth, have been thought to be particularly offensive and maleficent. This is the case largely because "dominion" has been understood to license doing whatever human beings wish to do with that over which they have dominion. Claus Westerman reminds us that dominion must be interpreted here in light of ancient understandings of kingship which held the king to be a mediator of blessings to the realm with which he was entrusted. Thus, Westerman notes that for the priestly writer of Genesis 1:1-2:4a there

> are alternatives which have fundamental significance for the future of mankind: will man exploit the forces of nature like a vandal who is quite indifferent as to what his act of destruction leaves behind, or will he, like a noble lord, conscious of his responsibility for the whole and its future, take care to see that the whole remains healthy as each new gain is made.[20]

Genesis 1:26a and 1:27a have also evoked criticism. Do they not, it is asked, show that human beings are the only real objects of divine interest? These two texts can yield this meaning only if "image of God" (*imago dei*) is understood to refer to the human soul. On this view, human beings *alone* are like God because they are spiritual and salvation means the triumph of this spirituality over the material world. As it developed, Christian speculation about the meaning of *imago dei* took on a rococo and spiritualized complexity--a complexity foreign to the meaning of the biblical text. Westerman notes helpfully that this speculation introduced an individualism into the text which led to disastrous consequences. He says that it

> was thought that we have here a declaration about man as such, as an individual. Consequently one looked for a special quality which had been given to man as the image and likeness of God. The point was missed from the very start, that the creation narrative was not saying anything about man as such by using this phrase...but was speaking of a Creation event. Man as the image and likeness of God had been cut off from the Creation event...[21]

Whereas the biblical text had intended to place human beings within creation acknowledging their particular relationship with God, a developing tradition of interpretation abstracted human being from creation.

The first creation narrative has also been accused of legitimizing anthropocentrism in that, so it is said, for this account human beings represent the culmination of God's creative activity. Motlmann has argued, however, that the real culmination of creation is not the appearance of human beings but the *sabbath* (Genesis 2:2-3).[22] Creation was not made for human beings as ends in themselves. Creation was made for the sabbath, that complete state of affairs in which *all of creation* will be blessed by God's universal *shalom*. Paul may well have this in mind in Romans 8:22-23. Rather than being anthropocentric this narrative is radically theocentric.[23]

As for the view that the biblical tradition is concerned only with history and God's activity in it and that nature is only a backdrop to this activity, this seems to be more a product of theological presupposition than of scriptural exegesis. The proponents of the "critical ecological wisdom" pay the "biblical theology" movement the compliment of accepting its reading of the biblical tradition as *the reading* of it. It is quite true that Israel confessed Exodus 20:2 ("I am the Lord your God, who brought you out of the land of Egypt, out of the house of slavery...") before it confessed Genesis 1:1. That is, Israel confessed--had they read Schleiermacher?--God to be Redeemer before it confessed God to be Creator. This does not mean, however, that God the Creator was a mere afterthought. Israel discerned that its Redeemer was also the Creator of heaven and earth; God did indeed break the bondage of Egypt but God also bestowed life and fecundity on all living things.   Israel's understanding of God as Lord of history was fulfilled only when it understood God as Lord of creation.[24] Thus, Westermann argues that "no concept of history that excludes or ignores God's activity in the world of nature can adequately reflect what occurs in the Old Testament between God and his people".[25]

As Moltmann argues in his book *God in Creation*, Christian theology can not accept the two creation accounts (Genesis 1:1-2:4a and 2:4b-25) as a complete picture of creation. The New Testament (John 1:1-4, Romans 8:18-23, and Colossians 1:15-20 for example) invites us to see creation in christological or, to use Moltmann's language, "messianic" terms. The word which emerges in the two creation accounts is not a completed or static entity but is actually in the process of being born (so Romans 8:22) and this creation has a christological shape. The immediate practical implication of this view is that the destiny of human beings and the destiny of creation are inseparable and inseparable because held together by Christ: "For the creation waits with eager longing for the revealing of the children of God...the creation itself will be set free from its bondage to decay and will obtain the freedom of the glory of the children of God" (Romans 8:19). Christ is the "firstborn of all creation" because "in him all things in heaven and on earth were created (Colossians 1:15-16) and Christ is the "firstborn of the dead" in order that he "might come to have first place in everything" (Colossians 1:18b).   The resurrection of Christ does not simply portend the salvation of human beings but the salvation of the cosmos because in Christ "all things hold together" (Colossians 1:17). Within the context of this vision it makes little sense to ask if Paul was interested in nature "for itself". Paul was interested in nature for the same reason he was interested in human beings--because both have their creation and redemption in Christ and, thus, in God.

Romans 8 contains a radical insight. There is an affinity between the suffering of creation and the suffering of God's people. Both creation and God's people are cruciform and, therefore, the first "eye-opening event for the cross-bearing Christian is to see that the great chorus of the groaning creation with whom he now feels a new affinity and responsibility".[26]

This brief foray into theological exegesis has, I think, substantiated the claim made earlier in this section that the ecological crisis is a crisis of the doctrine of creation and a crisis of soteriology. The crisis in the doctrine of creation comes in the form of an unwarranted anthropocentric reading of the first creation narrative (and of the whole biblical tradition) which results in the abstraction of human beings from their place in the created order and a radical attenuation of God's creatorship. The crisis in soteriology involves the refusal to see the destinies of human being and creation as linked, the result of a severe and unwarranted limitation of God's saving work. A genuine *interpretation* of the biblical tradition (as opposed to a forced reading of it) suggests that in order for nature to be ignored major elements of this tradition must be either disregarded or distorted.[27]

Contributing Factors to the Ecological Crisis

The issue of the intellectual "causes" of the ecological crisis with respect to Western thinking and the Christian tradition have already been mentioned. An inquiry into this subject might reasonably occupy an entire study in itself. The treatment of this issue here will of necessity be brief and, therefore, not completely adequate. Such an undertaking is necessary because anyone who wishes to develop an ecological theology will not want to retrace the intellectual path that led to the problem in the first place. While it is difficult to speak of the "causes" of the ecological crisis, three factors (not easily separated) will be discussed: the Christian tradition, science and technology, and the "turn to the subject".

The Christian Tradition as Malefactor

Mention has already been made of Lynn White's essay "The Historical Roots of Our Ecological Crisis" which maintains, it was noted, that the biblical tradition fostered the view that nature is simply something to be used by human beings and that this view gave rise to exploitative Western science and technology. Of course, this view has been criticized even by those who acknowledge that Christianity did foster an ambiguous attitude toward nature.[28] It was noted above that this view has found acceptance among some theologians who hold that the Christian tradition is so anthropocentric that it leads to the idea that the "natural world...is of an ontologically different order from man. Though man is part of nature and has been made of natural materials, he is lifted far above the rest of nature by his moral and personal character".[29]

Another form of this view focuses on theology in the strict sense of the term, that is the doctrine of God. On this view, Christian indifference or hostility toward nature is rooted in the doctrine of God. Kaufman argues that the Christian concept of God, as a symbol of ultimate value (and this is what God is for Kaufman), "is a means by which man gives ultimate metaphysical significance to the moral and personal side of his being" and this legitimated and reinforced the view that human beings were vastly different from and superior to nature which was not "personal" or "spiritual".[30] For Kaufman, the root problem is the doctrine of God in which God is thought of as a "metaphysical person". Thus, for him, the radical reconstruction necessitated by the ecological crisis will eschew personal images of God.

Sallie McFague partially agrees with Kaufman's analysis yet does not accept this conclusion. McFague argues that it is not the personal understanding of God that is at fault but the way in which God as person has been construed. In her view the primary models of the personal God which the Christian tradition has developed have been hierarchical and imperialistic and have led to dualism.[31] For McFague the traditional Christian concept of God has been monarchial and has led to an understanding of God's relation to the world which is characterized by, to use Kaufman's term, "asymmetrical dualism". This means that God and the world are distantly related, that God controls the world directly or indirectly, that God is radically separated from the world, and that what happens to the world is not of great (or any) consequence to God. Then too, because all power rests with God, human beings contribute nothing (or almost nothing) to their salvation; God does everything. The premise of the monarchial model is, in her view, that "God can be God only if we are nothing."[32] This picture seems to approach caricature and, in my judgment, is a one sided reading of the biblical and Christian tradition. Nevertheless, McFague's analysis is not without its strengths and she is particularly helpful in pointing out the *consequences* of the monarchial model of God. This model results in a way of thinking for which "God is wordless and the world is Godless" and which is "simply blank in terms of what lies outside the human sphere."[33]

This discussion (and on this point McFague is singularly helpful) should alert us to the fact that God's relation to the world is one of the central issues with which an ecological theology must deal. An assessment of the Christian tradition on this point will want, however, to avoid one sided readings of the doctrine of God. Nevertheless, a problem does exist and Gilkey is certainly correct when he remarks that once

> God was defined in theology as "pure actuality," "eternal being," "changeless," and thus quite devoid of potentiality, alterability, passivity, or temporality, it became virtually impossible, if not contradictory, to express intelligibly the obvious relatedness and mutuality of God to the changing world necessitated by the scriptural witness and by the structure of the Christian religion itself.[34]

"The Disenchantment of the World"

Science and technology, as has been noted, figure in as factors contributing to the ecological crisis. This is the case if for no other reason than that they have radically altered the relationship of human beings to the world. To whatever influence one attributes the rise of modern science and technology and whatever assessment one makes of their accomplishments, one must acknowledge that their influence has changed the relationship that human beings have with nature as well as our perception of nature itself and even our own self-understanding.

This point has been effectively been made by Martin Heidegger, who argues that in Greek thought technology (*techne*) was a mode of revealing (*aletheuein*); it referred not to manufacturing but to bringing forth, revealing, and the standing out of truth.[35] Understood in this sense, there is a similarity, now obliterated, between *techne* and *poiesis*. Modern technology, however, is of a very different character. It is a "challenging" (*Herausfordern*), an "ordering," and a "setting upon". Technology no longer allows presence to come forth out of concealment but is directed toward controlling and ordering things so that they are useful to human beings and fulfill human purposes. All things are seen in the mode of what

Heidegger calls a "standing reserve," as objects of potential use or value to human beings. Under what one might call the "technological attitude" (the phrase is John Cobb's) the human being "exalts himself to the posture of lord of the earth. In this way the illusion comes to prevail that everything man encounters exists only insofar as it is his construct."[36]

Heidegger's point is not that technology is evil but that it becomes so in the service of a particular mode of seeing the world and of understanding truth, the view just described which he designates as "enframing" (*Gestell*). This analysis should at least serve as a warning against the view that nature is a collection of things awaiting human use. Modern technology is dangerous in the sense that it creates the illusion of human control over all things, a control which is often accepted unreflectively as legitimate. As Heidegger makes clear, however, the "technological attitude" does not merely distort the human perception of nature but also has a corrosive and distorting effect on human self-understanding. It is precisely this that worries Heidegger most about technology:

> The threat to man does not come in the first instance from the potentially lethal machines and apparatus of technology. The actual threat has already afflicted man in his essence. The rule of enframing [*Gestell*] threatens man with the possibility that it could be denied him to enter into a more original revealing and hence to experience the call of a more primal truth.[37]

A similar way of assessing the effect of science and technology on the human perception of nature is provided by Morris Berman who sees Western consciousness moving in a definite direction through history. He maintains that the one thing which is "certain about the history of Western consciousness...is that the world has, since roughly 2,000 B.C., been progressively disenchanted, or 'disgoded' ."[38] Modern science and technology have played a major role in this "disenchantment". The loss of the sense of enchantment (a word the use of which Heidegger would certainly approve) came largely, according to Berman, when capitalism and modern industry found it convenient to appropriate the view that nature was dead. Modern science and technology found disenchantment to be convenient because it made it possible to subject nature to mathematics--a dead nature could be quantified and then exploited without scruple.

The point to be made here is that an ecological theology will have to attend to our *perception* of nature. If the world is to be reenchanted (or if something like this is to be achieved), human beings will have to reassess their relationship to nature and this will mean reassessing their perception of themselves.

As I see it, the ecological crisis has chiefly to do with an interpretation (which is actually a misinterpretation) of nature. It stems from a failure to understand the real character of humankind's relationship to the world. This is not to say that "reenchantment" should (or even can) involve a return to some former (and probably imaginary) view of the world as sacred and unambiguously good. Modern industrial economies, as bearers of both weal and woe, mean that the hope of returning to a view of nature held by a Taoist sitting in a bamboo grove is not a hope of reenchantment but one of self-delusion. Neither is this to say that a right interpretation of nature is a *guarantee* against ecological disaster. Mere theory has never been a sufficient buttress of correct practice because theories (and doctrines) can be corrupted or ignored.[39] Indeed, this is precisely what happened in the case of the Christian doctrine of creation. But this does not render attempts to interpret nature irrelevant. It simply raises the question of how such interpretations and perceptions are to be tested (and points to the *necessity* of their being tested) and the question of to what extent they are not simply theories (or ideologies) but genuine and truthful *convictions*. An ecological theology must insist that a doctrine of creation is only a truthful conviction when it supports an ethic of stewardship.

The "Turn to the Subject": The Eclipse of Nature

A third contributing factor to the ecological crisis is what has been called the "turn to the subject". This factor is not to be considered as completely distinct from the two previously discussed factors since it is certainly an element in both Christian tradition and modern science and technology.   The turn to the subject does not necessarily mean subjectivism but it does mean that, as in the philosophies of Descartes and Kant for example, the self is the point of reference for judging the world and not *vice versa*. It is my view that theology has ignored nature to the degree that it has not because, as stated earlier, it is anthropocentric at its foundations but because it largely accepted the modern turn to the subject which, while not without positive results, led to an *inability* on the part of theology to *think about nature*.

In a sense the turn to the subject was, within Christian theology, not completely a product of modern consciousness. In his *Soliloquies* St. Augustine says that he desires nothing else than knowledge of the soul and of God. The self, as his *Confessions* makes clear, is a subject of considerable importance to Augustine. But God and the self do not constitute a complete inventory of his theological interests. Augustine was interested in the theology of history (as can be seen in *The City of God*) and the creation accounts fascinated him endlessly and he devoted much attention to them (as can be seen in his *Literal Commentary on Genesis*). It is a long way from Augustine's remark in the *Soliloquies* to Ritschl's view that "nature was something that pressed upon man, something that man was called to dominate. The function of religion was to assist in achieving this dominance."[40] It will be necessary to meditate on how theology can to traverse this path.

One helpful view to take of contemporary theology is to see two paradigms at work in it. One paradigm might be called "subject centered" in that it focuses on the human subject and allows the doctrine of creation to fade into the background; the doctrine of creation becomes an appendage of theological anthropology. Theologies in this paradigm focus on christology, historical praxis, or hermeneutics.[41] It is not that these theologies are necessarily individualistic. For example, a theology in this paradigm, one which focuses on historical praxis, is J.B. Metz's political theology. Metz emphasizes that human existence is social in character and that social realities are objects of theological interest and necessarily so. But Metz, and many who have followed him, remain in the subject centered paradigm in that the emphasis falls on *human beings* as transformers of the world. The world is given over to human "creative transformation".[42]   World transformation for Metz means human liberation. John Cobb puts the matter helpfully when he says that Metz's theology is "sociological theology," which focuses on the transformation of human social realities, but not "ecological theology," which moves beyond anthropocentrism and sees the interrelatedness of all things, human and nonhuman.[43]

The second paradigm might be called "creation centered". Theology in this paradigm is emerging in a number of forms and is characterized by a movement away from anthropocentrism and an emphasis on God's "immanent presence within matter and the breadth of God's creative activity through natural processes."[44] In the following section examples of theology in this paradigm will be discussed. For the present, our focus will be on the subject centered paradigm.

The task of understanding how the turn to the subject came to exercise such an influence in Christian theology is a difficult one. Two views on this subject will be presented here, views which I think supplement one another. My purpose here is not to show that the turn to the subject must be utterly repudiated and its influence totally expunged, but to show that this turn needs to be critically assessed and modified.

Gustav Wingren has criticized contemporary theology for what he sees as its abandonment of the first article of the Creed (God as Creator) in favor of a monomaniacal concentration on the second article (Jesus as Redeemer). He maintains this to be true of Ritschl, Barth, Bultmann, and Bonhoeffer. For Wingren this concentration is sheer loss.[45] Wingren's premise is that creation and salvation, creation and gospel, exist in fundamental continuity and that if creation is neglected salvation collapses in upon itself. This is, he says, in fact what has happened.

Wingren takes the view that the turn to the subject has radically compromised the doctrine of creation and that this has led to, among other things, an impoverished understanding of salvation. The loss of creation faith is not simply a topic for polite discussion among theologians over sherry. Wingren claims that it

> should become clear to us today, as global problems, such as the destruction of the environment, the relations between rich and poor countries and energy policy come to preoccupy the community [the Church], that "salvation" in the Christian sense can not mean the deliverance of the individual from the chaos of earth. On the contrary...salvation comes to mean [for creation faith] the power of the Holy Ghost over chaos to form a healed world which includes man and nature.[46]

The disappearance of the doctrine of creation means a return to a Gnostic understanding of salvation, the very thing against which the orthodox Christian tradition argued as it took shape under the influence of Irenaeus. Wingren sees an incipient Gnosticism (not to mention a Marcionite view of scripture) in the theology of Bultmann in particular. His criticism of Bultmann can be summed up in these words:

> The body disappears. Not only does the body in the resurrection of the dead and in the resurrection of Christ on the third day disappear, but the social body, our connection to others, disappears as well. Salvation is thus, for Bultmann, individualistic in principle; it is the releasing of the individual self form the crowd...It is *Entweltlichung*.[47]

The source of the subjective turn (away from creation to anthropology), so far as European theology is concerned, is, for Wingren, Kierkegaard. In this reading Kierkegaard understood Christianity to be radically discontinuous with the world and with the Old Testament so that the continuity between creation and gospel was broken. Furthermore, Kierkegaard was simply not interested in anything but the individual and his or her "inwardness". To put it simply, Kierkegaard was for Wingren a "sophisticated pietist"--a phrase which is definitely not to be equated with Schleiermacher's designation of himself as a "Moravian, only of a higher order". Thus, Wingren observes of Kierkegaard, somewhat polemically, that "through out his life [he] fostered aggression against belief in creation...To him 'Christianity' was a breaking away from natural manifestations of life, a break with what 'one' does."[48]

But the reduction of Christianity to the second article, to christology, was the accomplishment, in Wingren's view, of Karl Barth. At work in Barth was the impulse to deny the continuity (which he sees in Irenaeus) between creation and redemption, between human nature as created and human nature as saved by God's grace. For Barth salvation can not be the restoration of the natural. Wingren comes to the conclusion that "the modern negation of the belief in creation has Karl Barth as its spiritual father: all others are secondary and have grown up in his shadow."[49]

George Hendry's analysis of this same problem is more encompassing than Wingren's though both are attempting to answer the question of why nature dropped off the agenda of theology and both locate the reason for this in the turn to the subject. Because it is more encompassing, Hendry's analysis is an appropriate supplement to (and, perhaps, corrective of) Wingren's.

In terms of contemporary theology, Hendry agrees with Wingren's assessment of Barth noting that Barth's christocentrism results in a virtual "unitarianism of the second person" (to use H. Richard Niebuhr's phrase). Hendry's view is, however, somewhat more nuanced that Wingren's in that he does not see Barth as being disinterested in creation but rather as being unable to give it an important role because of his theological method. One aspect of this method is the denial of the validity of natural theology. For Barth this meant that creation could have no independent theological significance from christology. Barth's view is well expressed when he writes

> The world with its sorrow and its happiness will always be a dark one to us, about which we may have optimistic or pessimistic thoughts; but it gives us no information about God as the Creator. But always, when man has tried to read the truth from sun, moon , and stars or from himself, the result has been an idol. But when God has been known and then known again in the world, so that the result was a joyful praise of God in creation, that is because He is to be sought and found by us in Jesus Christ. *By becoming man in Jesus Christ, the fact has also become plain*

and credible that God is the Creator of the world.[50]

Another aspect of Barth's method is a particular understanding of the relationship between theology and scripture. This also led, in Barth's case, to a weakened view of creation. Commenting on Barth's treatment of the doctrine of creation in *Church Dogmatics* III/3, Hendry says that

he [Barth] devoted the kernel of the book to an extended exposition of the creation narratives in Genesis, which provided the opportunity for a dazzling display of exegetical pyrotechnics, but did nothing to answer the question of a scientifically informed person who wants to know what light, if any, theology had to shed on the world of nature.[51]

Barth's answer to the scientifically informed person's question was, in the final analysis, "none at all". It is at this point that we can see that Barth followed a pattern of thinking which had its origin in Kant.

In Barth, the rejection of natural theology carried with it the tone of a bold theological offensive; in fact it was an acquiescence to a theological retreat, a retreat which had been going on for some time. In my judgment Wingren is only partially correct when he traces contemporary theology's subjective turn and consequent "flight from creation" to Kierkegaard. This turn must ultimately be traced back, as Hendry argues, to Kant. The general effect of Kant's *Critique of Pure Reason* was to expunge the cosmological element from theology leaving only the anthropological element. Of particular interest to this inquiry is the fact that Kant argued that creation could not be an object of knowledge; the doctrine of creation was one of theology's many luxuriant growths that would have to be pruned. But Kant's interests were not, as he saw them, anti-theological and he thought that ruthless pruning would ultimately save the theological tree. However, to shift metaphors, like the North American indians, theology lost control of most of its ancestral lands and was placed on a reservation and that reservation was the moral life of the *individual*. It became impossible to speak of God's relationship to nature, one could only speak of God in terms of the experience of the self. The net effect of this subjective turn was a state of affairs in which theology had nothing to say about the natural world which was now the virtual fiefdom of science and technology. Hendry observes that "critical reason, in Kant's hands, proved to powerful a solvent: it set people free from dogmatic prejudice, but it drove them back into Plato's cave, where they could see only flickering shadows and reflections of true reality."[52]

From the analyses of Wingren and Hendry it becomes clear that the turn to the subject resulted in the inability of theology to deal with nature. Kant's epistemology and his view of human beings as personal and moral agents opposed to a mechanistic and deterministic world had the dual effect of pushing God out of the world and pushing human beings into themselves. From this vantage point it can be seen that Barth's rejection of natural theology was in a sense an acquiescence to the *status quo*. The doctrine of creation really tells us nothing about the world but is an appendage to (or postulate of) faith in Jesus Christ. God is certainly the Creator of the world but this is merely an insight derived from christocentric faith.[53]

The turn to the subject led to a consistent anthropocentrism (though not necessarily, as Barth's theology shows, to subjectivism) which can be found, taking into account the differences of emphasis, in the theologies of Schleiermacher, Kierkegaard, Ritschl, Hermann, and Bultmann. What we see in all these theologies is that the "turn to the subject" leads to the "flight from creation".

The Case of Schleiermacher

Schleiermacher's theology could serve as a case study in this regard, a good example of theology in the subject-centered paradigm. The accusations of subjectivism and pantheism made against him miss the mark in my judgment. Schleiermacher is best understood when he is read as both partially accepting and partially rejecting critical philosophy. In *The Christian Faith* (*Glaubenslehre*) Schleiermacher accepts the view of the *Critique of Pure Reason* that properly speaking we have no *knowledge of God* at all (Proposition 50) while rejecting Kant's view that religion ("piety") is a postulate of morality (Propositions 3 and 4). Piety is *sui generis* and Christian doctrines are to be seen not as statements of fact or metaphysical assertions but as "accounts of the Christian religious affections set forth in speech" (Proposition 15). These religious affections have their origin in and receive their characteristic formation from a historically determinant community so Schleiermacher has absolutely no interest in "natural religion" or "religion within the limits of reason alone" (Proposition 10). The turn to the subject is certainly present in this theology but the subject to which we turn is a different subject than Kant's; Schleiermacher's subject is first and always an intersubjective subject--a subject in community.

But the turn to the subject makes itself known nevertheless. In Proposition 30 Schleiermacher says that all statements of Christian doctrine, which are utterances of the Christian religious self-consciousness, can be placed in one of three categories: "descriptions of human states," "conceptions of divine attributes" (though these refer only to a person's consciousness of his or her relationship to God), and "utterances regarding the constitution of the world" (though only in relation to human perception). Statements of the second and third kinds are permissible only as they have been developed out of the first kind which are "fundamental". Yet, Schleiermacher goes on to say that all theological statements *could be expressed in the first form* ("descriptions of human states") "*while the other two forms might be entirely set aside as superfluous.*"[54] Then why not do so? Schleiermacher's answer to this question is that Christian tradition militates against such a move because the resulting theology would "have no link with the past, and just for that reason would be of little practical use [to the Church]."[55]

Predictably, this anthropocentric approach results in a radical attenuation of the doctrine of creation and the eclipse of nature as an object of theological interest. Schleiermacher's doctrine of creation has two dimensions, one cosmological and the other anthropological. It is interesting to note that he regards the cosmological dimension of creation as a matter of "curiosity" foreign to piety (Proposition 39). This dimension of creation is reduced to a matter of information about how the world began and such information is not really information at all because, as he (echoing Kant) puts it, we "have no consciousness of a beginning of being."[56] In the end Schleiermacher reduces this dimension of creation to a regulative principle. The doctrine of creation stands as a principle which militates against any possible infringement upon the *human* feeling of absolute dependence but it has no real positive meaning.

Schleiermacher is very much interested in the anthropological dimension of creation which he discusses under the rubric of christology. In Proposition 100 he makes it clear that the appearance of Christ is the *completion of God's creative activity*. In this sense redemption is an aspect of creation (the Irenaean emphasis). Here, however, creation refers only to human beings in the sense that in Christ a fully completed human being has finally appeared. For Schleiermacher,

> the total effective influence of Christ is only the continuation of the creative divine activity out of which the Person of Christ arose. For this, too, was directed towards human nature as a whole...but in such a way that its effects are mediated through the life of Christ.[57]

The anthropocentric understanding of creation is accompanied by an anthropocentric account of salvation. As Schleiermacher understands it, salvation does not apply to the world of nature. For him eschatology refers to the consummation of the Church not the consummation of creation (because theology could not make statements on this topic that could be regarded as doctrinal). The exclusion of nature from the *ordo salutis*, an inevitable consequence of theology in the subject-centered paradigm, is another issue upon which an ecological theology must reflect. However, it should not be thought that Schleiermacher was a dualist in the sense of thinking that human beings and nature are two separate orders. While salvation does not apply to the world of nature, he notes that

> We shall do well to be on our guard against ascribing to divine wisdom the divine ordering of external and physical nature, as well as institutions for the all-round development of the human mind, in such a manner as to separate them from the sphere of redemption...everything in the world, in proportion as it is attributed to divine wisdom, must also be related to the redemptive or new-creating revelation of God.[58]

It is true that Schleiermacher established theology on a new footing, yet there was an immense price paid for this move. All theological topics could only be discussed in so far as they were related to human beings and their interests.

The preceding discussion should not be seen as an attempt to exculpate the Christian tradition from the charges leveled against it by Lynn White and others; such an attempt would be dishonest. There is an ecological indictment to be brought against the Christian tradition but it is not the indictment returned by White. At most, the Christian tradition's ecological sins are sins of omission rather than commission. The case of Schleiermacher confirms this. Here we see that the disappearance of nature from the agenda of theology was not the result of some world-denying impulse or dualistic antipathy to nature. The disappearance was due to a neglect of the doctrine of creation as embracing all of reality, a doctrine in which Christ is the "firstborn of all creation" (Colossians 1:15 and Romans 8:29) not simply the Lord of the human being's religious life. In the case of Schleiermacher incarnation, significantly, does not refer to an ontological reality (the Word of God *becoming enfleshed*) but is seen as an unfortunate metaphysical term which really has to do with Jesus's religious life, *his piety*.

The Ecological Crisis:
Theological Responses

It has already been noted that the ambiguity of the term "nature" was bequeathed to the West by Greek thought. This ambiguity was intensified when the term was appropriated by Christian theology for its own purposes. An account of the history of this appropriation, a current with many eddies, is beyond the scope of this study. However, it can be said, without risk of undue oversimplification, that nature may be used in three sense in theological discourse. Nature can be used to mean the whole cosmos as a created order dependent upon God. The word may also be use, secondly, to mean that which is proper to human being and may be distinguished from grace. Finally, nature can mean the world with an emphasis on the interrelatedness of human and nonhuman life. The three senses of nature may be distinguished as, respectively, the cosmological, the anthropological, and the ecological. These distinctions exist largely for analytical purposes and it should not be thought that one sense may be discussed in complete separation form the other two. I have tried to show, for example, that lack of attention to the first sense led to an ignoring of the third and an exaggeration of the importance of the second. Yet, in this study and specifically in what follows the third sense will be of primary interest, though the first will be kept in mind as well.

Attention was called previously to Cobb's distinction between sociological theology and ecological theology. The distinction between theology in the subject centered paradigm and theology in the creation centered paradigm has also been noted. In what follows I want to provide an account of the characteristic forms which ecological or creation centered theology is taking. Having discussed the reasons for the disappearance of nature from the agenda of theology, it is now time to see the ways in which a number of theologians are attempting to restore nature to that agenda and the changes in theology which this effort is producing. This will be done in preparation for an ecological reading of Karl Rahner's theology which is the central concern of this study. It goes without saying that it will be impossible to provide a complete account of the literature of ecological theology.[59] What I shall attempt to do is to discuss four models of ecological theology which have emerged with the conviction that such a discussion will convey essential insights and an adequate picture of the aims and methods of this kind of theology.

This discussion will proceed along lines already laid down. It will also provide a context for the following four chapters which develop an ecological reading of Rahner's theology. It has been noted that an ecological theology will have to reflect upon three issues or questions: (1) How is the relationship between human beings and the world to be understood? (2) What is the character of God's relationship with the world? (3) What place does nature occupy in the *ordo salutis*?[60] Each of the four models to be discussed will be analyzed in terms of the answers it gives to the first two of these questions.

A Feminist Model

It is not my intention here to suggest either that there is such a thing as *the* feminist ecological theology or that the theologians to be discussed here are in agreement on all points. My intention is only to draw a picture of an ecological theology that proceeds on feminist insights. In doing this it would be helpful to point out that feminist theology has long been concerned with nature and critical of anthropocentrism (or androcentrism). The reason for this is made clear by Rosemary Ruether when she notes that women

> must see that there can be no liberation for them and no solution to the
> ecological crisis within a society whose fundamental model of relationship
> continues to be one of domination...The concept of domination of nature
> has been based from the first on social domination between master and
> servant groups, starting with the basic relationship between men and
> women.[61]

For our purposes here, feminist thought has two valuable characteristics. It has insisted that the project of liberation must include the liberation of nature and it has been critical of various forms of dualism which understand human life to be antithetical to natural life.

How does a feminist theology deal with the question of human being's relationship to the world? Dorothee Söelle is most helpful in answering this question. She argues that belief in the doctrine of creation has become a mere sentiment; to believe in creation means to have "introverted, sentimental feelings about nature and its beauty."[62] This is the result of the almost complete spiritualization of creation faith which is the consequence of the turn to the subject. Such a spiritualization makes it difficult to see the continuity between the "spiritual" and the "material" and introduces a false dichotomy or dualism. Thus, creation faith which merely "believes in God" ("theoretical theism") leads to living as if God did not figure into the realities of human life ("practical atheism").[63] The ultimate consequence of the spiritualization of creation faith is that technology "has replaced the God of creation; it is the surrogate, all-powerful 'deity' whose might no one can escape."[64]

For Söelle, a theology that aspires to be ecological, to combine creation faith and liberation theology (Genesis and Exodus), will not neglect the "dust factor"--the fact that according to Genesis 2:7 there is an intimate connection between human beings and the earth. It is impossible to divide the world into the spiritual and the "merely material" because matter has a spiritual element and finite spirituality has a material element. The true character of the human being's relationship to nature can only be understood by an "embodied theology," the three salient features of which are (1) the idea that human beings were made from the dust of the ground, (2) the idea that the earth does not belong to humans but that human belong to the earth, and (3) the conviction that the earth is God's and not a human possession or the possession of *some humans*.[65] The "dust factor" means the end of such dichotomies as body and spirit and human and nonhuman. It also means the end of anthropocentric (or androcentric) hubris and "ecological imperialism".

For our purposes, what is most helpful about Söelle's analysis is its explication of the consequences of the "dust factor" for human work. If human beings are essentially alien to nature, if it is simply a material obstacle to spiritual progress, and if it is simply something to be used for "higher" (that is, human) purposes, then it follows that the purpose of work is to master nature. The consequences of this view, as has been noted, are made clear in Heidegger's essay "The Question Concerning Technology". This understanding of work is incompatible with creation faith which understands human beings as fundamentally related to nature through work (Genesis 2:15).

Creation faith has two important consequences for our understanding of work. First, work must be seen as a means through which human beings are reconciled to nature. This means that the "hope for reconciliation with nature through human work amounts to a rejection of the traditional, masculine aspiration to dominate the earth...Reconciling ourselves with nature through work is one of the great human projects before us."[66] Second, human beings must not regard themselves as passive subjects within creation. This view leads to a devaluation of human effort, not to mention a complete secularization of it. For Söelle, creation faith implies that human beings are to be co-creators with God, to participate in a creation which is not yet an accomplished fact. The doctrine of creation is not to be interpreted to mean that God's creative activity ceased at Genesis 3:25. To use biblical language, as human beings fulfill their assigned function with respect to the earth, which is to "till it and keep it" (Genesis 2:15), they participate in God's creative activity. This means that God's power is shared power.[67] Creation faith makes it impossible to see nature as a "standing reserve" (to use Heidegger's term) of raw material for human economic dynamism and it forces us to see our "tilling and keeping" of nature as an essential part of the human "spiritual" vocation.

Another important issue which needs to be addressed is that of God's relationship with the world. How would a feminist model deal with this question? The work of Grace Jantzen characterizes traditional Christian theism as based on "cosmic monarchial dualism".[68] By this she means that God's relationship to the world was understood in the classical Christian tradition to be analogous to the soul's relation to the body. Whereas the soul was understood, under the influence of Neoplatonism, as immutable, eternal, immortal, and essentially living, the body was seen as mutable, temporal, material, and essentially lifeless. This analogy lent itself to the view that just as the soul controlled the body, was completely independent of it, and was essentially distinct from the body, the same could be said about God's relation to the world.

A problem arose for theology, so Jantzen argues, when the anthropology underlying this view was rejected. What Jantzen calls "Platonic/Cartesian dualism" is no longer generally accepted as an accurate anthropology and this means that the understanding of God's relationship to the world based upon it is no longer valid. Her argument is complex and complete justice can not be done to it here. It is enough, for our purposes, to say two things. First, we can (and must) still have an understanding of God that is to some extent based upon our understanding of ourselves. Even though "the model of God based on human persons will undoubtedly need to be qualified in important ways" we must still use this mode because (*contra* Kaufman) "it is the best model we have."[69] Second, and consequently, the relation between the human being and the human body can still serve as an analogy for God's relationship to the world provided we accept a holistic anthropology. Such an acceptance will bring with it important theological changes because this analogy will no longer

> point towards a God existing independently of the world and interacting with it like a majesty from on high...Rather, the relationship between God and the world will be much more intimate, and his attributes of power and knowledge will not be forces externally applied.[70]

This is to say that in Jantzen's analysis the difficulties which Christian theology has experienced can be traced to the assumption that God is an incorporeal person, a concept she finds incoherent and unsustainable.[71]

The problem with the tendency to see God as an incorporeal person is, in her view, that it leads to the religiously inadequate idea that God has no real relationship to the world since it is through the body that a person is related to the world, both as a receiver of stimuli and as an agent. This has been long affirmed of humans but denied of God on the grounds that there is a point at which the analogy between God as personal and human beings as personal must be abandoned. Jantzen questions this view especially when it attributes a personal quality to God such as love and then maintains that God is also utterly impassive and immutable. Such a view speaks of God in personal terms but then proceeds to develop its assertions in the most impersonal of directions. For Jantzen God as personal is "central to theology" and that when there is a conflict between this view and the tendency to interpret personal characteristics in an impersonal, absolute direction, then "in a case of conflict, the conflict must be resolved in a way that heightens, rather than diminishes his [God's] personal nature."[72] This means, ultimately, that the universe must be seen as God's *body*.

It is not my intention to fully explicate what Jantzen means by saying this. This is because I intend to discuss the work of one theologian who has creatively appropriated this idea.[73] The important thing to note here is that this view may be regarded as a form of panentheism which certainly does accomplish Jantzen's goal of overcoming dualism even though it may create other theological problems. It is also important to say that she is not immediately interested in ecological theology though her understanding of God's relation to the world constitutes the foundation of such a theology in that it views nature as a direct manifestation of God's creativity. If this view is adopted, then this "doctrine of divine immanence takes on obvious significance with enormous impact on our view of nature, science and technology, the human body...to mention only a few areas too easily relegated to the 'secular'."[74]

Sallie McFague has essentially accepted Jantzen's idea of God's embodiment and her analysis of why it is necessary while applying this concept in more concrete ways with the expressed intention of constructing an ecological theology. She also agrees with Jantzen that traditional Christian theism is antithetical to an ecological theology.

The basic maxim of McFague's theological position can be seen in C.S. Lewis's view that images of the Holy easily become holy images--sacrosanct. My idea of God is not a divine idea. It has to be shattered time after time. He [God] shatters it Himself. He is the great iconoclast. Could we not almost say that this shattering is one of the marks of his presence?[75]

She argues that traditional images of God have undergone this metamorphosis, from images of the holy to holy images and, furthermore, that these images are all hierarchical, dualistic, and imperialistic in that God's relationship to the world is that of an external, dominating power. These images, which are all manifestations of what McFague calls the "monarchial model" of God, lead to both escapism (in that the world is not finally important) and irresponsibility (in that all power and initiative finally rest with God). In the final analysis, McFague finds the monarchial model of God inadequate because it does not reflect what she understands to be the Christian vision which is a "destabilizing, inclusive, nonhierarchical vision of fulfillment for all creation."[76]

Behind McFague's project is an important epistemological assumption which is that "religious and theological language is at most a foray attempting to express experiences of relating to God."[77] As does Schleiermacher, McFague holds that theological language refers not to God but to experiences of relating to God. It is unfortunate that the concept of experience is left rather vague. This epistemological assumption directly shapes her understanding of theology in that for her theology "is a kind of heuristic construction that is focusing on the imaginative construal of the God-world relationship" the task of which is to "remythologize Christian faith through metaphors and models appropriate for an ecological, nuclear, age."[78]

It is essential to understand the rudiments of McFague's project in order to understand her appropriation of Jantzen's idea of the world as God's body. While Jantzen sees the statement that God is embodied in the universe as a metaphysical one, McFague does not; for her this statement is an "imaginative picture" of the relationship between God and the world. This model, as McFague sees it, does not reduce God to the world but means that nothing exists outside of God and that God is intrinsically related to all things. The universe is "God's incarnation" which means that we are invited to see the "cosmos as God's bodily presence in all times and places" and that God cares for the world as one cares for one's body.[79] This means, finally, that God has a material stake in the fate of the earth and the health of nature since it is an expression of God's own being.

McFague goes beyond Jantzen in proposing three specific metaphors which further illumine God's relationship with the world. The three metaphors are mother, lover, and friend and correspond, respectively, to the three persons of the Trinity, which are understood generically as creator, redeemer, and sustainer.

As mother God's creative love is directed toward the nurturing and fulfilling of all life. As mother/creator God wishes that all species of life, not just the human, flourish.[80] For McFague God as mother helps reinterpret the doctrine of creation in a nondualistic way. If God is seen as mother, and the world as God's body, it is difficult to spiritualize creation and to subordinate nature to human ends because creation "is God's self expression, formed in God's own reality with the means to nurture and sustain billions of plants and creatures."[81] As mother/creator, God's relationship to the world is such that God is involved "in so arranging the cosmic household that the birth and growth of other [than the human] species will take place in an ecologically balanced way".[82]

In speaking of God as lover, McFague wishes to understand the motive for God's saving activity. The problem, she says, is that God's love has often been understood as disinterested and passionless. In this view, God does not, in any real sense, need or love creation. The motive for God's saving activity, for her, is God's love for and *need of* the whole creation, it being God's embodiment. God's saving activity is such that "God as lover in interested not in rescuing certain individuals from the world but in saving, making whole, the entire beloved cosmos that has become estranged and fragmented...threatened by death and extinction."[83]

The metaphor of God as friend emphasizes the fact that God is the companion of all life, the one who is freely bound to the world as sustainer. As the world's friend, God is the "one committed to it, who can be trusted never to betray it, who not only likes the world but has a vision for its well being."[84]

These three metaphors are intended to illuminate aspects of God's *one love.* McFague's intention is doing this is to lead us to see that we can not love God without loving the world. This is, in my judgment, the foundation of her ecological theology and is the most important consequence of seeing the world as God's body.

A Process Theology Model

Process theology has firmly challenged anthropocentric and atomistic views of the world because it is essentially biocentric and stresses the relatedness of all things. This challenge results in a very different understanding of the human being's relation to the world from the one engendered by seventeenth century science. This is because process thought presents a very different view of nature and in doing so forces us to reconsider our relationship to it.

John Cobb notes that Western thinking has seen nature as "a fundamentally inexhaustible and changeless stage on which we are to play our human drama" and, therefore, has "simply refused to see that the stage participates in the drama."[85] As has been noted, this is so because nature was seen as a lifeless mechanism which, in its dead regularity, was a foil for the spontaneity of human history. Because it was seen as merely a stage, nature had no intrinsic value. This anthropocentric attitude rests on a particular understanding of subjectivity--subjectivity defined as something which only human beings possess. Process thought denies this and advocates a shift to an "ecological attitude" which Cobb describes as "respect or even reverence for, and perhaps a feeling of kinship with, the other creatures" in the world of nature.[86]

Process thought argues that seventeenth century science was simply mistaken in thinking that matter was dead and that, consequently, nature was lifeless. The concept of nature it articulates is fundamentally non-mechanistic. All matter, even inorganic matter, is not inert or solid at all but is constituted by "energy events" organized in increasingly complex ways to form, in progression, atoms, molecules, cells, and complex life forms such as plants, animals, and human beings. These energy events are capable of having experiences and aims even if only unconscious ones. The more complex a life form is, the more intense its experiences and the more conscious its aims. For process thought, life is best understood not in substantial terms but as "occasions of experience" of greater or lesser degrees of complexity and richness. What this means is that *all life has some degree of subjectivity*, human subjectivity being the most complex kind of which we know. The most important consequence of this view is that it denies that only human beings have intrinsic value; it is the case, rather, that *all life* has intrinsic value even if in varying degrees. In other words, there is intrinsic value wherever there is subjectivity and subjectivity is relational not atomistic.[87]

Within this understanding of nature it is impossible to assume that all non-human life is simply of instrumental value; it is also difficult to neatly distinguish between human beings and "the environment". Cobb expresses this insight nicely when he says that the "whole universe is one vast ecological system". This means that the differences between human beings and nature

are differences within a single world, whether we call it nature, or history, or an ecological system. They do not make man an outsider. They do not

reduce the other products of the creative evolutionary process to mere
objects without intrinsic value. There is no dualism of man and his
environment.[88]

Process theology"s understanding of God's relationship to the world
is derived largely from its interpretation of the subject. Just as Jantzen
denied that there could be a disembodied subject, process theologians
deny that there could be a non-relational subject. The process critique of
classical theism holds that the latter understood God in personal terms yet
so qualified this understanding by asserting God's aseity and inability to
be affected by the world that the term "person" lost all meaning in relation
to God. Process theologians wish to understand God in personal terms
and insist that "that doctrine of God is always to be preferred which, other
things being equal, interprets his relation with the world more, rather than
less, like the way we interpret the relations of other entities."[89]
Furthermore, the process critique goes, classical theism understood God
in terms of a particular ideal of personhood--the self as sovereign over and
independent of its environment. In process thought no such self exists and
the highest form of selfhood is not that which is *a se* but that which is
ultimately and supremely relational. Classical theism, then, was the result
of a fundamental confusion; its understanding of God did not begin with
the crucified, servant Christ but with the pantocrator. This view is
expressed by Cobb who notes that the Church "gave unto God the
attributes which belonged exclusively to Caesar."[90]

Jay McDaniel describes process theology's understanding of God's
relationship to the world as "relational panentheism," which he contrasts
with "emanational panentheism". The latter view holds that the world is
a direct expression of God's being so that God's being and nature can not
finally be distinguished. Relational panentheism denies this and holds that
God and the world are not identical but that "the world is immanent with,
and present to, God even as God is immanent within, and present to, the
world."[91] God's immanence means that God is really related to all forms
of life while God's transcendence means that God is not simply the sum
total of all life forms.

The view that God is *ultimately and supremely relational*, the view
just described, has two implications which are of immediate interest here.
First, it means that God shares in the experiences of all forms of life and
that this experience either adds to or detracts from God's own consequent
nature. This means that there is an element of risk in God's life in that
being relational God is exposed to the pain of creatures. As McDaniel
helpfully points out, it is not just that God *knows* the pain and joy of

creatures but that God feels pain and joy *with* creatures. God is , in Whitehead's phrase, a "fellow sufferer who understands". It is God's purpose to lead each form of life to greater self-realization and richness of experience appropriate to it and to the whole creation and this purpose is "universal in scope and everlasting in duration".[92]

Second, this view means that God's power is not coercive but persuasive; God does not exercise unilateral control over all things. Process theology, following Whitehead, denies the doctrine of *creatio ex nihilo*. Since God created out of a pre-existent chaos, God is not the only source of creative power. Nature, as a dynamic and evolutionary system, has a creative power of its own through which God works.[93] God's power is that of the lure in that God offers relevant possibilities to all forms of life which entice each form toward a richer life. But these possibilities or initial aims need not be accepted completely or at all. While God's creative and providential power is limited, the extent of this power and its aims are not; God's purpose for human beings can not be spoken of apart from God's purpose for the whole creation. God's purpose for all life is what process theologians refer to as the "universal Christ" since this purpose is expressed in Christ. In other words, God's purposes are universally redemptive since redemption does not simply refer to human salvation but to the redemption and fulfillment of all life. McDaniel expresses this vision when he says that the

> cosmic Heart is active in the world as a universally felt lure, which is one way its love is experienced. It is also receptive of the world as an all-empathetic consciousness, which is the other way love is realized...Heart is the ultimate expression of relational power in the universe though the efficacy of its influence depends on worldly response, and it is the most vulnerable power in the universe.[94]

In other words, "God's life is...an adventure in the sense of being a risk, since God will feel the discord as well as the beautiful experiences involved in the finite actualizations" of the experience of each life form.[95]

A Catholic Incarnational, Sacramental Model

This model reflects a particular theological sensibility rooted in the Roman Catholic tradition, though many Protestant theologians have embraced what they call a "sacramental sensibility". As the guiding sensibility of an ecological theology, it means that the energy of the earth, living plants and animals, and human beings is unified by the Incarnate Word. Incarnation was not a self-corrective measure, a deus ex machina, or an afterthought but, rather, the ground and goal of the movement of the entire world process.[96]

Because of this theological fact, the earth "calls for our loving service". If the Incarnation is the "ground and goal" of creation, all of creation must have a final significance. While God is not to be identified with creation, the Incarnation reveals that creator and creation are not antithetical but that creation is a product of grace and is a graced reality. In the Incarnation the material world is sanctified and shown to have a permanent place in the *ordo salutis*. It thus becomes possible to speak, as does Teilhard de Chardin, of "holy matter".[97]

For this model, the human being's relationship to the world can be truly known only in light of the Incarnation. This is because the Incarnation alone tells us about the true character and destiny of the creation. By virtue of the Incarnation, we see that "*nothing* here below *is profane* for those who know how to see" but rather "everything is sacred" and that all aspects of the material world are destined to be brought into the "single, all-embracing work of the incarnation".[98] To use a term mentioned earlier, to see the world in light of the Incarnation results in its "re-enchantment" so that right "from the hands that knead the dough, to those that consecrate it, the great and universal Host should be prepared and handled in a spirit of adoration."[99]

Furthermore, in light of the Incarnation, human beings are led to have reverence for what John Carmody calls the "mystery of creation". The created world stands before human beings not as a reserve of useful material (a "standing reserve") but as an "initiative to pray" in that nature is given as "a gift from God's holy mystery, an expression of creative love". As developed by Teilhard and Carmody, this view has profound ethical implications. To abuse creation is parallel to profaning the Eucharist, the result of which is, according to Paul, that a person invites the judgment of God because of a failure to "discern the body" (I Corinthians 11:29). It is thus possible to speak of sinning against nature because one does not "discern the body". For Carmody, the abuse of nature represents an "egocentric denial of God" because the "ruin of nature and the denial of God go hand in hand, because both exalt human beings".[100]

The point just made about the Incarnation revealing the destiny of creation needs to be kept in mind. This model does not see creation in static terms but sees it moving towards a destiny prefigured by the

Incarnation. In the Incarnation the human and the divine, as well as the physical and the spiritual, are seen as joined in a mystical union. This means that the destiny of creation involves a point at which these two converge, though distinctions proper to each are not annulled.

Teilhard has devoted some attention to this point of convergence, calling it the "Omega Point" or the "Divine Milieu". At this point what he calls "ontogenesis" or "christification" occurs, which is to say that the world undergoes a "vast becoming what it is". The Incarnation is fully realized at this point.[101] The Divine Milieu as understood by Teilhard represents what might be called an "ecological eschatology" (a subject that will be taken up in the fifth chapter). This is so because the eschaton is understood to be that point at which *all creation* finds fulfillment *as an interconnected whole*. The whole of creation is the raw material for the New Earth of Revelation 21:1. In this eschatology the material world is not spiritualized away but radically becomes what God intended it to be. To use the language of the Apocalypse, it is not that human beings flee the earth to be with God but that God makes God's home on earth (Revelation 21:3).[102] This was all prefigured by the Incarnation which reminds us of the spiritual power inherent in matter by virtue of it:

> By means of all created things, without exception, the divine assails us, penetrates us and molds us...the palpable world, which we were want to treat with the boredom and disrespect with which we habitually regard places with no sacred association for us is in truth a holy place, and we did not know it.[103]

For this model any discussion of God's relation to the world must be approached with caution so that the mystery of God is fully respected. Just as the Incarnation is a mystery, in the sense that it can not be fully comprehended, so God's relationship to the world is a mystery. Nevertheless, just as the Son has a real relationship to Jesus's human nature in the incarnation, even if the Chalcedonian formula can not fully express it, so God has a real relationship with the world. This relationship is such that the world is an expression of God's mystery. This model wishes to deny both that the world is God's embodiment (because this would diminish the significance of the Incarnation) and that God is alienated from creation (because this would make the Incarnation impossible).

Thus, two emphases must be held together. On one hand, creation must be seen as that which God causes to stand forth from nothingness. Seen in this way nature appears as utterly gratuitous and *different from God*. Creation is the mystery of "ex-sistence". "Nature shows God's serious play, God's love of profusion, God's desire to hurl the divine Is! to the outermost galaxies."[104] On the other hand, creation must be seen as God's partial self-expression, the Logos. While nature is certainly not God, or even God's embodiment, God through the Logos is the innermost being and power of all nature's processes.[105] For this model, ultimately, God's relationship to the world can only be understood within the grand mystery that stands behind the mystery of the Incarnation, the Trinity. Thus:

> In creating the world, God made a beautiful place resonant with the unlimited resources of the Father, coruscant with the full intelligibility of the Logos, instinct with the healing love of the Holy Spirit. In the incarnation of the Son, God drew so close to the natural world as he could, uniting his [self-expression] to one of his creatures. In redeeming the world by the blood of Christ's cross, God showed the furthest reaches of divine love.[106]

Just as we can distinguish among the three persons of the Trinity, so we can distinguish between creation and the triune Creator. Yet in each case what must be emphasized equally with the *difference* is *community* and communion because "God is One as well as Three. God is one with creation, as well as apart from creation."[107]

As I hope to show in the fourth chapter, this is the model from which Rahner works. This is the case even if his position is more developed and less problematic than Teilhard's.

A Hegelian, Creator Spiritus Model

In discussing this model I am drawing upon the writing of two theologians whose work, while differing in particulars, reflects the includence of Hegelianism with special attention to the role of the Spirit in the life of the Trinity. Since Moltmann's position is more developed than Hendry's, most of what is said here will reflect Moltmann's emphases.

Moltmann's working out of what he calls an "ecological doctrine of creation" is found within his work *God in Creation*, which has already been mentioned. As he understands it, an ecological doctrine of creation

> implies a new kind of thinking about God. The center of this thinking is no longer the distinction between God and the world. The center is the recognition of the presence of God *in* the world and the presence of the world *in* God.[108]

In other words, it is Moltmann's aim to formulate a doctrine of creation which understands the human being's relation to the world and God's relationship to the world in such a way as to address the concerns of ecological theology.

In doing this Moltmann is building on a doctrine of the Trinity which he has articulated in *The Trinity and the Kingdom*, to which *God in Creation* is a sequel.[109] While the argument of *The Trinity and the Kingdom* is complex, it can be stated with concision. Moltmann argues that, fundamentally, all Christian theology is inescapably Trinitarian theology. This is the case because it is only the doctrine of the Trinity which allows us to understand God's relationship to the world. The doctrine tells us that the history of Christ is also the history of God. It also tells us that "through the Holy Spirit the history of Christ with God and the history of God with Christ become the history of God with us and hence our history with God."[110] Moltmann argues, *contra* Schleiermacher for example, that the doctrine of the Trinity is not a piece of speculation but really the heart of the Christian faith. It was the attenuation of this doctrine that resulted in a "monotheism of the absolute subject," a doctrine of God which denied that God was related to the world or could respond to it.[111] Once God was understood as one substance subsequently differentiated into three persons rather than a *koinonia* of three persons bound together in an eternal *perichoresis* of love, God was thought of as the *antithesis* of history, becoming, and finitude and could thus have no relationship with them. The bottom line for Molltmann is that such a view denies any real connection between God and the crucified Jesus and this renders all attempts at Christian theology null and void. In Moltmann's view, the doctrine of the Trinity means that *God's own being* is open to the world, to history, to human beings, and to nature.

What Moltmann argues for, in part, is a reinterpretation of all traditional divine attributes in light of his proposed Trinitarian doctrine. Briefly stated, this means that

> God is not unchangeable, if to be unchangeable means that he could not in the freedom of his love open himself to the changeable history with man and creation. God is not incapable of suffering, if this means that in the freedom of his love he [could] not be receptive to suffering over the contradiction of man and the self-destruction of creation. God is not perfect, of this means that he did not in the freedom of his love want this humanity and creation which he loves to be necessary to his perfection. God is not invulnerable, if this means that he could not open himself to the experience of the cross.[112]

The doctrine of the Trinity is Moltmann's way of speaking about the very life of God as dynamic and involved with creation. This means that God has a history and, indeed, Moltmann prefers to speak about the "Trinitarian history of God" rather than simply about the Trinity.

Both Moltmann and Hendry see the doctrine of creation in an eschatological light. This means that we can not view the world as it is as complete and that we know that the world is not complete in light of the resurrection. The key text for both is Romans 8:18-23 (though one might also mention Hebrews 2:5-9, 4:3-11, and 9:28) in which God's people and God's creation are linked both by their *present suffering* and their *future destiny*. The pattern of death/resurrection, and suffering/glory hold true for both human beings and the natural world.[113] As Moltmann puts it, "eschatology is nothing other than faith in the Creator with its eyes turned toward the future" and, to put it another way, faith "in the resurrection is...the Christian form of belief in creation."[114]

What this view accomplishes is important. It is nothing less than the overcoming of the traditional dichotomy between nature and history. Here, the kingdom of God is seen as the goal of creation; the consummation of history and the consummation of creation coincide. This is what Moltmann calls a "soteriological understanding of creation," meaning that it is impossible to understand the God of history apart form the God of creation because *creation* is the framework in which *history* takes place. Creation is not a static given but is itself involved in the process of salvation. This is the significance of the fact that the canon of scripture begins with the two creation accounts which precede the history of Israel and the Church and closes with the Apocalypse an its vision of a *new creation*.[115]

It is important to emphasize the point that the destinies of human beings and the world are inseparable. As has been noted, the turn to the subject resulted in an abandonment of nature to science and technology and a theological fixation upon human beings and their salvation. This view overcomes this disastrous development. Actually, Moltmann even refuses to speak of "nature" because for him this word designates creation as it was secularized and seen as something to be exploited or as "unclaimed property". For him, *creation* means a "spiritual ecosystem" which has a common destiny and in which human beings have an important place but are not its reason for being. To speak of the world as creation is to say that it is *God's creation* and must be respected as such.[116] Human beings are not the primary actors in the drama of creation because the world is, as Calvin said, the *theatrum gloriae Dei*.

For this model, the answer to the anthropocentrism induced by the turn to the subject is a theocentrism which emphasizes that creation is a community of which human beings are members, not masters. As has been stated, Moltmann argues that the human being as *imago dei* has been too much emphasized and emphasized to a degree unwarranted by the biblical text (Genesis 2:26). This emphasis has prevented human bings from seeing creation in its true (soteriological) light. Rather than being raw material for human projects, creation is eucharistic in that the proper response to it is gratitude and praise because creation is a "sacrament of God's hidden presence" and a "communication of God's fellowship," a fellowship which human beings share with all life.[117] The overemphasis on *imago dei* has resulted in a distortion of it and Moltmann, like Söelle, wishes to correct this by stressing the "dust factor". Therefore,

> it is important for the way the human being understands himself that he should not see himself initially as a subject over against nature, and theologically as the image of God; but haft he should first of all view himself as a product of nature and--theologically too--as *imago mundi*.[118]

When human beings in their relationship to the world are considered under the rubric of *imago dei* and *imago mundi*, it is made clear that they are neither to be absorbed into nature nor abstracted from it. To say that a human being is *imago mundi* is to say that this being sums up in its being the life of all other creatures and yet remains part of the community of creation. To say that a human being is *imago dei* is to say that this being is also open to the incarnation as the representative of creation. Yet, *imago dei* must be understood *eschatologically* in that human beings are not yet this image. Human beings only become *imago dei* after they are conformed to the image of Christ, conformed to the image of the crucified servant. The desire to conquer and dominate nature can not be supported by appeal to the *imago dei*.[119]

If human beings and the world of nature do share a common destiny, then speaking about humankind's unity with nature is more than poetic language or romantic fancy. If Romans 8:18-23 is at all correct, then, as Hendry says, both human beings and nature are involved in the process of death and resurrection. This means that the relation of human beings to creation should be one of profound *sympathy* for we are united with all creation in both *suffering and hope* (Romans 8:22). This faith receives its highest and most intense expression in the Eucharist

> in which representative elements of the world, by which our life is sustained, are brought in offering to God as a prayer that the consummation of our bodies through the incarnation, passion, and

resurrection of Christ may be continued and extended to the whole material world.[120]

As has been noted, this model wishes to avoid the idea that the world is God's body as well as the idea that God is alien to the world. In addition this model also wishes to avoid a mechanistic view of nature. It accomplishes all three aims by focusing on the Spirit in attempting to understand God's relationship to the world.

Moltmann argues that creation must be seen as an open system in which God as Spirit is always present, not as a closed causal system in which God occasionally intervenes. The Spirit pervades the whole of the world such that the

> whole creation is a fabric woven through by the efficacies of the Spirit. Through his Spirit God is also present in the very structures of matter. Creation contains neither spirit-less matter nor non-material spirit.[121]

This is because, as the efficacious power of the Triune God, the Spirit is directly involved in creation (Genesis 1:2). As Hendry explains it, this is because it is the essence of God as Spirit to go outside of Godself, to become embodied, and to loose Godself. Creation is an open system because it is a product of the Spirit. Both creation and salvation are accomplished in the power of the Spirit, through the Son by the Father because it "is the mystery of Spirit that it looses itself in its opposite itself in its opposite, and fulfills itself by bringing its opposite to fulfillment in itself."[122] Creation is different from God, not as an alien other but as the product of the Spirit's self-emptying. And just as the world was created in the Spirit so it will be consummated in the Spirit as well.

While there are some differences of nuance between Moltmann and Hendry's views, differences which have not been mentioned here, both are able to argue for God's difference from creation and God's radical presence within it because each holds a dynamic, rather Hegelian view of the Trinity. Thus, this model overcomes dualism, which is the object of the feminist model, without holding that the world somehow is God's body (which seems to be a nonsensical idea), and it affirms God's real presence to creation, which was the goal of the process model, while not abandoning God's absoluteness. As we shall see in the third chapter, Rahner follows this same Trinitarian, dialectical path.

The Thesis of the Present Study

From this brief survey, it should be clear that the term ecological theology designates not simply a theology that attempts to come to some evaluation and appreciation of the natural world but a type of theological method, a genre of theology. I think that it is possible to say that each one of the figures mentioned in the preceding discussion would understand ecological theology not simply as involving a minor adjustment in the theological agenda to accommodate the inclusion of nature as a worthy object of concern. Rather, each would see ecological theology as a particular way of conceiving the theological task itself. As I understand this effort, this conception at least involves a rethinking of the three questions mentioned earlier.

In the chapters which follow an analysis will be undertaken of the ecological dimension of Rahner's theology. To facilitate this, these three questions will be put to Rahner and his answers will be elucidated as far as possible. The thesis which will guide this analysis is that while Rahner is not explicitly responding to the ecological crisis as are the figures just discussed, his theology is profoundly ecological in that he brings to each theological problem and issue a fundamental vision which sees all reality, God, the world, and human being, as interrelated. Working from a profoundly non-dualistic metaphysic rooted in an interpretation of the Incarnation, Rahner develops a thoroughly ecological position which can respond to the questions of how we should understand human being's relation to the world, God's relation to the world, and the place of the material world in the *ordo salutis*.

Notes

1. Romans 8:22-23. Unless otherwise noted, all scripture quotations in this work are taken from the New Revised Standard Version of the Bible, copyright 1989 by the division of Christian education of the National Council of Churches of Christ in the U.S.A.
2. R.G. Collingwood, *The Idea of Nature* (New York: Oxford University Press, 1960), 29.
3. Ibid., 73. See also p. 111.
4. Ibid., 6.
5. Ibid. 91.
6. Ibid., 5. Emphasis mine.

7. Torture was indeed an unfortunate metaphor. Nature has been forced to divulge many of her secrets and at the end of this century there are many who wish that she would take back a few.

8. See F. C. Copleston, *A History of Western Philosophy*, vol. IV (New York: Image Books, 1994), 121-123.

9. I am thinking here particularly of Richard Rorty, *Philosophy and the Mirror of Nature* (Princeton, NJ: Princeton University Press, 1980).

10. Jürgen Moltmann, *God in Creation: A New Theology of Creation and the Spirit of God*, trans. Margaret Kohl (San Francisco: Harper and Row, 1985), 27.

11. Langdon Gilkey, "The New Watershed in Theology," in *Society and the Sacred* (New York: Crossroad, 1981), 5. See also in the same volume "Religious Dilemmas of a Scientific Culture".

12. This point is effectively made by Claus Westermann in *Creation*, trans. John Scullion (Philadelphia: Fortress Press, 1974), 1-3.

13. Moltmann, *God in Creation*, 36.

14. H. Paul Santmire, *The Travail of Nature: The Ambiguous Ecological Promise of Christian Theology* (Philadelphia: Fortress Press, 1985), 4. Santmire is critical of this view and does not, as I do not, accept it as a correct reading of the biblical tradition.

15. This view is reflected, for example, by Hendrikus Berkhof, "God in Nature and History," in *God, History, and Historians: Modern Christian Views of History*, ed. C.T. MacIntyre (New York: Oxford University Press, 1977).

16. Lynn White, Jr. "The Historical Roots of Our Ecological Crisis," in *Ecology and Religion in History*, ed. David and Eileen Spring (New York: Harper and Row, 1974).

17. Gordon D. Kaufman, "A Problem for Theology: The Concept of Nature," *Harvard Theological Review* 65 (1972): 350. This same essay can be found in Kaufman's book *The Theological Imagination* (Philadelphia: Westminster Press, 1981).

18. Ibid., 354-355. For Kaufman's "reconstruction" of the concept of God in light of this thesis, see for example his book *Theology for a Nuclear Age* (Philadelphia: Westminster Press, 1985), 30-46.

19. Santmire, *The Travail of Nature*, 1-12.

20. Westermann, *Creation*, 54.

21. Ibid., 56. Westermann's discussion of this on 57-60 is helpful. Moltmann carries this view one step further by saying that not only does *imago dei* not refer to a human essence (the soul) but rather to the relationship between God and human beings, but also the *imago* presented in Genesis is incomplete and will achieve completion only in the kingdom of God, the completion of the *imago* having been accomplished proleptically in Christ. See Moltmann, *God in Creation*, 215-233.

22. Moltmann, *God in Creation*, 31. See also 276-296.

23. It is important to note that within the Christian tradition the doctrine of creation acquires a christological focus but that this does not make it any less theocentric. One of the implications of the doctrine of the Trinity is that theocentricity and christocentricity can not be seen as opposites because Jesus

Christ *is* the Word of the Father (John 1:1-2) and it is *through* him that all things were created (John 1:3). Colossians 1:16 goes even further than this in affirming that "all things have been created *through* him and *for* him" (emphasis mine). Christ is the purpose for which creation has been made and this means that creation can only be really understood in light of God's ultimate purpose. Creation can not be seen only in the light of human purposes and to do so is the essence of what the Bible calls sin.

24. For a helpful exposition of Israel's "creation faith," see three essays by Bernard W. Anderson, "The Earth is the Lord's," "Biblical Perspectives on the Doctrine of Creation," and "Human Dominion Over Nature" in his book *From Creation to New Creation* (Philadelphia: Fortress Press, 1994).

25. Claus Westermann, *Blessing: In the Bible and in the Life of the Church*, trans. Keith Crim (Philadelphia: Fortress Press, 1975), 4.

26. James Rimbach, "All Creation Groans: Theology/Ecology in Saint Paul," *Asia Journal of Theology* 1 (1987): 389.

27. For a helpful "ecological reading" of the biblical tradition, see Santmire, *The Travail of Nature*, 189-218. See also Frank Moore Cross, "The Redemption of Nature," *The Princeton Seminary Bulletin* 10 (1989).

28. For a critique of White's position, see Robin Attfield, "Christian Attitudes Toward Nature," *Journal of the History of Ideas* 44 (1983).

29. Kaufman, "The Concept of Nature: A Problem for Theology," 353.

30. Ibid., 351.

31. Sallie McFague, *Models of God: Theology for an Ecological, Nuclear Age* (Philadelphia: Fortress Press, 1987), 19.

32. Ibid., 64.

33. Ibid., 65.

34. Langdon Gilkey, "God," in *Christian Theology: An Introduction to Its Tasks and Traditions*, Second Edition, ed. Peter C. Hodgson and Robert H. King (Philadelphia: Fortress Press, 1985), 95.

35. Martin Heidegger, "The Question Concerning Technology," in *Martin Heidegger: Basic Writings*, ed. David Farrell Krell (New York: Harper and Row, 1977), 295.

36. Ibid., 308.

37. Ibid., 309.

38. Morris Berman, *The Reenchantment of the World* (Ithaca, NY: Cornell University Press, 1981), 70.

39. This, in my opinion, points to one of the serious weaknesses of radical constructivist positions such a s Kaufman's. He seems to think that the right (and by this I take him to mean "useful" rather than true) concept of God will lead to right human action. But, on Kaufman's view, if we know God to be one of our constructs will this right action really follow? In the final analysis I think that it is possible to raise the serious question of whether what Kaufman is doing can really be called Christian theology. For a more fully developed version of the later thesis, see Carl E. Braaten, *No Other Gospel: Christianity Among the World's Religions* (Philadelphia: Fortress Press, 1992), 15-28.

40. Albrecht Ritschl, *The Christian Doctrine of Justification and Reconciliation*, trans. H.R. MacIntosh (Clifton, NJ: Reference Book Publishers, 1966), 191.

41. William French, "Subject Centered and Creation Centered Paradigms in Recent Catholic Thought," *Journal of Religion* 70 (January, 1990): 49.

42. Johannes Baptist Metz, *Theology of the World*, trans. William Glen-Doepel (New York: Seabury, 1969), 58.

43. John B. Cobb, *Process Theology as Political Theology* (Philadelphia: Westminster Press, 1982), 125.

44. French, "Subject Centered and Creation Centered Paradigms in Recent Catholic Thought," 65.

45. It should be noted that Wingren's analysis deals primarily with Protestant theologians and that his views are influenced by a long standing interest in Irenaeus whom he regards as the first Christian theologian of creation.

46. Gustav Wingren, *Creation and Gospel* (New York: The Edwin Mellen Press, 1979), 33.

47. Ibid., 34.

48. Gustav Wingren, *The Flight From Creation* (Minneapolis, MN: Augsburg Press, 1971), 51.

49. Ibid., 20.

50. Karl Barth, *Dogmatics in Outline*, trans. G.T. Thomson (London: SCM Press, 1949), 52. Emphasis mine.

51. George S. Hendry, *Theology of Nature* (Philadelphia: Westminster Press, 1980), 25. For an assessment of Barth's theology in terms of its ecological dimension (or lack of one), see Santmire, *The Travail of Nature*, 146-155.

52. Ibid., 37. See also 72.

53. Karl Barth, *Church Dogmatics*, III/1, trans. J.W. Edwards, O. Bussey, and Harold Knight, ed. G.W. Bromily and T.F. Torrance (Edinburgh: T and T Clark, 1958), 3, 31.

54. F.D.E. Schleiermacher, *The Christian Faith*, trans. and ed. H.R. Mackintosh and J.S. Stewart (Philadelphia: Fortress Press, 1928), 126. Emphasis mine.

55. Ibid., 127.

56. Ibid., 149.

57. Ibid. 427.

58. Ibid., 734-735.

59. Helpful for understanding the varieties of ecological theology are William M. Thompson, "Dappled and Deep Down Things: A Meditation on Christian Ecological Trends," *Horizons* 14 (1987) and Georges Wieruz Kowalski, "*Theologie de la Nature, Theologie de la Creation*," *Reserches de science religieuse* 72 (1984). For insight into problems faced by this kind of theology, see Jürgen Moltmann, "The Ecological Crisis: Peace With Nature," *Scottish Journal of Theology* 2 (1981) and *Evangelische Theologie* (Jan-Feb, 1977), the entire issue of which is devoted to the subject of nature as a theological issue.

60. I am using the term *ordo salutis* in an unconventional way and, thus, need to explain this usage. In conventional usage this term refers to the pattern of the process by which an individual passes from the state of sin to final salvation. There are, obviously, different accounts of this process. As I will use it in this

study, the term has a somewhat broader meaning. I use it to indicate the process by which God's salvation is realized in the *entire created order*, not simply in individual human lives. Rahner himself does not employ this term in this way. He does, however, use the terms "order of creation" and "order of redemption" and argues that the latter completely embraces the former. (This will be discussed in the fourth chapter.) I use *ordo salutis* in this broader sense to reflect Rahner's position.

61. Rosemary Ruether, *New Woman, New Earth* (New York: Seabury Press, 1975), 204.

62. Dorothee Söelle, with Shirley Cloyes, *To Work and to Love: A Theology of Creation* (Philadelphia: Fortress Press, 1984), 73.

63. Ibid. 72.

64. Ibid., 104.

65. Ibid., 28.

66. Ibid., 103-104.

67. Ibid., 39-40.

68. Grace Jantzen, *God's World, God's Body* (Philadelphia: Westminster Press, 1984), 70.

69. Ibid., 19.

70. Ibid., 9.

71. Ibid., see especially 34.

72. Ibid., 56.

73. See Jantzen's explication, especially 67-131.

74. Ibid., 127.

75. C.S. Lewis, *A Grief Observed* (New York: Bantam Books, 1963), 76. See McFague, *Models of God*, 37.

76. McFague, *Models of God*, 49. See also 65. For her description of the monarchial model of God, see 64-65.

77. Ibid., 39.

78. Ibid., 40.

79. Ibid., 72-73, 78.

80. Ibid., 103-108.

81. Ibid., 110-111.

82. Ibid., 120.

83. Ibid., 135.

84. Ibid., 165.

85. John Cobb, *Is It Too Late?: A Theology for Ecology* (Beverly Hills, CA: Bruce Publishing, 1972), 81.

86. John Cobb and David Ray Griffin, *Process Theology: An Expository Introduction* (Philadelphia: Westminster Press, 1976), 76.

87. Jay B. McDaniel, *Of God and Pelicans: A Theology of Reverence for Life* (Lousiville, KY: Westminster/John Knox, 1989), 76. See McDaniel's discussion of intrinsic value, 61-65.

88. Cobb, *Is It Too Late?*, 115.

89. John Cobb, *A Christian Natural Theology* (Philadelphia: Westminster Press, 1965), 195.

90. John Cobb, *God and the World* (Philadelphia: Westminster Press, 1965), 39.

91. McDaniel, *Of God and Pelicans*, 28. The process concern is to deny that God is external to the world and acts upon it from "outside". Thus, Cobb says that "God pervades the world and is manifest in all its parts." Cobb, *God and the World*, 80.

92. See Cobb, *God and the World*, 49-58.

93. McDaniel, *Of God and Pelicans*, 35-36.

94. Ibid., 143-144.

95. Cobb and Griffin, *Process Theology*, 61.

96. Albert C. Fritsch, *Renew the Face of the Earth* (Chicago: Loyola University Press, 1987), 29-30.

97. Pierre Teilhard de Chardin, *The Divine Milieu* (New York: Harper and Row, 1968), 106.

98. Ibid., 67. Emphasis Teilhard's.

99. Ibid.

100. John Carmody, *Ecology and Religion: Toward A New Christian Theology of Nature* (New York: Paulist Press, 1983), 72.

101. Teilhard, *The Divine Milieu*, 61; 123-124.

102. Teilhard does not use this metaphorical biblical language but it does express what he intends to say.

103. Teilhard, *The Divine Milieu*, 112.

104. Carmody, *Ecology and Religion*, 120.

105. Ibid., 125.

106. Ibid., 154.

107. Ibid., 122.

108. Moltmann, *God in Creation*, 13.

109. Jürgen Moltmann, *The Trinity and the Kingdom*, trans. Margaret Kohl (San Francisco: Harper and Row, 1981).

110. Jürgen Moltmann, *The Future of Creation*, trans. Margaret Kohl (Philadelphia: Fortress Press, 1979), 82.

111. Moltmann, *God in Creation*, 1.

112. Moltmann, *The Future of Creation*, 73.

113. Hendry, *Theology of Nature*, 206. Moltmann, *God in Creation*, 39.

114. Moltmann, *God in Creation*, 93, 66.

115. Ibid., 54-56.

116. Ibid., 118, 121.

117. Ibid., 70.

118. Ibid., 51.

119. See Moltmann's discussion of this in *God in Creation*, 215-227.

120. Hendry, *Theology of Nature*, 217.

121. Moltmann, *God in Creation*, 212.

122. Hendry, *Theology of Nature*, 171.

...the free spirit [human being] becomes, and must become, sensibility in order to be spirit, and thus expose itself to the whole destiny of this earth.[1]

Chapter 2

The Human Being: The Worldly Spirit

This chapter is an inquiry into Karl Rahner's understanding of the human being's relationship to the world. It is undertaken with the conviction that *what* he says about this subject is just as important as *why* he says it. We are interested in his metaphysical vision and the way in which this shapes Rahner's understanding of the relationship between human being and the world. Thus, this inquiry will concern itself to some degree with Rahner's metaphysics of knowledge and his metaphysical (essential) anthropology, though it by no means is a treatise on either of these two subjects. The procedure of this chapter will be to examine three of Rahner's major works which deal with our topic and to introduce collateral material when appropriate. It is hoped that by the conclusion of this inquiry a fairly clear portrait of Rahner's account of human being as a worldly spirit will have emerged.

Spirit in the World

Spirit in the World is deserving of close attention although what will be said here about this work can not be thought to constitute anything near a thorough study.[2] This work deserves close attention because in an important sense it is the key to all of Rahner's later writings. *Spirit in the World* was presented as Rahner's doctoral dissertation in philosophy in 1936 at Freiburg University. It was not approved because Rahner's supervisor Martin Honecker, who held the chair of Catholic philosophy at Freiburg, thought it an incorrect interpretation of Aquinas, whose metaphysics of knowledge (*Erkenntnismetaphysik*) the dissertation sought to explore.[3] Rahner, who did not receive the doctorate in philosophy, published his dissertation in 1939 and it was slightly expanded and reworked, with Rahner's approval, by Johannes Metz, to be published again in 1957.[4] Our interest in this work will focus on the book's understanding of the relationship between the human being and the world, though a brief discussion of the whole argument of this very complex work and its intellectual background are certainly in order.

Spirit in the World takes the form of an extended consideration of Aquinas's *Summa Theologiae* Ia, question 84, article 7 where the subject under discussion is whether or not it is possible for the intellect to know anything thorough understanding without referring to the phantasm (sense experience). In other words, the question under consideration is whether or not human beings have intellectual intuition, whether they can know things *without* sense experience. Of course, Aquinas answers this question in the negative and then raises the further question of how, then, metaphysics is possible. Rahner's treatment of this deceptively brief Thomistic text is not a historical inquiry which attempts to say how Aquinas answered this question. Rather, Rahner attempts in *Spirit in the World* a *Wiederholung* (in the Heideggerian sense), a retrieval or a "saying what was left unsaid". The effort in this work is to go beyond what Aquinas says explicitly in order to recover the process of inquiry and to take it further. This may explain why many Thomists (Honecker for one) did not and do not consider Rahner's position to be truly Thomistic. It is impossible to speak of Rahner's approach to Aquinas in *Spirit in the World* without mentioning the book's unmentioned conversation partners who are Kant, Hegel, and Heidegger.[5] One's assessment of Rahner's position depends largely on one's assessment of these conversation partners and the desirability of speaking with them.

Transcendental Thomism

The position which Rahner articulates in *Spirit in the World* stands within an intellectual tradition which is known as Transcendental Thomism, a Thomism which attempts to take Kant and the "anthropological turn" (*anthropologische Wendung*) seriously while remaining loyal to a particular interpretation of Thomistic metaphysics. Joseph Donceel helpfully hits upon the central theme of Transcendental Thomism when he says that it

> centers its attention upon that power in man which keeps longing for more knowledge of, more intimacy with the utterly mysterious Absolute. It is the dynamic of his intellect and the corresponding striving of his will, it is that in him which makes him, as St. Thomas said after Aristotle, *quodammodo omnia*, as it were everything.[6]

To amend a phrase of Paul Ricoeur designating his own hermeneutical project, Transcendental Thomism may be thought of as a post-Hegelian return to Aquinas through Kant and Heidegger (!). Aquinas's phrase *quodammodo omnia* is crucial in that it expresses the Transcendental Thomist conviction that the mind is in potency *to the whole of reality*, that being is fundamentally knowable, and that the human mind is characterized by a dynamism toward being. This is not a dynamic of spirit or mind away from the world (or sense experience) but toward being *through* its relationship to the world, never leaving the world behind. The human being is spirit-in-the-world (to use a shower of Heideggerian hyphens) in that while the human being is always and inevitably related to the world, the human mind has always already transcended the objects of the world. To borrow a helpful metaphor from Donceel, we can say that for Transcendental Thomism the human mind "looks like a mighty dome lacking a keystone. Where the keystone should be there is a gaping hole, opening upon infinity."[7] We are, then, to see the human mind as being something like the dome of the Pantheon. Likewise, the "human mind affirms the existence of God somewhat as the Hudson River, if it were conscious, would affirm the existence of the Atlantic Ocean: by irresistibly flowing toward it."[8]

It is generally agreed that the origin of Transcendental Thomism is to be found in the work of the Belgian Jesuit Joseph Márechal (1878-1944) who was himself influenced by Maurice Blondel. Márechal was one of the first neo-Thomist philosophers to take Kant seriously and to comment upon him favorably--to his imperilment. Márechal set out to examine Kant's challenge to metaphysics in a work that was entitled *Le point de départ de la métaphysique* and which was to consist of six volumes (or *cahiers*, notebooks, as Márechal called them), but only the first, second, third and fifth of which were published in his lifetime, the fourth being published posthumously and the sixth never materializing at all. *Cahier* III is a surprisingly fair study of Kant while *Cahier* V, the most important for our purposes, is an attempt, as its title (*Le Thomisme devant la philosophie critique*) implies, to confront Thomism with the Kantian challenge to metaphysics.[9] In his attempt to refute Kant's claim that the mind does not know reality itself when it knows objects and to vindicate the Thomistic claim that in knowing human being reaches absolute reality implicitly, Márechal

> discovered that, despite the prevailing cosmocentric and objectivist mood of thought of St. Thomas, that thought contained elements which could be transposed without great difficulty into the anthropocentric and subjective approach of modern philosophy. Aquinas himself occasionally used the transcendental method, which Kant seemed to have introduced into philosophy. Thomism could only gain by becoming aware of this, its own component.[10]

In his *Critique of Pure Reason*, Kant had denied precisely what Márechal and Transcendental Thomism want to affirm, that the human mind has an openness to *being itself* and that this openness serves as the foundation or, to use Marechal's phrase, the point of departure, of metaphysics. Kant limited knowledge to that which had its foundation in a synthesis of phenomenal experience and the formal categories of reason (*Vernunft*) which organize that experience in an *a priori* way so that it is rendered intelligible. In arguing this point, Kant rejected the thoroughgoing empiricism and skepticism of Hume. Yet Kant did retain an empiricist emphasis in the sense that for him the *a priori* epistemological apparatus of the mind does not by itself produce any real knowledge but simply has a formal and regulative function. Sense experience remains crucial. Without the categories supplied by the mind sense experience would be blind and meaningless, but without sense experience knowledge would be empty of content. Yet for Kant what the human mind knows is greatly dependent upon its own *a priori* categories, so that knowledge is not a matter of knowing things as they are in themselves but of phenomenal experience of objects as organized by the categories which transcend experience and can thus be described as transcendental. The word transcendental takes on somewhat of a new meaning here in that in Kant the term designates that which precedes experience as its *condition of possibility*. In as much as Kant argued that knowledge of the world is dependent to a large extent upon what the human mind does with phenomenal experience, that what is in the mind is not simply a copy of what is "out there" but an *accomplishment* of the mind itself, he made an "anthropological turn".

Kant was not quite the arid and dogmatic rationalist that some accounts make him out to be. While he argued that the categories which made knowledge possible could not be applied to an object transcending sense experience (and that the attempt to do so would simply result in a "transcendental illusion"), Kant acknowledged that the human mind is never content simply to confine itself to sense experience. Reason continually gives rise to the transcendental ideal, that is it seeks the all encompassing unity within which all possible experience is contained. For Kant, metaphysics and onto-theology have their roots in this natural but, from Kant's perspective, regrettable tendency. Sheehan helpfully observes that while Kant certainly denied that metaphysics exists as a science, he granted that it exits as a "natural disposition". For Márechal this was one of the many *aporiai* in the Kantian position. How could Kant accept the fact that the mind *inevitably* and *universally* sought that which was beyond phenomenal experience yet ignore this when coming to an understanding of what constitutes knowledge? Could Kant's position be not so much completely wrong (as most neo-Thomists maintained) bur rather *radically incomplete*? For Transcendental Thomism any complete account of the human being as knower will have to take into consideration the fact, acknowledged by Kant himself, that, in Kant's words, "human reason...proceeds impetuously, driven on by an inward need, to question...Thus in all men, as soon as their reason has become ripe for speculation, there always existed and will continue to exist some kind of metaphysics."[11] In this recognition of Kant's, Márechal saw Aquinas's view that the human mind is *quodammodo omnia*, in a certain way everything.

While it is not possible here to render a complete account of Márechal's critique of Kant, a few remarks along these lines need to be made. Márechal rejected Kant's agnosticism about knowing reality as it is in favor of the Thomistic teaching that being is ultimately knowable and that the intellect is in potency to being in its totality (and thus is *quodammodo omnia*). Intelligibility is a transcendental property of being so that whatever *can be* can be *known*. Indeed, for Thomism being and knowing ultimately coincide as can clearly be seen in the being of God. Because God is *actus purus*, pure *esse* with no *potencia*, God knows all things through God's own being, so that in God the act of being and the act of knowing coincide. Thus, knowledge is dependent upon the intensity of the knower's being. This view gives Transcendental Thomism a very different perspective on epistemology from that adopted by Kant and those who followed him. For Kant, objectivity was the norm of knowing. Knowing was a matter of the mind "in here" establishing a relationship with objects "out there". For Transcendental Thomism self-intuition is the norm of knowing. The knower's "object" is the knower's own being through which the knower knows in proportion to his or her own intensity of being. Knowing occurs because ultimately knower and known are one. In other words, knowledge occurs to the extent that the being of the known is immanent in the being of the knower.

Of course, human knowing is quite different from divine knowing. Márechal was not advocating an idealism but a Thomism which had a strong empiricist bent. In human beings knowledge and being do not coincide because humans are finite and always becoming. Because intensity of being determines a knower's power to know, and because human beings are finite, their knowledge is finite--but even for them the principle that being is potentially intelligible holds true. More about this point will be said later. For now, it can be said that Márechal accepted *on Thomist grounds* Kant's view that human beings do not possess intellectual intuition, that all human knowledge is mediate not immediate and that human beings do no know objects which transcend sense experience. In coming to this conclusion Márechal accepted the turn to the subject.

For Márechal human beings have knowledge not through intellectual intuition (immediate, without sense experience) but through affirmation (mediate, requiring sense experience). "Affirmation is the mode of objectification for a non-intuitive intelligence."[12] Human beings know objects through the medium of sense experience yet rise above this experience in concepts. In this going beyond experience what is known in experience is objectified and objectified because it is seen against the backdrop of a larger reality, *being itself.* The affirmation that *this* particular object *is what it is*, is possible only because the particular "this" is always already transcended and placed against the horizon of being itself. Márechal argued that this tendency of the mind to transcend particular things (each "this") in a dynamic toward the totality of being (as the horizon of knowledge) is the *condition of possibility* of knowledge as such and that Kant had mistakenly evaluated this dynamic as leading to "illusion". Put another way, the fact that the objects of the world never seem to exhaust the capacity of the intellect seems to vindicate for Márechal the Thomistic view that being is the ultimate (though formal) object of human knowledge against the Kantian restriction of human knowledge to phenomena.

Márechal's position was not another blind stumble into transcendental illusion. He did not claim that the human intellect was a jet that eventually left the runway of sense experience as soared into the clouds of a transcendental beyond. Absolute being never appears as an *object* for the human intellect; it is never known directly but is only co-known with knowledge of the world and of worldly objects. The mind is neither a prisoner in the Kantian epistemological dungeon nor a metaphysical athlete capable of an ontological leap from sense experience to objective knowledge of being in general. Thus, Transcendental Thomism claims that there is explicit knowledge of God only in revelation and even this knowledge is limited because it must conform to the categories of the human mind if it is to be understood. Yet, outside of revelation, God is known *implicitly* in each act of knowledge as that towards which all knowledge is finally oriented. A good shorthand way to characterize the position of Transcendental Thomism on this question is to say that for it human beings are *capax Dei* because they are *capax entis*. Márechal's conclusions help explain why the phrase "metaphysics of knowledge" has been used in connection with Thomist epistemology. For Aquinas and Transcendental Thomism epistemology is inevitably a metaphysics of knowledge because human knowledge is inevitably knowledge of being, even if only implicitly.

One final word needs to be said about Márechal's critique of Kant. Perhaps his greatest achievement was to replace Kant's essentially static understanding of the mind with a dynamic one.[13] The fact that Hegel had done just this does not diminish Márechal's accomplishment. This dynamism has already been hinted at in our discussion. Aquinas understands the intellect as in potency for being as such and Márechal argues that the whole process of human knowing is borne along by a dynamic in which the intellect seeks to actualize this potency. It is impossible to understand human knowledge without taking into account this ontological dynamism. The existence of this dynamism makes it possible to argue that God could not be merely a postulate of practical reason because a

> real dynamism demands that its goal or term also be real. It follows therefore that, if the mind's real striving toward the Infinite Absolute is one of the *a priori* conditions of the speculative reason's objective judgments, God's real existence is an *a priori* condition of possibility for any categorial judgment of the speculative reason...far from showing that the idea of God is merely a regulative ideal for speculative reason, a transcendental reflection on human knowledge manifests that God's real existence is an *a priori* condition of possibility for any speculative judgment whatsoever.[14]

"Metaphysics"

I hope that this brief discussion of Transcendental Thomism has brought out what is, for our purposes here, one of its major features. Transcendental Thomism insists that for human beings God and the world are not opposites and that human beings are inevitably and intrinsically related to both. Furthermore, each conditions (from the human standpoint) the other. Being in general as the ultimate *telos* of the human spirit makes knowledge of the world possible and there can be knowledge of being in general only through knowledge of the world. When Transcendental Thomism speaks of spirit it does not mean a worldless or immaterial ghost. Spirit is not the opposite of the world but is always, as has been noted, *spirit-in-the-world.*

As has been mentioned, Rahner's *Spirit in the World* attempts to discuss how metaphysics is possible given the fact that human knowledge is inevitably sense knowledge. As in Márechal's *Cahier* V, we have here Thomism confronting critical philosophy and the claim being made that the turn to the subject is not foreign to Aquinas. It might help to begin our discussion where Rahner ends his, that is with an attempt to say what metaphysics is. This subject was implicitly raised when Márechal's approach to being in general was discussed earlier but the subject now deserves explicit consideration.

In taking the anthropological turn, Transcendental Thomism also produced a refashioned version of metaphysics which is very much reflected in Rahner's work. For Rahner, metaphysics is not, to use Sheehan's phrase, "news from nowhere". It is not a vision from another world or knowledge of objects beyond this world such as God. The "more" (*meta*) of *metaphysics* is not the more of a non-sensible world. Rahner wishes to argue that there is metaphysical knowledge of a kind which does know God implicitly but that God, as Márechal insisted, is never an object in the usual sense of this term, and that this is why no concept of God is ever adequate.[15] Rahner's approach to metaphysics can best be characterized by saying that it

> promises to deliver no intuitions of pure being, no secular beatific vision of *esse qua esse*. If it makes any claim to be universal, necessary knowledge of a "more", it either will claim that this is already operative in man's worldly knowledge, bereft of intellectual intuition, or will give up or modify the claim.[16]

Rahner's approach to metaphysics reflects the emphasis of Kant that one can not speak about knowledge without speaking about the knower (the human being), recognizing that the *knower* determines *apriori* what can be known, and the emphasis of Heidegger that one can not separate metaphysics from the being who inevitably asks the metaphysical question--human being (*Dasein*).[17] Ontology is metaphysical (essential) anthropology. The human being "exists as the question about being" and the question "is the 'must' which he himself *is* and in which being as that which is questioned presents and affirms itself, and at the same time, as that which withdraws itself."[18]

In *Spirit in the World*, following Márechal, Rahner is concerned to show that the question of the possibility of metaphysics is inseparable from the question of how human beings know anything at all. To inquire into the conditions of possibility of knowledge (to engage in transcendental questioning) is inevitably to have to deal with metaphysics. Rahner takes this position because in his interpretation this is the position taken by Aquinas. The "point of departure" for the question of metaphysics is the question of human knowing or, to put it another way, "a metaphysical realm manifests itself through the light of the intellect."[19] What this means is that "metaphysics is only the reflexive elaboration of all human knowledge as ground, which as such is already and always posited simultaneously in this knowledge from the outset."[20] And what is posited simultaneously with all human knowledge from the outset, that which makes knowledge possible, is an *implicit knowledge of being itself.* Yet, metaphysics has the character of an *anticipation* of being rather than a *grasp* of it. This is the thesis which *Spirit in the* World undertakes to demonstrate by transcendental deduction. The question of how human beings have any knowledge of the world is inseparable from the question of metaphysics because

> the light of the intellect is given first of all only and exclusively as a condition of the possibility of physics, of the science which has to do with "mobile being", hence with the quiddities of material being. But this means that the light of the intellect can be shown to be the opening up of the metaphysical realm only by showing that it is only as such a disclosure that it can be the condition of the possibility of physics.[21]

In other words, the realm of metaphysics is open to human beings not as they leave the world but only as they are *in the world* and as they reflect upon their experience *of the world*. For Rahner, it makes no sense to speak of confining one's intellectual interests to the "real world of the here and now" because human knowing always already has transcended that world though it always begins with it. Yet, it also makes no sense to speak of knowing a purely spiritual realm because transcendence is available to human beings only through their experience of the world. Thus,

> God shines forth only in the limitless breadth of the pre-apprehension [*Vorgriff*], in the desire for being as such by which every act of man is borne, and which is at work not only in his ultimate knowledge and his ultimate decisions, but also in the fact that the free spirit becomes, and must become, sensibility in order to be spirit, and thus expose itself ot the whole destiny of this earth.[22]

Having glimpsed Rahner's conclusions, we will now look briefly at how he comes to them because this reveals a great deal about his understanding of the human being's relationship to the world.

Knowing as the Self-Presence of Being

It has already been noted that for Transcendental Thomism being and knowing are an original unity and that this view is based on the Thomistic teaching that whatever can be can be known. The fundamental determination of being is being-able-to-be-known; knowledge is the self-presence of being (*Erkennen is Beisichsien des Seins*).[23] A being knows and is knowable to the extent that it is self-present (*Beisichsein*) which means that knowledge is a function of a being's intensity of being (*Seinsmochtigkeit*). Of course, as has been noted, this is eminently the case with God.

But human beings are not God in that their being is not being in its fullness and, thus, they are not completely self-present. This is simply a way of saying that human beings are finite and that their knowledge is radically different from God's. Human finitude is seen in the fact that human beings *ask about being* (the metaphysical question); for human beings being is inevitably questionable (*Fragbarkeit*). Human beings ask after being because they are not completely present to it, yet the fact that they do ask after it indicates that they are always already present to being in some way. This is why metaphysics is inevitable. The fact that human beings are finite creatures yet also have an anticipatory (*vorgriefenden*) knowledge of being is an indication of their place in reality: "Man is the mid-point suspended between the world and God, between time and eternity".[24]

What does this tell us about human beings as knowers? It tells us, most importantly, that human beings are neither purely spiritual nor purely corporeal. (Rahner does not understand the difference between these two terms in a dualistic way, as we shall see.) This means that the human being is not "a ghost in a machine or an angel in an animal, and his 'faculties' of intellection and sensation cannot be understood by investigating, respectively, pure spirit or beasts."[25]   To use the conceptuality of *Beisichsein* (self-presence), the human being must be neither completely self-present (as God is) nor completely self-absent (as a thing of no self-consciousness is) but rather must be characterized, to use Sheehan's phrase, by the term "pres-ab-sence".   Human being *is* a continual movement between relative self-presence and relative self-absence, a movement stretching toward being in its fullness though never attaining it. This means that human being is fundamentally *kinetic* in that it is always involved in a stretching-ahead-of-self (*Sichvorstrecken*).[26] For a position which operates within a Thomistic framework, the ontological fact that a being is neither completely self-present nor completely self-absent can only mean that such a being is dependent on sense experience for its knowledge, yet in its knowing there is always a "more"; such a being would attain the self-presence that it does *through its self-absence*. For Aquinas the faculty of self-presence is the intellect while the faculty of self-absence is sensibility. One of the major concerns of *Spirit in the World* is to discern the relationship between these two faculties.

Sensibility

Rahner first examines sensibility, the faculty through which human being is *praesentia mundi*. In doing so he makes it clear that any philosophy (and *Spirit in the World* was a philosophy dissertation) which proceeds upon Thomistic presuppositions must rid itself of any "closet Platonism"--there can be no thought of innate ideas or intellectual intuition of non-sensible realities. There is only one knowing proper to human beings and this is a "knowing-presence-with-the-world" (*ein wissenden Bei-der-Welt-Sein*).[27] A being which is completely self-present does not need receptive knowledge of the world for such a being (God) knows all thing through its very being. Human being, not being completely self-present, does need receptive knowledge of the world and this is sensibility and sensibility means corporeality:

> Therefore, if there is to be any knowledge at all of another as the fundamental and first knowledge, if the world is to be the first and only intuition of man, the human intuition must be sensible, the being of the one intuiting must be the being of the other, of matter.[28]

Although I simply present Rahner's conclusion here, he comes to it through a transcendental deduction. The world is the human being's proper environment ("proper object" in Thomas's language) and this, for Rahner, is not a temporary arrangement but remains the case, as we shall see in the fifth chapter), even after death.

Through sensibility the human being is given over to the world in the mode of *receptivity*. As sensible, human being is a being-with-the-other rather than a being who is self-present. This is an ontological fact and one of the conditions of possibility for human knowledge as such. The world is open to human being only through sensibility, that is, the body and its senses.

Intellect

If sensibility were the only faculty of knowledge, the human being would be incapable of any self-presence, which means incapable of judgment and objective knowledge. It can not be that the human being is simply given over in total abandonment (*Verlorenheit*) to the world, for this being does return to itself through intellect and sets itself against the world as a subject. It is in this return (*reditio in se ipsum*) that human knowledge finds its fulfillment (*Vollzug*) and attains a degree of self-presence (*Insischselberstandigkeit*) or self-possessed existence. The intellect is the faculty through which the human being stands in *oppositio mundi*.

If "human knowledge is objective reception (*Hinnahme*) of the other, of the world," then intellect must be understood as the condition of possibility of rendering "reception of the world" (in sensibility) objective.[29] In other words, sensibility only renders the world in terms of "this thing" and it is only through the operation of the intellect (the agent intellect to be precise) that each "this" is known in terms of "what". The agent intellect is the faculty of the one human intellect which renders the phantasm (sense experience) *intelligible*. For Aquinas intelligibility involves the liberation (Rahner's word is *Loslosung*) of form from matter whereby the *species sensibilis*, the phantasm, becomes *species intellibilis*. Objective knowledge occurs when a "this" is known under the aspect of universality as a "what". What is the condition of possibility for the agent intellect's abstracting the universal from the particular of the phantasm and of the intellect's knowing the particular under the form of the universal?

Rahner's answer to this question occupies a lengthy chapter and is arrived at through a series of transcendental deductions. The answer is based on Aquinas's view that, according to Rahner, every "judgment attains to *esse*, mediately or immediately...or, expressed more precisely, to what really exists, to *ens*."[30] The condition of possibility of knowing the universal is that the intellect always already surpasses the particular of sensibility and thus the particular is known to be a *limited particular*, one of many possible instances of a single "what" or *universal*. Rahner argues that in Aquinas there is an *excessus ad esse* which means that the intellect always already surpasses particular objects in the world because it tends toward being in general. For Aquinas, while all human knowledge is based on the phantasm the *formal* object of human knowledge is being itself. The *excessus ad esse* is the condition of possibility of any human knowledge whatsoever. Rahner refers to this *excessus* as "pre-apprehension" or "anticipation" (*Vorgriff*) of being and characterizes it as the "movement of spirit towards the whole of its [intellect's] possible object, for it is only in this way that the limitation of the individual known can be experienced."[31] It is for this reason that any inquiry into the condition of possibility of human knowledge must deal with metaphysics.

It needs to be mentioned again that the anticipation (*Vorgriff*) of being is not a grasping of being itself. Being is only present to human being as a *horizon within which all objects appear*; being in general does not appear itself as one of those objects. This means that human knowledge is never completely fulfilled and always remains a "striving after". In human beings being as such never attains complete self-presence. And God as Being Itself is not known as an object but is only *implicitly* and *simultaneously* affirmed (*implicite metbejaht*) with knowledge of objects within the world. Thus, the *Vorgriff*, the *excessus ad esse*, is not a grasp but an *anticipation*. The theological consequences of this position were mentioned in our discussion of Márechal and it is worth noting that Rahner incorporates Márechal's position into his own. In every act of knowledge the existence of an Absolute Being is affirmed along with knowledge of the world because (1) the horizon of the anticipation is the totality of the possibly real and (2) the affirmation of any particular being implies affirmation of the Being on which it is actually dependent. Therefore, it is in

> this sense, but only in this sense, [that] it can be said: the pre-apprehension [*Vorgriff*] attains to God. Not as though it attains to the Absolute Being immediately in order to represent it objectively in its own self but because the reality of God as that of absolute *esse* is implicitly affirmed simultaneously by the breadth of the pre-apprehension, by *esse commune*.[32]

The Conversion to the Phantasm

It should now be clear in what sense metaphysics is possible and necessary for Rahner. It should also be clear that in knowing, even in metaphysics, the world is never left behind. This point is reinforced when Rahner discusses Aquinas's concept of *conversio ad phantasma*. If in sensibility the human being is self-absent and in intellect is partially self-present, then the concept of *conversio ad phantasma* designates the fact that the one human knowing is constituted by both *simultaneously*. Human being is bivalent in that intellection (the spiritual faculty) and sensibility (the corporeal faculty) are two moments of one process:

> Our being with the here and now of the individual things of the world through sensibility is of such a nature that as such and in its concrete possibility it is already and always being with being in its totality through intellect, and vice versa.[33]

Conversio ad phantasma means that human knowledge is always knowledge of the world but that *within* this knowledge there is inevitably a "more"; it "is the term designating the fact that sense intuition and intellectual thought are united in the *one* human knowledge".[34] The human process of knowing is a spiritual-sensible unity:

> The conversion to the phantasm is not merely a turning of the spirit to sensibility which is logically prior to the actual knowledge of the universal and makes it possible, but is precisely that movement of the spirit in which the sensible content [sensible species] is informed, as it were, by the a priori structures of the spirit, by its "light" [intelligible species], that is, is seen within the absolute being which the spirit pre-apprehends, and is thereby known in its universality. Abstraction and conversion to the phantasm are two sides of the one power.[35]

The Self-Realization of Spirit

In attempting to answer the question of how metaphysics is possible given that all human knowledge is inevitably sense knowledge, Rahner offers some important indications of how human beings are related to the world. Thus far we have seen that the human being's relation to the world as a knower is essential in that all human knowledge is fundamentally knowledge of the world. The world is the human being's proper environment in that human knowledge finds its fulfillment (relative self-presence) through the world, through sensibility. In discussing the *conversio ad phantasma* we have come upon one of Rahner's most important emphases, the desire to understand things in their unity. Rahner is pushing toward seeing the spiritual and the corporeal dimensions of knowing as two moments of one unified process. The world view which emerges from *Spirit in the World* is thus profoundly non-dualistic. This fact will become even more clear when we examine more closely the relationship between sensibility and intellect.

Because human being is not completely self-present, it is fundamentally potential being. While the human intellect is *quodammodo omnia*, in potency to all being, it must have sensibility to *realize* this potential. Using a term from Aristotle and Aquinas, Rahner says that in a sense the human intellect as a whole can be fundamentally characterized as *possible intellect* in that this intellect "is present to itself [only] in the knowledge of the other".[36] Human knowing requires the other of the world to realize itself. The human intellect is characterized by a dynamic, a striving (*Streben*) toward being in its fullness and this striving passes through and remains within the world. But this point has a wider application than to the human being as knower; human being itself is potential striving to realization, and the *telos* of this striving is being in general. It is upon this basis, this feature of metaphysical anthropology, that Rahner bases his conviction that anthropology must inevitably arrive at theology. The picture that emerges of human being from *Spirit in the World*, and is further developed in all of Rahner's later thought, is of a being who is *kinetic*, who is in the process of becoming. Thus, Rahner's anthropology is more precisely characterized as a doctrine of becoming-a-person (*Personwendung*). And just as human knowledge can not attain self-realization apart from the world, the same may be said of human being itself. While Rahner does not develop this theme fully in *Spirit in the World* (which, after all, was a study of Aquinas's metaphysics of knowledge), the groundwork is laid for an understanding of human being as radically relational.

In the discussion of the *conversio ad phantasma* it was noted that Rahner sought to understand intellect and sensibility as a unity by seeing them as two moments in one process. But more can be said about their relationship than this. Like Thomas, he thinks of spirit or intellect as ontologically, though not temporally, prior to sensibility. And yet spirit allows sensibility to emanate from itself *as an unfolding of its own potential.* Finite human spirit

> must produce sensibility, because in itself it is only desire (possible intellect). But insofar as it produces sensibility as a condition of its own

fulfillment, it retains it from the outset...as its power under the law of a pre-apprehension [*Vorgriff*] of *esse*.[37]

Thus, the necessity of the conversion to the phantasm rests on an ontological foundation, namely the nature of human being, a being whose relationship to the world is essential. Spirit produces sensibility for itself as is formal cause:

> The human spirit releases sensibility from itself in such a way that it has already and always gathered it in again also, and this in such a way that sensibility accomplishes its own work as that of spirit. Insofar as the spirit releases sensibility from itself as a faculty for itself, the spirit appears alongside sensibility, as it were, as a power different from and coordinate with it, and having its own foundation which, subsequently, so to speak, converges with the foundation of sensibility in the one human knowledge.[38]

For Rahner, it is impossible to think of finite spirit (human being) apart from the body and the world. There can be no return to the view in which the body is a (dispensable) container for the soul. Finite spirit always already produces sensibility by formal causation. Spirit and sensibility are not incidentally related because spirit produces sensibility *as another form of itself*. In the human being spirit is always already corporeal and the body always already spiritual.

Rahner's doctrine of *Personwendung* contains a radical insight, one which is crucial for the subject we are attempting to explore. As finite spirit, the body, matter, and the world are the things through which human beings find fulfillment and self-realization. This means that in "love [striving for God], as well as in knowledge, matter is not spirit's obstacle but its way to itself and to others, to all persons, including the infinite" and that human being is spirit only as spirit-becoming-in-matter so that

> matter is an essential part in the very becoming of man as spirit. Man is not first pure spirit who then becomes "finitized" by an unfortunately necessary relation to matter; man is first finite as spirit (material because finite, not finite because material) and thus can become at all only through matter.[39]

Spirit in the World lays the foundation for a metaphysical vision which takes seriously two inseparable aspects of human being--transcendence over the world and essential relatedness to it. This vision is non-dualistic and ecological in the sense that it strives to see reality as an interconnected whole.

A Word on Method

Before concluding this discussion of *Spirit in the World* it might be helpful to remark on Rahner's use of philosophy even though this does not directly bear on the chief interest of our inquiry. The person who reads *Spirit in the World* without theological commitments or without some commitment to Christian philosophy in the Thomist tradition may find it unsatisfactory and might misjudge Rahner's intentions. From Rahner's perspective, *Spirit in the World* is a work of philosophy but this does not mean that it is theologically neutral, theologically innocent, or a presuppositionless inquiry. Sheehan, who criticizes Rahner's ontology from a Heideggerian vantage point and maintains that what Rahner has achieved is the transformation of Aquinas's ousiological thinking into transcendental thinking, is, in my judgment, correct (in a certain way) in concluding that for all Rahner's "dedication to the transcendental turn and to the question of being, it [*Spirit in the World*] already knows the answers before it starts. It is, in the broadest sense, an 'apologetic work,' an exercise in *fides quarens intellectum*."[40]

The fact that Rahner seems to "know all the answers" before he starts does not make *Spirit in the World* a subterfuge; it is not a theological Trojan horse the purpose of which is to surreptitiously convey theological convictions past the defenses of the intellect in the guise of philosophy. As *Foundations of Christian Faith*, Rahner's only "systematic" work, makes clear, Rahner's intention is not to begin at a neutral starting point in search of answers to theological questions. Rather, he is concerned with the intellectual justification of faith, the use of philosophical arguments to justify theological claims.[41] This is not to say that the aim of Rahner's theological method is simply to justify whatever Christians believe or the Church teaches. The characterization of Rahner as a "Denziger theologian" is completely misguided.[42] Very often , Rahner's theological justifications have the result of transforming what he has just justified. The intellectual justification of faith is not the mere repetition of the content of faith.

This is not the place to dwell extensively on this issue, but a word does need to be said to defend Rahner against the charge of intellectual dishonesty, a charge implicit in Sheehan's comment. This is especially important in light of the fact that one of Rahner's central concerns is affirming the Christian faith in an intellectually honest way.[43] For Rahner, philosophy is a moment within theology in that the human being has a self-understanding *prior* to being addressed by revelation. Revelation does not come to a subject who is a *tabula rasa*, nor does revelation come as something completely discontinuous with or alien to human experience. Rahner's doctrine of grace will not allow this. (*Hearers of the Word*, which will be discussed next, attempts to deal with this issue.) Philosophy is "a previous, transcendental as well as historical self-comprehension of the man who hears the historical word of God."[44] This means that philosophy and theology can not refer to two completely separate forms of knowledge because both involve the one human subject who is always implicitly referred to God. Rahner takes the Thomist view that philosophy and theology must be seen on a continuum for which "revelation is the highest entelechy and norm of this knowledge [philosophy], unified in the unity of the one subject."[45] Revelation presupposes philosophy and is its complete fulfillment. Rahner's inquiry can proceed as it does in *Spirit in the World* with complete intellectual honesty despite the fact that as a "philosopher" he seems to "have all the answers in advance" because of his conviction that

> it is correct to say that in every philosophy man already engages inevitably and unthematically in theology, since one has no choice in the matter-- even when one does not know it consciously--whether he want to be pursued by God's revealing grace or not.[46]

These remarks, of course, do not set aside the whole of Sheehan's comments and are not intended to do so. They do, hopefully, at least suggest that the issue here is not Rahner's intellectual honesty but his concept of philosophy and whether "Christian philosophy" is a real possibility (Heidegger, for one, did not think that it was) and not simply a fabrication of theologians. This is an issue which can not be dealt with here.

Hearers of the Word

The problem addressed by *Hearers of the Word* was actually raised in *Spirit in the World*.[47] It has been noted that Rahner sees human transcendence (spirit) as being bound up with the world. If what he says about human knowing is true, that this knowing is essentially bound up with the human being's relation to the world and is always a knowing-in-and-through-the-world, this has profound implications for understanding God's revelation to human beings. Revelation can not be the momentary transportation of the human subject to an otherworldly beyond. Thus, Rahner concludes *Spirit in the World* by arguing that

In order to be able to hear whether God speaks, we must know that he is; lest His word come to one who already knows, He must be hidden from us; in order to speak to man, *His word must encounter us where we already and always are, in an earthly place, at an earthly hour.*[48]

The question is, then, that of how the human being, who is a spirit that realizes itself in the world and through the world and whose relationship to the world is, therefore, essential and not extrinsic, can be understood to be a recipient of God's revelation, a "hearer of the word".

Metaphysical Anthropology

For our purposes what is most interesting about this work is the way in which Rahner develops the anthropology outlined by *Spirit in the World*. The anthropology worked out there is metaphysical or essential anthropology. The transcendental method is used here to deduce the essential features which contstitue human being as such. Such an anthropology, in Rahner's rendering, reveals that the human being must be understood as a being who is open to and searches for revelation and that there are conditions under which revelation must occur if the human being is to "hear" it. While it is not necessary to recapitulate the metaphysical anthropology in its totality, it can be said that for Rahner

> man is the existent thing, possessing a spirituality that is receptive and open to history, who stands in freedom and as freedom before the God of possible revelation which, if it occurs, appears in his history (as the supreme actualization of that history) *in the word.* Man is the one who listens in his history for the word of the free God. Only this is what he must be. Metaphysical anthropology has thus reached its conclusion when it has comprehended itself as the metaphysics of a *potentia oboedientialis* for the revelation of the supernatural God.[49]

Or, to put it another way, Rahner's task is to show that no understanding of the human being is adequate which does not recognize the presence of a *potentia oboedientialis* for revelation in the human being. As Rahner understands it, this effort is philosophical (in the sense just discussed) and not a theological one; he characterizes *Hearers of the Word* as a "philosophy of religion" not as a work of theology. Within Rahner's Thomistic framework this is completely understandable. Within this framework, a philosophy of religion can argue that the human being is *a priori* and essentially disposed toward divine revelation and can discuss the transcendental conditions under which revelation can occur and can argue these points on properly philosophical grounds. For Rahner, the integrity of philosophy is not compromised when it is used to serve theological ends for reasons just mentioned. In this service "philosophy will not attempt to do anything but philosophize...precisely by doing so it will become a *praeparatio evangelii* and lead beyond itself" and it "does away with itself by working itself out in its own field and destroying its own title to be the first existential rationale of human existence"--which means that philosophy "dispenses with itself by elevating itself to a higher plane".[50]

Perhaps yet another way to understand this work is to say that it represents a piece of what Rahner calls "formal and fundamental theology". Such a theology is formal in that it "works out the 'formal' and permanent structures of saving history (basic relationship between God and creation; general concept of personal revelation in word and deed; concept of redemptive revelation)" and fundamental in that "it presents these formal categories as means to the understanding of saving history".[51] Formal and fundamental theology is not theology proper in that it does not deal with the *content* or revelation but discusses the formal conditions under which the content of revelation must be understood.

Rahner clarifies the aim of his metaphysical anthropology by distinguishing it negatively from two influential theological positions which he identifies as two "Protestant philosophies of religion". The first position maintains that revelation is the objectification of what is already present in the human being; the content of revelation is actually the "natural, non-historical religious structure of man himself".[52] Rahner maintains that Schleiermacher is the exemplar of this view. (Actually, it might be more fair to attribute this view to someone like Schubert Ogden than to Schleiermacher.) The second position holds that revelation is completely unexpected and *beyond expectation*. While he does not mention any names here, Rahner is clearly thinking of Barth. Rahner agrees with Barth that the *content* or revelation can in no way be anticipated by human beings, because this would limit God's freedom of self-disclosure. Yet he in no way shares Barth's (and Kierkegaard's) contempt for the "religious *a priori*". In denying that the human being has a fundamental openness to revelation, Barth ignored an essential feature of the human being. Thus, while Rahner is not unsympathetic to Barth, he finds that the latter's theology is built on faulty foundations. Rahner's rejection of these two types of "Protestant philosophy of religion" reveals a great deal about his own project and his reasons for their rejection derive directly from *Spirit in the World*. In Rahner's view, it can not be that

"God is either the inner meaning and possibility of the world and no more ["Schleiermacher"] or the sheer contradiction of man and his world ["Barth"]."[53] The human being's essential relatedness to the world in sense experience and corporeality means that God's self-disclosure can never be known in advance because God is not a worldly object. On the other hand, the human being's transcendence in *Vorgriff* is a transcendence toward being as such, a transcendence which anticipates, without possessing, being in its fullness or God. As has been noted, the human being for Rahner is *capax dei* because this being is *capax entis*.

Two particular features of Rahner's metaphysical anthropology are relevant to this inquiry. His understanding of human freedom and his understanding of human historicity both help elaborate a definite understanding of the human being's relation to the world.

Human Freedom

In discussing the kinetic nature of human being it was noted that this being is in the process of becoming, of realizing itself. It was also noted that this self-realization is inseparable from the world, that finite spirit realizes itself in the body and the body's relation to the world. In *Hearers of the World*, Rahner radicalizes this insight. This radicalization is partly due to the fact that his understanding of freedom undergoes some development. In *Spirit in the World* Rahner understands freedom mainly in cognitive terms. (This, of course, is understandable given the nature of the work.) Because of the *Vorgirff* human being transcends particular objects in the world and thus is not simply immersed in them. This fact is the foundation of human freedom and objective knowledge through which is effected the return to self. Freedom is considered here largely in terms of the *realization of human knowledge* in knowledge of the world through concepts. Rahner develops this further by exploring the way in which freedom is the self-realization of the *human being as such*. Freedom is not to be understood in terms of discrete acts which accomplish this or that, but rather in terms of the "fulfillment of one's own nature, a taking possession of oneself...a coming to oneself, a self-presence in oneself."[54] In each free act the person enacts his or her existence in a certain way so that the self is the cumulative product of its free acts. This means that morality is far more that a matter of doing this or that good or bad act; it is a matter of *becoming good or bad*. Theologically speaking, with each concrete action the human being either draws closer or moves away from God.

Knowledge Fulfilled in Love

This radicalization is also due to the fact that Rahner develops his concept of knowledge in *Hearers of the Word*. Because of its cognitive orientation, *Spirit in the World* tends to portray the intellect as a neutral faculty. In addition to this, human transcendence is seen as "automatic" and self-sustaining. *Hearers of the Word* works a moving beyond this position. Human transcendence in knowing is never automatic or self-sustaining because the character of this transcendence is shaped by human volition. Human transcendence is shaped decisively by the human being's decision to accept or reject his or her own existence in the world. The fundamental decision to affirm existence or to not affirm it is possible both because human beings are free and because, despite the fact that human existence and the world exist apart from our individual decisions with regard to them, there is a *contingency* about human existence in that it *need not be at all*. The absoluteness of the world must derive from the fact that it is a creation of God and its contingency must be due to the fact that it is a *free creation* of God; God need not have created it.

How is it possible to affirm human existence and the world and not regard them as alien things imposed upon us? Creation is a free, personal (and continuing) act and it can only be affirmed in the way that any such act can be affirmed--through love. The affirmation of such an act

> happens when one tries to understand the free action of the other not after it has already been carried out, but when one takes part in the performing itself, or by ratifying it lets it, as it were, emerge from oneself.[55]

It is impossible, Rahner says, to understand human existence and the world from an objective standpoint. Only as the human being ratifies his or her individual existence and that of the world by affirming them as belonging essentially to him or herself, can one really *know* one's existence and that of the world. It is at this point that we can see in what direction Rahner's understanding of knowledge has developed. He has taken an Augustinian turn in that knowledge turns out to be (if it may be so expressed) a function of love. It is not enough merely to affirm that creation is a fact, we must also "ratify it in our love for it, thus re-experiencing it, as it were, in its origin and production...In the first analysis, knowledge is but the luminous radiance of love."[56] Knowing is not a function of an automatic and self-sustaining transcendence but a function of love, a *fundamental decision* about reality as a whole. Human transcendence only actualizes itself fully in love because in affirming the world, in accepting one's existence and that of the world, one implicitly affirms God, the creator of the world and source of one's existence, who is the source and proper term of human transcendence. This means that all human knowledge must ultimately be understood as love of God such that at the "heart of knowledge stands love from which knowledge lives".[57]

One more point needs to be made before Rahner's development of human freedom and his development of human knowledge are drawn together. The fundamental decision to affirm the world (to love it), to allow one's transcendence to be borne along by its ground and *telos* in love, can not be understood as a purely spiritual act. The human being's love for God never stands by itself but expresses itself through the fundamental attitude human beings take up with respect to the world and their fellow human beings.[58] The human being's relationship to the world can not be separated from the human being's relationship to God in that the latter is realized through the former.

The Human Being, The World, and God

Drawing Rahner's developed understanding of freedom and knowledge together we come to an important insight which bears directly on our topic. Just as human beings do not have a neutral knowledge of the world, in that the world is always known in the mode of acceptance or rejection, so human beings have no neutral knowledge of God. God is never known first, as one element of human knowledge, and then affirmed in love or denied. Rather, the way the human being "knows and understands God is always also carried by the order or disorder of his love".[59] The attitude that the human being takes toward the world determines the extent to which human transcendence will find its fulfillment in God through love and this will determine the extent to which human being is fulfilled in its becoming. In other words, if the human being's relationship to the world is disordered, the result will be a disordered relationship to God and a failure of human being to find its real fulfillment. In complete consistency with the metaphysical anthropology of *Spirit in the World,* in *Hearers of the Word* Rahner concludes that the "concrete way in which man knows God is from the start determined by the way man *loves and values the things which come his way.*"[60]

For Rahner it is impossible for human beings to have a corrupted relationship with the world and a proper relationship with God. Because human beings realize themselves in their free acts, and because these free acts follow from a certain attitude taken toward the world and one's own existence, the acts which proceed from a corrupt relationship to the world lead to a human existence that moves away from God, a move that might be called the "unrealizing" or diminution of human life. Of course, this is Rahner's way into the doctrine of sin but I do not propose to discuss this complex subject here.[61] What I do want to emphasize is Rahner's stress on the interconnectedness of the world, human existence, and God. If the human being is a finite spirit which realizes itself in matter (the world, the body), then the ill treatment of the world can only be seen as a refusal to love the God who created it. This is true, for Rahner, by *transcendental necessity* despite what may be said verbally about loving God. Rahner's position can be understood as a paraphrase of I John 4:20. The treatment of the world as a "standing reserve" (a things merely useful for human purposes) is irreconcilable with loving God because if we can not love creation which we can see we can not love its creator whom we can not see. To see the world as simply something to be used is to be unable to see its essential mystery and to be blind to the Mystery which stands behind it.

It is important to note that Rahner comes to this position not by attempting to identify God with the world, or by asserting that the world is God's body, but through an analysis of human knowing and human becoming. Human knowing and becoming are ultimately realized in love and for Rahner there is an "order of love" because God is both the source and goal of human transcendence in love. This "order of love" is such that human being must love the finite as a way to the infinite. This view has the effect of militating against the spiritualization of creation. It is not the case that Christian faith can be reduced (as some might wish) to "concern for the world"--but such a concern can never be absent from it.

Rahner's analysis helps us to see why merely secular concern for ecological problems will always be frustrated. Secular ecological thinking (even in Christian guise) seems to want to speak about the "sacredness" of the world but is not really able to do so. Because it can not think in this way, secular ecological thinking must always fall back on merely pragmatic concerns (that the survival of human beings is ultimately contingent upon the fate of nature, for example). But as G. K. Chesterton observed, human beings have many pragmatic needs and one of them is to be something more than a pragmatist. With Rahner we may suspect that what really motivates "secular" environmentalism is an inchoate sense of the "sacredness" of the world which is really more than just that. In a sense, secular environmentalism has an "anonymous" doctrine of creation, a more potent doctrine that the "explicit", though etiolated, one embraced by many Christians.[62]

Historicity

Human historicity is an important feature of Rahner's metaphysical anthropology. He arrives at the concept of historicity by way of an transcendental inquiry into where revelation occurs. Should the human being seek for revelation in the inwardness of his or her own being or in a realm outside space and time? From our discussion of *Spirit in the World* we can immediately see why Rahner rejects both these options as false. To think that revelation could occur in human inwardness or in a realm beyond the world would be to misunderstand human spirituality as Rahner has portrayed it. Such thinking overlooks the fact that "man is spirit in such a way that, in order to become spirit, he enters and he has ontically always already entered into otherness, into matter, and into the world."[63] Because the human being is not completely self-present, human knowledge is always *receptive* knowledge, sense knowledge, mediate knowledge, knowledge of the world. If revelation does not occur within the world, the human being can have no access to it. But this does not say enough in terms of specifying where revelation does occur. As a being who is not completely self-present and as a being whose knowledge is fundamentally sense knowledge, the human being is a *material spirit*. As a material being not completely self-present, the human being is fundamentally a being *in the process of becoming:*

> This is to say that man as a material being is constantly in movement, never limited to the present actuality, always open to further determination, oriented toward a future of new enactments, etc., it is to say that man *becomes.*[64]

The fact that this being is fundamentally material means that it is essentially *spatial* and the fact that the human being is a becoming being means that it is fundamentally *temporal*. Space and time are transcendental features of matter and, thus, of human being as well. It is not the case that there is first a human being who is then subsequently placed in a spatial and temporal setting. *Spirit in the World* shows how the human being is essentially *spatial* in that, as finite spirit, the human being can not become what it is apart from the world and the body. *Hearers of the Word* makes it clear that *temporality* is not extrinsic to the human being because temporality is "the inner protracting of the thing itself [human being] in the realized totality of its possibilities."[65]

Human existence is fundamentally historical in the sense that it is essentially *spatial, temporal, and free*. Human historicity consists in the fact that not only does the human being live in space and time but also in the fact that human being *realizes itself* through free acts in space and time. If revelation is to occur, it must occur in history because "man is a historical being, who as *spirit* may come to know *every* being and is a spirit *endowed with senses and living in history*."[66]

For Rahner human historicity is not primarily a matter of the self-realization of the individual in history. It is simply not true that the transcendental method leads to a nonhistorical, individualistic view of human existence. The realization of the self as a free person acting in history can not be understood apart from the whole of humanity. The human being can only realize itself by entering into relationships with the Thou of the other. There is an essential solidarity among human beings because individual fulfillment is dependent upon the fulfillment of humanity as a whole and this is because history has a common origin and a common eschatological destiny.[67] It is impossible to appreciate Rahner's understanding of human historicity without realizing that it means "more than time, more than that we become persons in space and time. It means that personal becoming happens within community; i.e., is through, by, and with other persons."[68] In discussing Rahner's development of the concepts of knowledge and freedom, I have tried to show that the human being's relationship with the world can not be separated from its relationship with God. In his development of the concept of historicity it becomes clear that the human being's relationship to the world is also inseparable from its relationship to other human beings.

The picture which emerges here is that of a complex ecology of relationships, an ecology in which spiritual and physical, individual and communal, the human and the world, and the world and God are intrinsically related. This is the case even though this picture emerges out of a metaphysics of knowledge and a metaphysical anthropology.

Hominization

The epigraph at the start of this chapter is from *Spirit in the World* which argues that, as finite spirit, the human being requires sensibility (the body) to realize itself, to become what it is essentially. Because this is so, because the human being is intrinsically related to the world, this being "thus exposes itself to the destiny of the earth."[69] For Rahner this is not a fact to be accepted with resignation while simultaneously wishing that it were not so. A merely secular or "pagan" affirmation of the unity of the destinies of the human being and the world could lead to despair because the world can be a dark place. Christianity has a different perspective on the unity of these two destinies because while it acknowledges the darkness it knows an even greater light--the Resurrection. For Rahner the Christian can love the earth in spite of its darkness because Christ

> rose, not to show that he was leaving the tomb of the world once and for all, but in order to demonstrate that precisely that tomb of the dead--the body and the earth--has finally changed into the glorious, immeasurable home of the living God...[70]

In *Hominization* Rahner attempts to elaborate on the idea that the human being is "exposed to the destiny of the earth" as a way of addressing the question of evolution. This book and a later essay based upon it are perhaps Rahner's most explicit treatments of the relationship between the human being and the world.

The Challenge of Evolutionary Thought

Evolutionary thought has exerted a great influence on theological reflection as this reflection considers the relationship between human beings and the world. While there has been a tendency for much evolutionary *thinking* to become evolutionary *dogma* (a materialist and immanentalist ideology), in that a scientific hypothesis has been transformed into an absolute metaphysical principle (by those who deny the validity of metaphysics!), evolutionary thought has had a generally salutary effect on theological refection.[71] Some of this influence was portrayed in the previous chapter, particularly in the discussion of the process model. The Catholic incarnational model has been influenced as well, primarily through Teilhard, and Moltmann attempts to take evolutionary thinking into account in developing his position. Prescinding from the thorny thicket that surrounds the question of human origins, evolutionary thinking manifests itself in these models at least by suggesting that biological life is a *unified process*, that life is not static and is very much an interconnected whole. This suggestion exposes ideas such as the view that human beings are not part of nature and the view that nature is a dead stage for human history to criticism. In other words,

> Theologians are encouraged by evolutionary theory to consider humanity's place in the universe *more correctly*: to pay close attention to the vagaries of natural and historical process; to value the process itself as well as its possible outcome (its "how" as content as well as its "why" as goal); to conceive in a new way the immense extent and variety of our

common destiny in a universe which is billions of years old.[72]

If nothing else, evolutionary thinking has made it clear that nature has a history of its own. The crucial theological issue which this thinking raises is how and to what extent human being and the history of nature are related. In the first chapter it was noted that some theologians do not consider this an important question while others maintain that it is a question in which the biblical and Christian tradition does not have any interest. It will be remembered that I argued against both of these views as incorrect. It is now time to focus on Rahner's treatment of this issue.

The Human Being as a Creature of the Earth

In *Hominization* Rahner makes it clear that most theological opposition to evolutionary thinking derives from the fact that it seems to diminish human uniqueness, resulting in the view that the human being is simply a highly complex animal. In his judgment this view goes too far and ignores the fundamental fact of human self-transcendence or spirituality. Of course, Rahner does not approach this issue as an interesting question requiring a somewhat intellectually satisfying answer, an answer simply generated from the theologian's own creativity (a theologoumenon). He begins with the Church's (Pius XII's) teaching that a moderate view of evolution may be adopted (in that it does not contradict Christian teaching) but that it must be accepted that the human soul is an immediate creation of God. In a sense, then, *Hominization* deals with a double problematic. On one hand, it seeks to deal with the question of evolution. On the other hand, it also seeks to deal with the Church's teaching on evolution in that while this teaching, from Rahner's perspective, is essentially correct, it presents a conceptual problem and requires interpretation (and development). That is, it seems to affirm that bodily human beings are a product of the earth while spiritually they are a creation of God. In Rahner's judgment clarification is needed in order to avoid giving the impression that the human being is composed of two disparate realities. Thus, Rahner devotes quite a bit of attention to discussing the metaphysical relationship between spirit and matter and attempting to work out (or, in light of *Spirit in the World*, further develop) an ontology of becoming which attempts to understand evolution in relation to God's (unique) quasi-formal causality. In short, it can be said that *Hominization* provides a good vantage point from which to observe Rahner's theological method at work.

Any theologically credible understanding of evolution will have to take two facts about the human being seriously. In an important sense the human being is a product of the world. The human relationship to and dependence upon the biosphere is undeniable and should not be spiritualized. Nevertheless, a theological anthropology which wishes to remain theological can not assert that human beings are simply highly developed animals. Rahner agrees with (and does not simply give assent to) the Church's teaching that from the standpoint of revelation only a moderate view of evolution can be adopted. Thus, Rahner holds that the human being does indeed have a genetic relationship to the biosphere but that to acknowledge this fact does not account for the *whole reality* of the human being.[73] If there was a tendency previously in theology to overemphasize human uniqueness, there is perhaps now a tendency in ecological theologies, by way of reaction and correction, to overemphasize human continuity with nature. Rahner agrees that

> If we believe in a redeeming creator as the final ground of human history which comprehends and includes the evolutionary process (not merely intentionally but actively), if we hope for communion with God as the only fulfillment of evolutionary history which deserves that name in its proper sense...Humanity cannot finally be described in terms of nature alone; on the contrary, nature can only be fully understood with reference to humanity.[74]

If it is a mistake to abstract the human being from its environment, it is also a mistake to not see the environment in light of human being. This is not necessarily an assertion of hubristic anthropocentrism; it can be simply a recognition of the fact that in human life God's creative activity has crossed an important threshold on its way to fulfillment.

For Rahner, the Genesis accounts of creation (which he characterizes as "historical etiologies") reveal two important truths about human being. They show that the human being "is a partner [with God] without parallel on the earth and radically distinct from the animals" while at the same time affirming that this creature "springs from the earth".[75] And even though the human being has a relationship with God, "this direct relation...must itself be realized in a way that involves an origin from this earth."[76] Any idea that the human being is somehow an alien in the world or that it must seek its fulfillment outside the world must be resisted as a "Platonic temptation" and not accepted as a genuine part of Christian belief. The human being "despite the irreducible specificity of his nature, originates from the earth, was formed out of the already existing universe" and because it does really belong to the world, it must not be seen "as an alien in it, but as from the start earthly and of this world."[77]

Without quite saying it, Rahner suggests that many theological anthropologies formerly found evolutionary thinking repugnant because these anthropologies fail to take seriously the idea that the human being is a creature of the earth and that its destiny is linked to that of the earth. In other words, Rahner agrees with Söelle that the "dust factor" has not been taken with due seriousness. What needs to be noted is that Rahner takes the "dust factor" seriously not because he is consciously attempting to formulate an ecological theology but because of his ontology, the outline of which has been sketched. This is an important point in that it shows that what makes Rahner's thinking ecological is not the fact that he sets out to address the ecological crisis but the fact that his fundamental theological vision is itself ecological in that it strives to see the world in terms of the whole. Thus, Rahner objects to the "Platonic view" (as he calls it) of the relationship between the soul and the body not because of the consequences (as significant as they are) of such a view but because this view rests on a mistaken ontology:

> We reduce it [the idea that the human being has its origin in the earth] to insignificance and remove its ontological and theological sting, by construing it as though it said that man's body was taken from the earth and in doing so we think of "body" as meaning just what fits into the framework of our standard and superficial ideas, and as something that has nothing to do with the "soul".[78]

A mistaken ontology assumes that spirit and matter are two disparate realities and it, consequently, never really understands the human being's relation to the world. But an equally mistaken ontology can assume that it is unnecessary to speak of spirit when speaking of the human being. Such an ontology would have an equally incomplete picture of the human being's relation to the world. Of course, ontology begins with the subject who asks the ontological question--the human being. For Rahner any attempt to understand the human being's relationship to the world will have to deal with the relationship between spirit and matter, and any attempt to do that will have to understand how these two elements are related in the one human person. As has been noted, this issue is discussed in *Spirit in the World*. The results of this exploration are brought to bear on the problematic of *Hominization*.

It is impossible to regard the distinction between spirit and matter as being an "absolute metaphysical heterogeneity". It is a fundamental mistake to see the human being as a conjunction of spirit and matter, a conjunction in which the two elements are extrinsically related. As *Sprit in the World* makes clear, spirit and matter are the "realization and accomplishment of one essence".[79] For Rahner, matter

> is a limited component or factor in this spirit [human being] itself. And
> the spirit distinguishing it from itself, itself posits it by formal causality as
> rendering possible its own achievement of its identity. For the spiritual
> soul...does not possess two completely different functions but in both its
> partial functions it has only one, namely, to fulfill its unitary nature as
> spirit..[and] its corporeality in...not something alien to spirit but a limited
> factor in the accomplishment of spirit itself.[80]

The human being is a creature of the earth not simply in the sense that it
happens to have a body and happens to live in an environment called the
biosphere. It is not the case that the body and the bisophere can at some
point be left behind for a more "spiritual" environment. The human being
realizes and fulfills its spirituality precisely in the body and in the
environment. When Rahner says that creation comes into its fulfillment
in the human being he does not mean that the human being has left the
world behind for better things so that the world then fades into
insignificance. While the human being is "radically distinct from any
animal" it is distinct "in such a fashion that he carries with him the whole
inheritance of his biological pre-history into the realm of his existence
remote from the animals."[81] If the human being is the fulfillment of
creation it is so not in the atomistic sense of being a creature completely
different from the rest of creation but in the sense that it bears within its
life the whole creation and recapitulates it.

While Rahner's discussion of this issue is more complex than I have
made it out to be, the point at which the discussion arrives should come as
no surprise. Rahner comes to the conclusion that it is impossible to
separate human being from the history of nature because nature and human
being are one in terms of their *beginning* (creation) and their *telos*
(consummation). This is what Rahner means when he says that the human
being is exposed to the "destiny of the earth". If the human being is
fundamentally a creature of the earth (though not simply this) and if as
finite spirit the human being requires the material world to realize itself,
then the human history of salvation can not be something completely
separate from the history of nature. Thus,

> if one wanted to conceive the material world in its physical and biological
> sphere as a kind of neutral stage on which is enacted the history of
> spiritual persons, of their culture, salvation and damnation and the process
> of eternal perfecting, one cannot even do justice to the Christian
> understanding of faith.[82]

If one accepts Rahner's metaphysical anthropology, one has to conclude with him that sin and salvation can not refer to the corruption and restoration of an a-cosmic relationship between a disembodied human creature and God. One implication of this conclusion is that

> the climax of salvation history is not the detachment from the world of man as a spirit in order to come to God, but the descending and irreversible entrance of God into the world, the coming of the divine Logos in the flesh, the taking up of the material world so that it itself becomes a permanent reality of God in which God in his Logos expresses himself to us for ever.[83]

This aspect of Rahner's christology will be explored in the fourth chapter; for now it should suffice to say that for him the Incarnation indicates that the world, the world of nature and the flesh, is the place of salvation.[84]

Rahner's understanding of the consummation or perfection of creation also helps us to see that salvation history and natural history must be seen as a unity. Consummation does not mean the liberation of the spiritual from the material. If finite spirit must realize itself in matter, matter must play a role in its perfection. In other words, in the perfecting of creation the human being's relationship to God does not become a-cosmic or otherworldly precisely because what is perfected is *creation*:

> There is to be such a thing as a perfected state of created reality in which what is material will, however altered, persist as such and will be an enduring element in the perfection of the total reality...the perfected material reality must be a factor related to the perfection of spirit itself, not something that is there "as well," in addition to spiritual perfection.[85]

Because spirit and matter and human being and world can not be understood apart from each other in Rahner's ontology, it is impossible to understand creation and consummation only in a spiritual sense. Rahner's statement that the human being is "exposed to the destiny of the earth" does not, as it stands, express the truly radical nature of his position because the statement seems to allow for some other alternative. In fact, for Rahner, there is no alternative. The "dust factor" is not a new emphasis to be adopted (in light of present theological concerns) but an essential component of any theological anthropology which wishes to claim the title of Christian.

Human Responsibility for the World

One final point needs to be made about Rahner's understanding of the relationship between the human being and the world. In our discussion of *Hearers of the Word* it was noted that the reality of the world as God's creation can only really be known in love. The world can only be loved as a creation of God and God can only be loved through the world. Because human transcendence in knowledge and love has God as its ground and goal, all specific acts of knowing and loving have God as their ultimate reference. Because we love "the one who never regretted the creation of such a world of guilt, malediction, death, and fruitlessness" we can also "love the earth together with God."[86]

The human being is not presented with an either/or choice of loving the world or loving God; the relationship between God and human beings can never be thought of as a-cosmic or worldless. This relationship with God and the world is characterized, for Rahner, by freedom and responsibility. With respect to God, Rahner agrees with Schleiermacher that the human being is absolutely dependent upon God but disagrees with his view that this relationship has no reciprocity. For Rahner, the human being is related to God as a partner who is able to enter into a relationship with God or to ignore God, becoming less human in doing so. And while the human being is a creature of the earth, it has some freedom with respect to its environment.

But to say that the human being is free with respect to the world is not to say enough; as God's *partner*, the human being is related to the world in the mode of *responsibility*, responsibility for its own development and responsibility for the ordering of its environment. The process in which this takes place is called "hominization".[87] While it may be potentially misleading, it can be said that there is a sense in which the human being is, after a fashion, a co-creator with God. While Rahner argues for the unique place of the human being in creation, he never separates this exalted status from the responsibility which accompanies it, a status which is a *gift from God*. Hominization does not mean that the human being emerges from nature and thereafter is at liberty to dispose of it in any way it deems necessary. If the human being is co-responsible for the world, it is co-responsible *with God* and cooperates in the fulfillment of *God's purposes*. Perhaps this point can best be put by saying that our

> unity with the material universe from which God's free initiative we have sprung is transformed into responsibility. Nature must be understood to have a real independence of humanity and yet there is a work of salvation

to be done in her.[88]

To speak of the human being's responsibility for the world is to get to
the heart of the human-world relationship as understood by Rahner. He
is aware (as is Heidegger) that the human being's relationship to the world
has been drastically changed by science and technology. Human beings are
not simply dependent upon the world but are capable of *changing* it. The
world is increasingly a world arranged and engineered by human beings
and this means that nature has lost most of its numinous character for
modern people. While nature was once viewed as an immediate
expression of the activity of the gods (or God), it is now seen as something
that human beings use for their own benefit. Of course, as was noted in
the previous chapter, the results of this changed relationship are at best
ambiguous. But Rahner wants to make the point that our relationship to
nature can not be what it was and both secular and theological
romanticisms about nature will not transport us back to a numinous nature
and a world free of modern technology; after crossing the threshold of
science and technology, any "romantic yearning" for a "pure nature, for its
numinous rule, its pristine beauty and fruitfulness, is and remains
romanticism."[89]

One way, then, to read Rahner is to see him in disagreement with the
implicit strategy of some ecological theologies (especially those of the
feminist model) to "renuminize" nature by identifying it in some way with
God (by claiming that the world is God's body, for instance). The
relationship between the human being and nature brought about by science
and technology can not, for all its negative qualities, be seen as totally
contrary to Christian faith. It must be seen, Rahner asserts, that "this
development springs from the very nature of Christianity itself and is a
necessary moment in its own history."[90] This is not to say that the
despoliation of nature is a phenomenon inspired solely or primarily by
Christianity, no matter what vulgar opinion might want to assert to the
contrary. It is to say that Christianity does not see nature *qua* nature *as* a
direct expression of God nor does it view the human being simply as a part
of nature, not distinct from it:

> Nowhere more than in the Christian religion is man the free partner of
> God, so much so that he does not passively undergo his eternal salvation
> but must *achieve it in freedom*...man, understood in a Christian sense, is
> someone who is conscious of being in a most radical way a subject of
> freedom and directly present to God. Man in the Christian sense is
> someone who has really understood that nature, which means everything
> surrounding him, is not God but merely a creature of God which is lower

than man who is a partner of God himself.[91]

Rahner's point, on this reading, is that Christianity has emphasized that the human being is God's covenant partner and that the world of nature is an aspect of creation which can be changed and used within limits; nature is not a direct expression of God and should not be treated as such. In this sense Christianity has demystified the world.

If human responsibility for the world can not be based on the world's holiness, it can be founded on the theological fact that as human beings assume more control over themselves and the environment their responsibility for the world increases proportionately. Power must always be considered within the context of responsibility. For Rahner--and this is not difficult to see if we remember what has been said about freedom-- the Christian enters into a relationship with God not through a numinous encounter with nature but through the acceptance of freedom and responsibility for his or her life and acceptance of responsibility for the world as God's covenant partner. The world is not *sacred* but it is *sanctified*. It can be said that

> this relationship [between God and human beings] is realized whenever man discovers that he has more responsibility because he and the world around him are left more than ever to his own decisions, when freedom is experienced as responsibility...it is realized, whenever such a responsibility is really accepted and when this accepted responsibility is absolute...[and accepted] as inescapable and eternally valid. This is because the last, absolute reason for all responsible freedom and power-- for that inescapable, silent listening as to how we should act responsibly-- is called God.[92]

The world of nature is not sacred in the strict sense. But this does not mean that it is mere raw material for human dynamism. The world is experienced by human beings as the creation of God, as that to which they are intrinsically related and as that from which they have come and in which they remain. But human beings, for Rahner, do not so much experience God in nature as such but rather experience God in their *responsibility for it*; it is in the proper (faithful) discharge of this responsibility that human beings realize their status as God's covenant partners and thus realize themselves as human beings.

While *Spirit in the World*, *Hearers of the Word*, and *Hominization* have different aims, it is clear that a fairly consistent picture of the human being's relationship to the world emerges from them. I have characterized this picture or vision as "ecological" because of its rejection of such dualisms as matter--spirit, human being--world, and soul--body in favor of a position which sees an essential relationship between matter and spirit, human being and the world, and soul and body. The composite picture created by these three works is ecological in the same way that the theologies examined in the preceding chapter are ecological--in the sense of seeing the world as a unity to which human being has an essential relationship as "child of the earth" as one who shares its destiny.

We shall have occasion to mention this subject again in the fifth chapter and then again, by way of conclusion, in the final chapter.

Notes

1.   Karl Rahner, *Spirit in the World*, trans. William V. Dych (New York: Herder and Herder, 1968), 406. Rahner's understanding of the human being as worldly spirit is well expressed in an essay from which the title of the present essay is drawn: "The reality beyond all the distress of sin and death is not up yonder; it has come down and dwells in the innermost reality of our flesh. The sublimest religious sentiment of flight form the world would not bring the God of our life and of the salvation of this earth down from the remoteness of his eternity and would not reach him in that other world of his. But he has come to us himself. He has transformed what we are and what despite everything we still tend to regard as the gloomy earthly residue of our spiritual nature: the flesh." Karl Rahner, "A Faith That Loves the Earth," in *Everyday Faith*, trans. W.J. O'Hara (New York: Herder and Herder, 1968), 83.

2.   For a thorough examination see Thomas Sheehan's excellent book *Karl Rahner: The Philosophical Foundations* (Athens, OH: Ohio University Press, 1987). Also helpful, but much more brief, are George Vass, *Understanding Karl Rahner*, vol. I, Heythrop Monographs (London: Sheed and Ward, 1985), 31-45; Louis Roberts, *The Achievement of Karl Rahner* (New York: Herder and Herder, 1967), 7-31; Barrie A. Wilson, "The Possibility of Theology After Kant: An Examination of Karl Rahner's *Geist in Welt*," *Canadian Journal of Theology* 7 (1966); and Andrew Tallon, "Spirit, Matter, Becoming: Karl Rahner's *Spirit in the World*," *The Modern Schoolman* 48 (January, 1971).

3.   Honecker would have probably disagreed with Vaas's judgment that Heidegger's "influence can be reduced to a terminological saturation of Rahner's writing with the oddities of Heidegger's language." Honecker saw Rahner's work as granting too much to modern philosophy, especially to Kant. See Vass, 27. However, Honecker would certainly have concurred with Vass's view that "Rahner is indeed not a *Thomist* and he can hardly claim the authority of Aquinas for his philosophy." See Vass, 43. Along similar lines, see Denis J. M. Bradley, "Rahner's *Spirit in the World*: Aquinas or Hegel," *The Thomist* 41 (April, 1977).

4. Karl Rahner, *Geist in Welt: Zur Metaphysic des endlichen Erkenntnis bei Thomas von Aquin* (Innsbruck: Rauch, 1939) and (Munich: Kösel, 1957).

5. Throughout his career, Rahner rarely discussed his interpretation of Heidegger or the latter's influence upon him explicitly. Rahner did, however, publish an article in which he provides an interpretation of Heidegger's project. See Karl Rahner, "The Concept of Existential Philosophy in Heidegger," trans. Andrew Tallon, *Philosophy Today* 13 (1969). Sheehan's discussion of Heidegger's influence is helpful, see *Karl Rahner*, 103-124. With respect to the influence of Aquinas, see for example Karl Rahner, "On Recognizing the Importance of Aquinas," in *Theological Investigations*, vol. 13, trans. David Bourke (New York: Crossroad, 1983) and Gerald A. McCool, "Karl Rahner and the Christian Philosophy of St. Thomas Aquinas," in *Theology and Discovery: Essays in Honor of Karl Rahner*, ed. William J. Kelly (Milwaukee, WI: Marquette University Press, 1980). For assessments of Heidegger's relationship to Rahner and to theology in general, see Thomas F. O' Meara, "Heidegger and His Origins: Theological Perspectives," *Theological Studies* 47 (June, 1986); John R. Williams, "Heidegger and the Theologians," *Heythrop Journal* 12 (July, 1971); and William J. Richardson, "Heidegger and Theology," *Theological Studies* 26 (March, 1965).

6. Joseph Donceel, *The Philosophy of Karl Rahner* (Albany, NY: Magi Books, 1969), 18.

7. Ibid., 16.

8. Ibid., 14.

9. Joseph Márechal, *Le point de départ de la métaphysique, Cahier 111: La Critique de Kant*, 3rd edition (Brussels: L' Editions Universelle, 1944); *Cahier V: Le Thomisme devant la philosophie critique*, 2nd edition (Brussels: L' Editions Universelle, 1949). An English translation of about half of *Cahier* V can be found in *A Márechal Reader*, trans. and ed. Joseph Donceel (New York: Herder and Herder, 1970), 65-231.

10. Joseph Donceel, "Transcendental Thomism," *The Monist* 58 (1974): 71.

11. Quoted from Sheehan, *Karl Rahner*, 25.

12. Ibid., 82.

13. See Francis S. Fiorenza's introductory essay in *Spirit in the World*, "Karl Rahner and the Kantian Problematic," xxxvii.

14. Gerald A. McCool, "Karl Rahner's Philosophical Theology," in *A Rahner Reader*, ed. Gerald A. McCool (New York: Crossroad, 1975), xv. For more on Transcendental Thomism, see Leslie Dewart, "Transcendental Thomism," *Continuum* 6 (1968); Johannes Baptist Metz, *Christliche Anthropozentric: Uber die Denkform des Thomas von Aquin* (Munich: Kösel-Verlag, 1965); and Otto Muck, *The Transcendental Method*, trans. W.D. Seidensticker (New York: Herder and Herder, 1968).

15. Fiorenza, "Karl Rahner and the Kantian Problematic," xliii-xliv.

16. Sheehan, *Karl Rahner*, 174.

17. There is a great deal of similarity between *Spirit in the World* and Heidegger's *Kant and the Problem of Metaphysics*, trans. James Churchill (Bloomington, IN: Indiana University Press, 1962). Heidegger carries out a *Wiederholung* of Kant showing that Kant's intention was to lay a foundation for metaphysics in the

transcendental imagination, a horizon of transcendence which is the condition of possibility for the knowledge of any object. Within this horizon, being is known unthematically. See Anne Carr, *The Theological Method of Karl Rahner* (Missoula, MT: Scholar's Press, 1977), 19-32.

18. Rahner, *Spirit in the World*, 58.

19. Ibid., 391. "Metaphysics is seen to be both possible and necessary, even for an intellect whose proper concepts are confined to the essences of sensible objects, because in every judgment the intellect transcends the world of space and time to touch at the term of its *a priori* drive the infinite unity, truth, and goodness of the unconditional Absolute, in whose reality every finite object of its affirmation must participate. Gerald A. McCool, *The Theology of Karl Rahner* (Albany, NY: Magi Books, 1969), 8.

20. Ibid., 390.

21. Ibid., 391.

22. Ibid., 406. As Rahner uses it, *Vorgriff* can also be reasonably translated as "anticipation" or even "reaching out". Dych has chosen to translate it as "pre-apprehension" which is a bit misleading. However it is translated, it is important to notice that the term indicates that the intellect does not have direct knowledge of being in general but only anticipates, reaches out after, it in every act of knowing.

23. Ibid., 69.

24. Ibid., 407.

25. Sheehan, *Karl Rahner*, 184.

26. Hence the possibility of translating *Vorgriff* as "reaching out".

27. Rahner, *Spirit in the World*, 63.

28. Ibid., 82.

29. Ibid., 132.

30. Ibid., 169. "...spirit is the potentiality for the reception of all being...and the active desire for it...Every operation of the spirit, whatever it may be, can therefore be understood only as a moment in the movement toward absolute being as toward the one end and goal of the desire of the spirit." Rahner, *Spirit in the World*, 283.

31. Ibid., 145.

32. Ibid., 181.

33. Ibid., 66.

34. Ibid., 238. "Conversion to the phantasm and abstraction are moments of a single process and are inseparably related to each other in a relationship of reciprocal priority." Rahner, *Spirit in the World*, 266.

35. Ibid., 278.

36. Ibid., 244.

37. Ibid., 289.

38. Ibid., 240.

39. Andrew Tallon, *Personal Becoming* (Milwaukee, WS: Marquette University Press, 1982), 46, 75. This book originally appeared as *The Thomist* 43 (January, 1979).

40. Sheehan, *Karl Rahner*, 311.

41. See especially Rahner's "Philosophy and Philosophizing in Theology," in *Theological Investigations*, vol. 9, trans. Graham Harrison (New York: Seabury, 1972).

42. For an example of this attitude, see Hans Küng, "To Get to the Heart of the Matter II," in *Homiletic and Pastoral Review* 71 (July, 1971): 28-29. For insight into the transformative effect of the transcendental method on doctrine two essays by Rahner are helpful: "Theology and Anthropology," in *Theological Investigations*, vol. 9 and "Foundations of Belief Today," in *Theological Investigations*, vol. 16, trans. David Morland (New York: Crossroad, 1983). For an overall assessment of Rahner's approach to doctrine, see Mary E. Hines, *The Transformation of Dogma: An Introduction to Karl Rahner on Doctrine* (New York: Paulist Press, 1989).

43. See Karl Rahner, *Foundations of Christian Faith*, trans. William V. Dych (New York: Seabury, 1978), 1-25 and "Intellectual Honesty and Christian Faith," in *Theological Investigations*, vol. 7, trans. David Bourke (New York: Seabury, 1977).

44. Karl Rahner, "Philosophy and Theology," in *Theological Investigations*, vol. 6, trans. Karl-Heinz and Boniface Kruger (New York: Crossroad, 1982), 73.

45. Ibid., 74.

46. Ibid., 79.

47. Karl Rahner, *Hörer des Wortes: Zur Grundlegung einer Religionsphilosophie* (Munich: Verlag Kösel-Pustet, 1941) and 2nd edition, ed. J.B. Metz (Munich: Kösel-Verlag, 1963). The first edition is available in partial English translation by Joseph Donceel in *A Rahner Reader*. The second edition is available in English translation as *Hearers of the Word*, trans. Michael Richards (New York: Herder and Herder, 1969). This translation is generally regarded as being defective. Hereafter, the English translation of the first edition will be referred to as *Hearers of the Word* (1) and the English translation of the second edition as *Hearers of the Word* (2).

48. Rahner, *Spirit in the World*, 408.

49. Rahner, *Hearers of the Word* (2), 162.

50. Rahner, *Hearers of the Word* (2), 24. "Philosophy, as genuine philosophy, is Christian when, as fundamental theological anthropology, it looses itself in theology." *Hearers of the Word* (1), 175.

51. Karl Rahner and Herbert Vorgrimler, *Dictionary of Theology*, trans. Richard Strachan, et. al. (New York: Crossroad, 1985), 179. See also Karl Rahner, "A Scheme for a Treatise on Dogmatic Theology," in *Theological Investigations*, vol. 1, trans. Cornelius Ernst (New York: Crossroad, 1982), 19.

52. Rahner, *Hearers of the Word* (2), 113.

53. Ibid., 26.

54. Rahner, *Hearers of the Word* (1), 39. See also Karl Rahner, "Theology of Freedom," in *Theological Investigations*, vol. 6 and "Theology of Freedom," in *Grace in Freedom*, trans. Hilda Graef (New York: Herder and Herder, 1969), 203-225.

55. Ibid.

56. Ibid., 40.

57. Ibid., 41. See also Rahner, *Foundations of Christian Faith*, 65. For Rahner, knowledge is fulfilled in love because the ultimate object of human knowledge, God, can not be grasped in knowledge but can only be approached in the mode of self-surrender; this is love. In order to be fulfilled, knowledge must pass over into love, to, as it were, loose itself. Ultimately, the same is true in the case of one's own existence and that of the world. For Rahner, both of these are ultimately mysteries not capable of being grasped. The human being is confronted with the choice of accepting these mysteries in love or not. Any position on the self, the world, and, ultimately, God that does not accept this fundamental truth is bound to be, for Rahner, superficial and inadequate.

58. As an example of the fruit of this insight, see Rahner's essay "Reflections on the Unity of the Love of Neighbor and the Love of God," in *Theological Investigations*, vol. 6.

59. Rahner, *Hearers of the Word* (1), 44.

60. Ibid. Emphasis mine.

61. See Rahner, *Foundations of Christian Faith*, 90-115.

62. The differentiation between the "anonymous" and the "explicit" plays an important but often misunderstood role in Rahner's theology. See, for example, "Atheism and Implicit Christianity," in *Theological Investigations*, vol. 9.

63. Rahner, *Hearers of the Word* (1), 51.

64. Tallon, *Personal Becoming*, 88.

65. Rahner, *Hearers of the Word* (1), 53.

66. Ibid., 63.

67. For a discussion of this, see Rahner's essay "Theological Reflections on Monogenism," in *Theological Investigations*, vol. 1. Though Rahner later abandoned monogenism, he continued to hold that humanity had to be seen as having a common origin, history, and destiny.

68. Tallon, *Personal Becoming*, 88.

69. Rahner, *Spirit in the World*, 406.

70. Rahner, "A Faith That Loves the Earth," 80.

71. "In this 'evolutionary' world of becoming there are, however, essential differences between various beings and therefore their evolution is itself intrinsically heterogenous. Natural history, the history of mind or spirit, of the person, of human societies, of salvation, all display essentially different kinds of 'evolution'. It wold be a philosophically and theologically false evolutionism to claim that the categories of biological evolution can be transferred in precisely the same sense to 'evolution' of man as such, to history in the proper sense, and to claim that his history can be interpreted and explained on the basis of such categories. Any evolutionism would be unacceptable from the philosophical and theological standpoints...which affirmed, not within the limits set by scientific method but in an apodictic statement extrapolated so as to refer to the whole of reality, that there are no essential differences within the empirical world." Karl Rahner, "Evolution, Theological," in *Sacramentum Mundi: An Encyclopedia of Theology*, vol. 2, ed. Karl Rahner, et. al., trans. W.J. O'Hara (New York: Herder and Herder, 1968), 289.

72. Leo J. O'Donovan, "Making Heaven and Earth: Catholic Theology's Search for a Unified View of Nature and History," in William J. Kelly, ed. *Theology and Discovery: Essays in Honor of Karl Rahner* (Milwaukee, WS: Marquette University Press, 1980), 279.

73. Karl Rahner, *Hominization: The Evolutionary Origin of Man as a Theological Problem, Quaestiones Disputate* 13, trans. W. J. O'Hara (New York: Herder and Herder, 1965), 62.

74. O'Donovan, "Making Heaven and Earth: Catholic Theology's Search for a Unified View of Nature and History," 296.

75. Rahner, *Hominization*, 40.

76. Ibid.

77. Ibid., 22.

78. Ibid.

79. Ibid., 19. "Man comes quite unashamedly from the earth and is therefore seen even in scripture, without detriment to the fact that he is also known to be the spiritual, responsible partner of God, called directly by God, as...the product of this material cosmos, without scripture thereby allowing this one man in the paradoxical duality of his origins to break up into quite independent realities called spirit and matter." Karl Rahner, "The Unity of Spirit and Matter in the Christian Understanding of Faith," *Theological Investigations*, vol. 6, 160.

80. Ibid., 58. "...the Christian dogma of the creation of 'good' matter and of spirit and the rejection of any kind of dualism and gnosticism which sees matter as something a-divine or anti-divine and anti-spiritual, means the affirmation of an innermost and ultimate unity and relationship of spirit and matter." Rahner, "The Unity of Spirit and Matter in the Christian Understanding of Faith," *Theological Investigations*, vol. 6, 157.

81. Ibid., 108.

82. Rahner, "The Unity of Spirit and Matter in the Christian Understanding of Faith," *Theological Investigations*, vol. 6, 157.

83. Ibid., 160.

84. "Always and everywhere, man is regarded by Christianity, precisely in the history of his relationship to God, as a bodily, material and social being who can always only have this relationship to God in the material constitution of his existence." Ibid., 161.

85. Rahner, *Hominization*, 51.

86. Rahner, "Theology of Freedom," *Theological Investigations*, vol. 6, 193.

87. See Rahner, *Foundations of Christian Faith*, 168-170.

88. O'Donovan, "Making Heaven and Earth: Catholic Theology's Search for a Unified View of Nature and History," 296.

89. Rahner, "The Man of Today and Religion," *Theological Investigations*, vol. 6, 9.

90. Ibid., 10.

91. Ibid.

92. Ibid., 15.

The true radicalism of the doctrine of God can only be the continual destruction of an idol, an idol in the place of God, the idol of a theory about him...God only appears when he is accepted simply, humbly and unselfconsciously in worship and obedience and when he is not torn to pieces in all the talk of reflection.[1]

Chapter 3

The Mystery of God: Absolutely Transcendent and Absolutely Near

The present chapter is an investigation of Rahner's understanding of God's relation to the world. While it does not constitute a complete study of his doctrine of God, it does, I think, capture the essence of that doctrine. Since this is the case, one important fact about Rahner's doctrine of God does need to be mentioned so that this essence may be fully appreciated. In speaking about God, Rahner's intentions are essentially mystagogical and his whole doctrine has a distinctive Ignatian tone. This fact can not be exhaustively explored here but must, at least, be mentioned. The present chapter does not aspire to be an examination of Rahner's mystagogy or an example of it; it merely attempts to show how his doctrine of God allows him to construe God's relation to the world in a thoroughly ecological way.

This aspect of Rahner's doctrine of God needs to be mentioned if for no other reason than the fact that it is possible to form the impression that his theology is "academic" in the worst sense of the word--abstract and concerned mainly with the internecine disputes of scholars. Such an impression would be formed against the weight of the evidence which consists of Rahner's many writings on the Church, the Christian life, and spirituality.[2] But it would be a mistake to think that expressions of

Rahner's "practical" interests are confined to these writings. Sheehan's view that Rahner is an apologetic theologian has already been noted. One might go further, I think, and say that even in his more technical works Rahner is not only an apologist but also a mystagogue.

Prologue: Mystagogy and the Mystery of God

Mystagogy, of course, has to do with "initiation into the mysteries" of the Christian faith. The term was first used by the mystery religions and was taken over by Christians for their own purposes. To say that Rahner's doctrine of God is mystagogical is to say that its intention is not so much to say new things about or to propose new concepts of God but draw out the intellectual and spiritual implications of the fact that God is the Absolute Mystery. The foundations of Rahner's mystagogy are actually laid in *Spirit in the World* and all that he has to say on this subject ultimately goes back to this work. For Rahner, there is a fundamental human experience of God which grounds all the various concepts of God. This being the case, the goal of a mystagogical theology should not be so much to add new concepts of God to the already existing collection as to revise all concepts of God in light of the fact that God is not a categorial reality. Part of this mystagogy involves drawing attention to the inherently mysterious character of human experience and to suggest points of contact between this openness to mystery and what Christians confess about God (when they properly understand God's mysteriousness). Knowledge of God is not finally gained by forcing God into ready-made categories and concepts but is found only in an act of self-surrender to God's incomprehensible self-giving. Thus, Rahner says that

> the religious man...already possesses the totality of what can and must be
> pondered by theology. For genuine and fundamental knowledge consists
> in the unreserved surrender to the self-communication of the Mystery...[3]

Mystagogy has succeeded not so much when a person embraces a new or different concept of God as when a person has engaged in an act of self-surrender to God as the Absolute Mystery. The consequence of this view follows logically:

> This being so, we cannot really proceed in a revolutionary manner, as if
> the men of old did not know the God of whom we speak. We can only
> claim to use the speech of reflection about him in such a way that it

introduces *us* better to the faith which was already there. And this we
must do with the painful and sobering thought that when we have poured
out our part of knowledge into the ocean of the incomprehensible God, we
have really poured it back into the ocean whence we drew it in the first
place."[4]

The Ignatian element in Rahner's doctrine of God should not be
ignored; it is not merely something thrown in to give the appearance of
orthodoxy. Rahner shares the Ignatian emphasis on the ever greater
realization of the "mysterious and inconceivable greatness of God" and on
the "overwhelming experience of God as ever greater".[5] Thus, Rahner's
mystagogy aims neither at creating new concepts of God nor at repeating
the old ones but, rather, it aims at penetrating more deeply into the
fundamentally mysterious character of human experience, an experience
which can be characterized as openness to an always-ever-greater-
Mystery.

With its emphasis on God's absolute mysteriousness and the necessity
of self-surrender to the Absolute Mystery, mystagogy appears to be the
theologian's ideal intellectual trick, a strategy for disarming the mind,
confusing it, and then foisting God upon it. This is certainly not Rahner's
intention.   His intention is something more along the lines of
Schleiermacher's--he attempts to show that an analysis of fundamental
human experience can at least suggest points of contact with God.
Mystagogy is not an *ersatz* inductive process which purports to begin with
bare experience and leads (surprise!) inevitably to God by force of
necessity--this would be an intellectual subterfuge. Rather, mystagogy
presupposes that God is self-communicating love and seeks to show that
this self-communication can be discerned in human experience. It shows,
in other words, that the mystery of human being points to the Absolute
Mystery of God.

Nor is mystagogy a subterfuge in the sense of discouraging critical
thinking about the doctrine of God. Its function, as I understand it, it
precisely to force us to think critically about our doctrines of God and
their accompanying concepts and images.   Mystagogy checks our
continuous tendency to make God into a categorial reality and to thus
dispense with God's mysteriousness, leaving us not with God but with an
idol.

While this is not the place to give a complete account of Rahner's
mystagogy, a few general remarks about it need to be made. Rahner's
mystagogy is, not surprisingly, a "transcendental mystagogy". As such
it is not "an initiation into something external or the production of a new
experience" but is rather "the disclosure of an experience that is already

present although in a hidden way."[6] This means that the mystagogue

> must concentrate on inaugurating people into an experience of God that is always present, on awakening in them the sense of mystery which already pervades their existence, on gently inviting them to reflect on the genuine depths of their experience.[7]

The method of Rahner's mystagogy can be expressed by its goals and these in turn reveal a great deal about Rahner's doctrine of God. Since this is the case, I propose to briefly discuss each goal. Such a discussion will better situate us to appreciate Rahner's understanding of God's relation to the world.

(1) Mystagogy aims to show that God is an intrinsic and necessary aspect of the experience of every human being.

As we saw in the previous chapter, in *Spirit in the World* Rahner attempts to show that there is an implicit and necessary knowledge of God in all particular acts of knowing. Rahner attempts to show that this implicit and necessary knowledge of God is the condition of possibility of all knowledge whatsoever.[8] At least one of the implications of this conclusion for mystagogy is that God can never be considered to be a discrete element in human experience, one element, however important, among others which some happen to have and others do not. Just as God is not a categorial object--one thing in the world of things--the experience of God is not categorial either. The significance of this for Rahner's understanding of God's relationship to the world will be discussed later. For now it can be noted that, as indicated by *Spirit in the World*, the experience of God (transcendence) is the condition of possibility of being a self and experiencing oneself as a subject. In the language of Rahner's metaphysics of knowledge, self-transcendence is a necessary moment in the finite human being's self-presence. In other words,

> The transcendentality of man in knowledge and freedom, as it reaches up to absolute being, the absolute future, the inconceivable mystery, the ultimate basis enabling absolute love and responsibility to exist, and so genuine fellowship...is at the same time the condition which makes it possible for the subject strictly *as* such to experience himself and to have achieved an "objectification" of himself in *this* sense all along.[9]

Because of this, Rahner refuses to accept as valid secular anthropologies which see the human being as self-enclosed and autonomous.[10] This is also why he concludes that 'anthropocentricity' and 'theocentricity' in theology are not opposites but actually one and the same thing seen from different perspectives.[11]

Of course, the experience of God as transcendence in knowledge, freedom, and love is such that it can be overlooked or repressed. The contemporary mystagogue will be aware of this and will attempt to show that

> the ultimate depths and the radical essence of *every* spiritual and personal experience (of love, faithfulness, and so on)...thereby precisely constitutes [also the] ultimate unity and totality of experience, in which the person as spiritual possesses himself and is made over to himself...we can only point to the experience, seek to draw another's attention to it in such a way that he discovers within himself that which we only find if, and to the extent that we already possess it.[12]

Because God is not a categorial object mystagogy can not be the effort to indoctrinate people about God as if God were a new bit of knowledge to be taken in. Any contemporary mystagogy, as Bacik argues, must be transcendental mystagogy. Such a mystagogy, however, will not confront its audience with new or more readily accessible concepts of God. This is not what is needed.

> What is needed is an initiation [mystagogy], an "inauguration" into an experience of God that is ultimate and basic...if any   understanding has been achieved of that reality which we have already designated as man's transcendental reference to the *mystery called God*, if this transcendental reference is not once more confused with the concept corresponding to it and objectifying statements about it, if we do not speak of this transcendental reference in merely abstract and formal terms, but rather point it out to man in his concrete life (for it is precisely *here*, in his own life, that he makes this experience all unnoticed and all undefined, whether he wills it or not) then it is no mere empty talk to speak of the possibility of its necessity for inaugurating him into an ultimate experience of God.[13]

The first goal of Rahner's mystagogy points to the second. The inevitability of the experience of God points toward the inevitable presence of mystery in human life.

(2) Mystagogy aims at showing that human experience inevitably involves the experience of mystery.

From Rahner's perspective, the reason why a transcendental mystagogy is required is the fact that modernity has so limited what it is willing to regard as valid human experience and knowledge. In the modern philosophies of Descartes and Kant, for example, the emphasis falls on the *limitations* of human experience and knowledge, confining them to what is certain and manageable. In other words, the scientific ideal of knowledge has been accepted as the norm for all knowledge. This emphasis has precipitated a crisis which is still with us. This crisis is due to the fact that the experience of God resists scientific domestication and is therefore regarded as an illusion or less than real. Of course, one way to address this problem would be to develop concepts of God that are more in keeping with this positivist sensibility. Rahner is convinced, however, that this endeavor will bear little fruit.

As might be concluded from our discussion of *Spirit in the World*, Rahner challenges this positivist position rather yield to it.[14] If Rahner's conclusion that all human knowledge is made possible by an *excessus ad esse* in which being itself is intended but not grasped as an object is correct, then in an important sense all human knowledge is based on mystery, something which can never be fully understood. Thus, a contemporary mystagogy will attempt to show that the reverse of the positivist position is actually the case. It will attempt to show that "clear and distinct ideas" are not the norm of human knowledge but rather its real norm is mystery:

> Radically and intrinsically man is not a being who employs the *idea clara et distincta* (in the sense Cartesian rationalism), nor is he the subject of an absolute system in which alone he and reality in general attain their conscious identity definitively (in the sense of German idealism). The unlimited transcendentality of the infinite human subject in knowledge and freedom, theory and practice, consists in going beyond any comprehensible statement and raising further questions put to it and being lead into precisely what we call mystery.[15]

If this is correct, it will be impossible to see mystery as that dubious residue which remains when that which is sure and certain is distilled from human experience. Rather, mystery must be seen as the "innermost essence of transcendence in cognition and freedom, because it is the condition of the very possibility of cognition and freedom as such."[16]

The accomplishment of this requires something of a "transvaluation of values" since positivism still has an established place in contemporary thinking. As difficult as this transvaluation may be, Rahner is convinced that there is no alternative for

> as long as we measure the loftiness of knowledge by is perspicuity, and think that we know what clarity and insight are, though we do not really know them as they truly are; as long as we imagine that analytical, co-

ordinating, deductive and masterful reason is more and not less than
experience of the divine incomprehensibility; as long as we think that
comprehension is greater than being overwhelmed by light inaccessible,
which shows itself as inaccessible in the very moment of giving itself: we
have understood nothing of the mystery and of the true nature of grace
and glory [which is the experience of God].[17]

This brings us to the final, and for our purposes the most important, goal
of Rahner's mystagogy.

(3) Mystagogy aims to show that the true knowledge and experience
of God consist in recognizing God as the Absolute Mystery which
communicates itself.

This goal reveals the truly radical nature of Rahner's mystagogy.
Aquinas's words could well serve as the motto Rahner's enterprise:
"Man's utmost knowledge of God is to know that we do not know him."[18]
This is not to say that Rahner embraces skepticism with respect to
knowledge of God.[19] We do know and experience God because God
communicates Godself to us, but even in this self-communication we know
God precisely as the *Absolute Mystery*. The ultimate goal of mystagogy,
as the term suggests, is to lead people to this realization and to evaluate all
concepts of God in light of this fact. Ultimately, all concepts of God
derive from this experience (whether it is thematic or not), but Rahner is
convinced that these concepts continually lead us away from God because
they are grounded in categorial experience. Therefore,

> One can only speak correctly of God when he is conceived of *as the
> infinite*. But he can only be grasped as such when we return to the
> transcendental illimitation of every act, since merely to remove this limit
> of the finite as such is not enough to bring about an understanding of what
> the *absolutely and positively infinite* means. All conceptual expressions
> about God, necessary though they are, always stem from the
> unobjectivated experience of transcendence as such: the concept from the
> pre-conception [*Vorgriff*], the *name from the experience of the nameless*.[20]

This goal follows, of course, from the first two in that Rahner's
characterization of God as the Absolute Mystery is intended to militate
against the tendency to think and speak of God as one object among
others, even if the greatest. Of course, this way of thinking can not be
totally abandoned nor totally expunged from theological reflection
because it is an inherent part of human knowing as such. But theologians
must always be aware of its limitations and the necessity of never resting
content with it.[21] As long as this awareness is not present, even Christians
(who experience God explicitly) will not understand the true nature of the

God they worship:

> ...for the average Christian God is not the one who in an incomprehensible
> and improbable outpouring of his love communicates himself with his
> inmost reality to his creatures who, without being consumed in the fire of
> divinity, are able to receive God's life, his very glory as their own
> perfection.[22]

In a very real sense, it is possible to say without fear of exaggeration or
distortion that God as the Absolute Mystery which communicates itself in
its own reality expresses the very essence of the Christian faith; it is the
one mystery to which all Christian doctrines ultimately point. All that
Rahner has to say about God's relationship to the world does not, in the
final analysis, go beyond this--if one may speak in this way. It will be the
concern of the balance of this chapter to explore what this statement means
in detail. But it is not Rahner's intention as mystagogue to lead someone
to this as an intellectual recognition or idea. We will not understand
Rahner's doctrine of God unless we see that it is intended to lead to an
attitude, one which

> in traditional terminology, is called adoration, total commitment in which
> man falls into silence, in which the word he addresses to God is merely a
> prelude to his silence, in which he veils his countenance before the
> majesty of the ineffable mystery, and in which he is aware of that contrary
> to all appearances today man cannot contend with God.[23]

Of course, it could be said that Rahner's understanding of God as the
Absolute Mystery which communicates itself in its own reality could be
interpreted in a categorial way. Some attention will be devoted to this
matter later. For the moment, it need simply be noted that for Rahner even
this understanding, at which his mystagogy arrives and with which it
begins, must finally be plunged unreservedly into the "divine darkness"
and to do this is "to enter this bliss which is authentic and unique, and to
enjoy it as the nourishment of the strong."[24] I will attempt to more
precisely characterize Rahner's understanding of God's relation to the
world, but as I do so it needs to be remembered that everything which he
says about God must always be seen as in the process of disappearing into
God's "brilliant darkness". Rahner is very much aware that when we
speak of God we are faced with a choice, a choice we must make:

> In his heart of hearts, there is nothing man can know better than that his
> knowledge, ordinarily so called, is only a tiny island in the universe of the

unexplained. He knows better than anything else that the existential question facing him in knowledge is whether he loves the little island of his so-called knowledge better than the ocean of infinite mystery.[25]

The Immanence of the Transcendent God

In the preceding section it was noted that Rahner does not wish God's relationship to the world to be understood in a categorial way. The concern of this section will be to show how he interprets this relationship in light of this conviction. In the process of doing this, the thesis will be advanced that Rahner's understanding of God's relationship to the world must be characterized as "dialectical" in that God both radically transcends and is radically present to the world. In other words, God is both radically transcendent and radically immanent *at the same time.*

The Transcendence of God

As our survey of the various models of ecological theology showed, the concept of transcendence and how to best understand it is a significant problem. Interpreted along certain lines, "transcendence" can simply be shorthand for "not really related to the world". Yet whatever difficulties have attached themselves to the concept of God's transcendence, no Christian theology can really dispense with it entirely. As the preceding section indicated, Rahner offers an explanation of why God's transcendence has become a seemingly insoluble problem. The problem is insoluble if one views God transcendence (and other attributes as well) as being somewhat separate and prior to God's essential incomprehensibility. The problem is insoluble because God's incomprehensibility and status as Absolute Mystery are overlooked and God's attributes are then interpreted in a categorial way. Thus, transcendence becomes that immense distance between God and the world. The problem is compounded when God's absoluteness is also given a categorial interpretation; God becomes an extremely distant, unchanging *thing* "out there". Of course, in such an interpretation, immanence and transcendence are not two moments in a dialectic (as they are for Rahner) but logical and polar opposites. This difficulty is certainly present in classical theology but even some of the ecological theologies we have discussed do not entirely escape this difficulty despite the fact that they depart from classical presuppositions. Jantzen's attempt, for example, to understand God's relation to the world as analogous to a person's relation with his or her own body still sees the God-world relationship in categorial terms.

In order to avoid the difficulties involved in categorial understandings of transcendence, Rahner develops a position which he characterizes as "dialectical". The essence of this position was mentioned in the preceding section but it was not appropriate to attempt a further characterization there. When speaking of God's transcendence, it is not enough to say that God creates a world which is *different* from Godself; one must also say that God gives Godself *in God's own reality* to this world. God as really distinct from the world is really present to it in God's own proper reality. This means that the transcendent God "has his fate in and with the world." If immanence and transcendence are seen as the two foci of an ellipse, we can begin to see why Rahner refers to his position as "dialectical":

> For a Christian understanding of God, in which God and the world are not fused together but remain separate for all eternity, this is the most tremendous statement that can be made about God at all. Only when this statement is made, when, within a concept of God that makes a radical distinction between God and the world, God himself is still the very core of the world's reality and the world is truly the fate of God himself, only then is the concept of God attained that is really Christian.[26]

How may we properly speak of God transcending the world or being *radically different* from it? The traditional way of answering this question has been in terms of the distinction between Creator and creation--God is the Creator and everything else is creation and as such is finite and radically dependent upon and radically distinct from God. For Rahner, this view is correct *in principle*, the problem is, however, that the Creator-creature relationship has consistently been seen in terms of inner-worldly efficient causality in which a cause produces an effect that is distinct from itself in the sense that what is produced is a *different entity*. When this approach is adopted (in one of many forms) the God-world relationship is understood to be a categorial one and this, as we have seen, is what Rahner wishes to avoid because of the insoluble conceptual problems this understanding produces. Understood in categorial terms, the God-world relationship begins with the assertion of the duality of God and the world, an assertion which introduces the conceptual problem of how these disparate realities can possibly be related.[27] Attempts to address this problem have never been wholly satisfactory. Such attempts ultimately result in the view that God's relationship to the world is merely external.[28] Attempts to overcome the difficulties entailed in this way of thinking move ineluctably in the direction of pantheism which does overcome dualism but merges God and the world. For Rahner, as long as the God-world relationship is understood in categorial terms, theology, like the Israelites criticized by Elijah, will "go limping with two different [inadequate] opinions" (I Kings 18:21).

Thus, Rahner wishes to develop a mediating position between dualism and pantheism, a position which does not see these two views as mutually exclusive but as each containing a partial glimpse of the truth. Dualism correctly perceives that God is radically distinct from the world and can not be identified with it because this reduces God to being just another object in the world. Pantheism correctly perceives that God is intimately related to the world.[29] Yet both fail to grasp the crucial point that the *difference* between God and the world is not to be seen as an extrapolation from functional relationships between categorial entities. Creatureliness designates the unique relationship between God and the world, a relationship that does not exist between worldly objects and so must be understood transcendentally rather than categorially. In other words,

> creation and creatureliness do not mean a momentary event, namely, the first moment of a temporal existent, but mean the establishing of this existent and his time itself, and this establishing does not enter into time, but is the ground of time.[30]

As creator, God is, and must be, different from creatures but this difference must be understood in an non-categorial way, a way that is appropriate *to God*:

> The *difference* between God and the world is of such a nature that God establishes the *closest unity* precisely *in the differentiation*. For if the *difference itself comes from God*, and, if we can put it this way, is itself identical with God, then the *difference* between God and the world is to be understood quite differently than the difference between categorial realities.[31]

In other words, there is (*contra* pantheism) a real difference between God and the world, but the difference is not a categorial one because it is a difference-in-unity in that God *Godself* established the difference. If one might so put it, *God* is the difference between God and the world. Of course, if we were speaking about the relationship between two categorial objects this would make no sense; but we are not speaking about a categorial relationship. This means that (*contra* dualism) God is not an object alongside the world as its antithesis. God is different [from the world] in the way in which this difference is experienced in our original, transcendental experience. In this experience the peculiar and unique difference is experienced in such a way that the whole of reality is borne by this term and this source [God] and is only intelligible *within* it. Consequently, it is precisely *the difference which establishes the ultimate unity between God and the world*, and the *difference* becomes intelligible only in this *unity*.[32]

The difference between God and the world is not a difference *from* God (as if God were one object from which the world might be differentiated) but a difference *within* God, a difference constituted by God.

Rahner's position requires some amount of intellectual acrobatics to comprehend. This is not to say that there is something artificial about it or that it is disingenuous. If his position is difficult to grasp we simply need to remember what has been said about Rahner's approach to the doctrine of God. Yet, however difficult it might be, it should be clear now what was meant earlier when I referred to Rahner's position as being dialectical--God's difference from the world and God's intimacy with the world must be seen as two moments within the one God-world relationship. Any attempt to focus on one without the other inevitably leads back to categorial thinking and its intractable difficulties.

God and the World in Dialogue

Because God's relationship to the world is dialectical, it is not enough to speak of the world as "creation" for this gives the impression that creation is an end in itself. We must, rather, speak of creation and God's self-communication "as two moments and two phases of the *one* process of God's self-giving and self-expression, although it is an intrinsically differentiated process."[33] This helps us to better understand the difference between God and creation. The difference is simply a moment in God's total relationship with the world. Put another way, the difference between God and the world, as explained above, is simply the presupposition of God's self-communication to the world. Thus, "what is earlier in time [creation] can be and can become precisely *because* it is the condition of the possibility of what comes later in time [God's self-communication]."[34] The unity between creation and God's self-communication consists in the fact that "both come about because they are supported by the one God" and God "simply wants one thing, viz. to communicate himself."[35]

Since God's relationship to the world is in fact dialectical, it is proper to characterize this relationship as a *dialogue*. In describing the relation between God and the world as a dialogue, Rahner intends to call attention to the fact that both partners are free with respect to each other. On one hand, the world places no constraints upon God in terms of limiting God. Even though, as was noted in the previous chapter, human beings are so constituted so as to be open to revelation, the *potentia oboedientialis* in no way determines the content of revelation nor does it constrain God to provide revelation. For Rahner, God must be seen as both personal and free though he is always at pains to emphasize that God's personality and freedom can not be understood in a categorial way.[36] There is a certain amount of actualism in Rahner's theology as can be seen in his emphasis on theology attending to what God has *actually done*. It is possible to speak of God as free and personal only because this is the way in which God has actually been experienced and revealed. Of course, this actualism and the emphasis on God's freedom are mutually reinforcing:

> God's decision [to reveal Godself] is personal and free, a moment in a dialogue with men already constituted in being. In so far as God's actually evinced speech to man always meets a human being for whose nature and existence God's revelation can never become a self-evident constituent...it is clear that Revelation is always a free event, free even when and indeed in so far as man is presupposed as something given. It is not just because man himself is an act of God's freedom that God's word and his saving Acts are free; this metaphysical freedom is not to be confused with God's freedom within the world already in being.[37]

On the other hand, the world is free in relation to God. God's freedom with respect to the world in part means that God is completely independent of the world. God is self-sufficient and self-subsistent, though these qualities must not be interpreted undialectically.[38] To speak of God's self-sufficiency, freedom, and independence of the world is not, for Rahner, to speak of the relationship between an all-powerful cause (God) and a powerless effect (the world); to do so would be to fall back into categorial thinking and to see the relationship between God and the world as being of efficient causality. In such a relationship there could be no real dialogue. For Rahner, the world is a free partner with God and this *freedom* does not conflict with it *absolute dependence* upon God. Of course, other theologians have drawn different conclusions based on the judgment that these two things do conflict. Some have decided in favor of the world's absolute dependence to preserve God's freedom (Schleiermacher, for example), while others have modified the world's absolute dependence to preserve *its* freedom (process theology, for example). But in Rahner this conflict does not exist. The idea of *creatio ex nihilo*, if properly interpreted, correctly designates the status of the world. For Rahner, this means that on one hand God

> cannot be in need of the finite reality called "world", because otherwise he would not really be radically different from it, but would be part of a larger whole [and on the other hand the world] can have absolutely nothing which is independent of [God].[39]

Creatio ex nihilo also must mean, on the other hand, that this "radical dependence must be ongoing; and therefore not just affect the first moment of creation, for what is finite is related now and always to the absolute as its ground."[40] In other words, God continually bestows the world upon itself.

For Rahner, the world's freedom with respect to God is founded on its absolute dependence upon God. In categorial thinking, the more something is dependent upon something else, the less free it is. Dialectically considered, radical dependence upon God and autonomy before God *grow in direct not inverse proportion*. This is due to the unique relationship between God and the world which itself is dependent upon God's unique causality:

> For it is only in the case of God that it is conceivable at all that he himself can constitute something in a state of distinction from himself. This is precisely an attribute of his divinity as such and his intrinsic creativity: to be able, by himself and through his *own* act *as such*, to constitute something in being which by the very fact of its being radically dependent (because *wholly* constituted in being), also acquires autonomy...with respect to the God who constitutes it in being.[41]

Because God's relationship to the world is not one of efficient causality (even in the sense of being created from nothing), the world is really God's free partner in dialogue not in spite of its absolute dependence but precisely *because of it*. This is because of God's unique causality which Rahner designates as *quasi-formal*. The concept of causality is, obviously, based on categorial relationships. Rahner recognizes this and takes the position that of all the forms of causation which we know, it is best to understand God's causality as being *analogous* to formal causation.[42] In recognition of this fact he uses the term *quasi*-formal causality to describe the causality appropriate to God as the Absolute Mystery:

> The relationship of God to the world in which God is mystery, therefore, can only consist in the fact that it is constituted by God himself and not by any created reality distinct from himself. In other words this means

that over and above his "intrinsic" status as mystery, God can be mystery only in virtue of a quasi-*formal* causality in which he makes not some entity different from himself, but rather himself (in his freedom and abiding sovereignty) is the specification of the creature.[43]

God and the world are in dialogue in so far as God addresses a world which is free to listen or not to do so. God has freely chosen this relationship and so it should not be seen as a limitation forced upon God. The relationship between God and the world is dialogical in a *real* sense:

> God's activity in the course of saving history *is not a kind of monologue* which God conducts by himself; it is a long, dramatic dialogue between God and his creatures, in which God confers on man the power to make a genuine answer to his Word, and so makes his own further Word *dependent upon the way in which man does in fact freely answer.*[44]

Perhaps another way of indicating the truly dialogical character of God's relation to the world is to use a metaphor which Hans Urs Von Balthasar has developed so fruitfully.[45] God's relationship to the world is a *drama*:

> History is not just a play in which God puts himself on the stage and creatures are merely what is performed; the creature is a real co-performer in the human-divine drama of history. And so history has a real and absolute seriousness, and absolute decision, which is not to be relativized as far as the creature is concerned with the remark--at once true and false-- that everything rises from God's will and nothing can resist it.[46]

God's Immanence as Self-Communicating Love

Rahner's "dialectical" understanding of God's relationship to the world means that while God must, in the specific way discussed above, be *distinct* from the world, God must also have a *real relation* to the world. This real relationship is not to be understood in the mode of inner-worldly causality but in the mode of quasi-formal causality. It will be the concern of this section to provide an exposition and interpretation of this important point.

Rahner's conviction that God has a real relationship with the world is expressed in his view that God communicates Godself in God's own reality to the world. God's difference from the world (creation) is simply the presupposition of this self-communication. Rahner's position is neatly summarized when he says that the Christian revelation claims that

God, whom Christianity radically distinguishes from the world as free creator, is the God who has in his own most proper reality, and not merely by the mediation of created realities, as inmost dynamism and definitive goal offered and communicated himself to the world in its spiritual creatures so that the otherness of the world can be understood as the condition of possibility of the self-communication of God; creation exists as the presupposition of grace, and revelatory history actually takes place as an element of the history of God himself.[47]

It would thus be wrong to think of God's relationship to the world as being an inner-worldly efficient causal relationship. In other words, God should not be thought of as a first cause or unmoved mover. To be sure, God is the primordial ground of all reality but God is also the *telos* towards which this world moves and the dynamic by which it thus moves. God's relationship to the world can not be external to the world because God is the world's fulfillment and its innermost entelechy.[48]

It is possible to say that Rahner's doctrine of God is really a doctrine of grace. This may be a slight overstatement of the matter but it is true that for him God and grace are really synonymous in the sense that Rahner shares the patristic understanding that grace is the presence of God.[49] The two are synonymous in that when he speaks of God's self-communication in grace, as he does in the passage just cited, Rahner means that it is *God's own reality* that is communicated. Through God's self-communication in grace to the world, *God Godself* becomes the *telos* and the innermost dynamic of the world which moves it towards its end while remaining distinct from the world. For Rahner, the primary sense of grace is, to use the scholastic term, uncreated grace--*God's own divine reality*. Grace is not a secondary power through which God works but God's own real presence. Because this is so, the causality exercised by grace is unique. In uncreated grace

> God communicates himself to the man to whom grace has been shown in the mode of *formal* causality, so that this communication is not then merely the consequence of an efficient causation of created grace [producing something fundamentally different from God]...with Scripture and the Fathers the communication of uncreated grace can be conceived of under a certain respect as logically and really prior to created grace.[50]

God's self-communication in uncreated grace is Rahner's way of speaking about God's immanence in creation; God is immanent in creation in God's own reality as the world's *telos* and fulfillment and as the innermost dynamic of the world. In this way God is the world's quasi-formal cause. In this relationship of quasi-formal causality, God and the world exist at once in the highest state of union and the greatest state of distinction.[51] In Rahner's dialectical understanding of God's relationship to the world , God is both a God of radical nearness and a God of radical transcendence.[52]

Rahner's position allows for a real relationship between God and the world. It also insists that God created the world precisely to have a real relationship with it in self-communication. But it must be remembered that Rahner qualifies God's formal causality by adding the prefix "quasi" to call attention to the fact that this causality is not to be understood in categorial terms.   As was noted in the discussion of the dialogic relationship between God and the world, Rahner does see the God-world relationship, within limits, as a personal one. But because he insists on the non-categorial nature of this relationship, he does not accept the view adopted by the feminist and process models that the God-world relationship must be understood *as far as possible* along the lines of human relationships. For Rahner, God's relation to the world in the mode of quasi-formal causality is *unique* because God is unique; to take any other position would be to fall into categorial thinking. In as much as God is related to the world in the mode of quasi-formal causality, God does not simply cause something different from Godself but, while remaining distinct from the world, becomes the constitutive principle of the world.

This *real relationship* must not be seen, from Rahner's perspective, as a *reciprocal* relationship. This is the case because as distinguished

> from the intrinsic, essentially constitutive causes which are found elsewhere in our experience, this intrinsic, formal causality is to be understood in such a way that the intrinsic, constitutive cause retains in itself its own essence absolutely intact and in absolute freedom. The ontological essence of this self-communication of God as the possibility of this self-communication remains obscure in its uniqueness...only the absolute being of God can not only establish what is different from himself without becoming subject to this difference from himself, but can also at the same time communicate himself in his own reality without losing himself in this communication.[53]

The paradigmatic instance of God's quasi-formal causality is the Incarnation, which (as we shall see in the fourth chapter) actually grounds Rahner's understanding of God's relationship with the world because

> here...God stands in a certain connection with something else and yet remains wholly transcendent to it, i.e.. He is active and yet this fact in no

way reacts upon him nor gives him a fresh determination...[54]

God's relationship to the world does not introduce new determinations into God's being, determinations which God Godself has not brought about. Rahner is not arguing for a doctrine of God's static immutability; to understand God's immutability as being similar to that of an unchanging object would be a serious error and a transgression into categorial thinking. Rather, he is simply stressing the point that God's relation to the world is not a categorial one and that so far as possible theologians should avoid speaking as if it were such.[55]

One of the concerns present in Rahner's doctrine of God is the concern to move away from scholastic theism and its tendency to become eristic. This movement can be seen in his long exegetical essay "*Theos* in the New Testament," to which we have already referred. The motive force behind Rahner's concern was the new Catholic emphasis on biblical studies which was particularly present after Vatican II, an emphasis which Rahner himself helped to foster. He is concerned to show that scripture does not present a "static, metaphysical monotheism" but speaks forthrightly of a personal God who is understood primarily as the One who has entered into a covenant relationship with a particular people.[56] There is not discussion here of God's metaphysical attributes but rather an *encounter* with God whose outstanding characteristic is loving faithfulness. In words that could have been written by Barth, Rahner notes that

> [the] Lord...is not described [in scripture] in the empty indistinctness of an impalpable metaphysical concept but remains in his absolute transcendence of all earthly things concretely and unambiguously *He*, yet as he wished in his sovereign freedom to show himself, in the course of the unique history of his covenant with his People.[57]

From this Rahner concludes that any theological formulation of God's relationship to the world which hopes to be at all scriptural will see I John 4:8 as the best summation of what scripture teaches about God. Scripture, for Rahner, proclaims the *radical immanence* of God when it understands God as love. Love is not one of God's attributes deduced logically from a concept of God, but rather a designation of what *God essentially is*, based upon God's activity in history.

God's relationship to the world can be said to be fundamentally characterized by love for two reasons. First, as has been noted, God is fundamentally free with respect to the world. God is under no external compulsion in relation to the world. This is essential because for Rahner love must always be a free act which expresses essentially the one acting and in which the lover realizes him or herself in relation to the beloved. Second, God's relationship to the world can really be said to be one of love in that God communicates Godself to the world, God opens *God's own innermost life* to the world in a act of radical self-giving. In this act of self-bestowal to the world God does not "constitute some other being, different from himself [a created mediation of God], but imparts himself, and thereby effectively manifests himself as the *agape* that bestows itself."[58] Because he fundamentally understands God as self-bestowing *agape*, Rahner is critical of the idea that revelation is simply verbal and that grace is a secondary power granted to human beings by God. He is insistent that both revelation and grace have their root in the same thing, God's real presence in creation. This real, intimate relationship can be seen, Rahner claims, in what scripture says about the work of the Spirit:

> So the Spirit of God, who is the realization in us of God's personal love and in whom God has unfolded to us his ultimate depths, is the spirit of adoption (Gal. 4:4-6), who gives testimony to our adoption (Rom. 8:15). In this way we are taken up into the most intimate community of life with the God of whom it is said that no one has seen him or can see him (Jn. 1:18; I Tim. 6:16)...[59]

We have already noted that for Rahner creation is simply the presupposition of God's self-communication. What this means of course is that love is the ground and unifying goal behind all of God's acts and that which fundamentally governs God's relationship with the world. This is an important point in that it reminds us of the fact that God's ultimate intention is to have an intimate relationship with creation. This relationship is one of love in which God is creation's fulfillment and the means to that fulfillment. Since this is God's ultimate intention, it must be said that the world was created to be open to just this--the self-communication of God in love. The openness between God and the world is, in a manner of speaking, a reciprocal one. Not only does God communicate Godself in God's own reality to the world, but also

> the whole of creation in the *de facto* order imparted to it is from the outset posited as the condition enabling God to impart himself to the non-divine by becoming the addressee and recipient of this self-utterance of his.[60]

Rahner's understanding of God's relationship to the world is clearly reflected in his interpretation of the Trinity. It might even be said that it is *derived* from his interpretation of the Trinity in that the Trinity is the *Christian* way of understanding God and God's relationship to the world.

Holding as he does the view that God in God's own reality is present in the world, Rahner is critical of treatments of the Trinity which see this doctrine as an end in itself and therefore do not relate it to salvation history or the experience of grace. In his view, the Trinity has become problematic because of this approach. Rahner's chief criticism of traditional formulations of the Trinity is especially directed at what he calls "textbook theology"--theologies which do not tell us precisely what the doctrine was formulated to say, which is that God's own inner life is open to the world and that the mysteries of Incarnation and grace are proper mysteries because both involve God in *God's own proper reality*. For formulations of the Trinity which do not make this clear, Rahner says that it is if the Trinity "has been revealed for its own sake, or that even after it has been made known to us, it remains, *as a reality*, locked up in itself. We make statements about it, but as a reality it has nothing to do with us at all."[61] The Trinity thus slides from the center of Christian belief to the periphery (and maybe beyond that) because it fundamentally has nothing to do with us; we merely say things about it. The blame for this development is assigned to the Augustinian (Western) interpretation of the Trinity because this view results in a Trinity "which is absolutely locked within itself--one which is not, in its reality, open to anything distinct from it" and, what is more, it results in a Trinity "from which we are excluded, of which we happen to know something only through a strange paradox."[62]

The Augustinian concept of the Trinity results, Rahner holds, in a Trinity unrelated to the world because of the way in which it understands the unity of the three persons. This understanding is not dialectical but sees unity consisting in the *one divine essence* which precedes the three persons, a divine essence which is seen as a static, "thing-like reality".[63] For Rahner, the Greek (Eastern) view of the Trinity, like the Greek view of so many other things, is more attractive; God's reality subsists precisely *in three persons*. The unity of the Trinity is not that of an undifferentiated thing but a *tri-unity*, a unity which is threefold:

> ...we must say that the Father, Son, and Spirit are identical with the one Godhead and are "relatively" distinct from one another. These three as distinct are constituted only by their relatedness to one another...[64]

The unity of God's inner life is not a static unicity but rather a dynamic tri-unity which consists in the *perichoresis* of the three persons. God is open to the world and our threefold experience of God in history corresponds to real distinctions in God's own life. For the Augustinian concept of the Trinity the relationship between economic Trinity and immanent Trinity was always problematic, whereas for the Greek understanding of the Trinity the economic and immanent dimensions of the Trinity were closely held together--the Trinity is the *Christian* way of speaking about God's relation to the world.

Rahner can claim that God's inner life is open to the world because he adopts the Greek view of the Trinity and thus contends that *the immanent Trinity is the economic Trinity and vice versa.* The doctrine of the Trinity is not simply a doctrine about God, not merely a revelation of something we otherwise have no contact with or experience of. Rather, the doctrine expresses, for Rahner, the Christian conviction that what happens in salvation history is a real mediation of God's own inner life. The doctrine of the Trinity is the center of the Christian faith because it gives voice to Christianity's central claim, that God communicates Godself in God's own reality to the world as its fulfillment. Seen in this way, this doctrine is a mystery in the strict sense, in that it speaks of God in God's own proper reality not of a logical or mathematical difficulty. This interpretation moves the Trinity from the periphery to the center of the Christian life because it holds that

> ...this incomprehensible, primordial, and forever mysterious unity of transcendence through history and of history into transcendence holds its ultimate depth and most profound root in the Trinity, in which the Father is the incomprehensible origin and the original unity, the "Word" his utterance into history, and the "Spirit" the opening of history into the immediacy of its fathomless origin and end. And precisely this Trinity of salvation history [the economic Trinity], as it reveals itself to us by deeds is the immanent Trinity.[65]

Rahner's dialectical view of the Trinity thus reflects and enunciates his conviction that God both transcends the world and at the same time is really present to it. God is really present to the world in the mode of love because God's bestows Godself on the world and this is the significance of saying that the economic Trinity is precisely the immanent Trinity:

> God gives himself so fully in his absolute self-communication to the creature, that the "immanent" Trinity becomes the Trinity of the "economy of salvation," and hence in turn the Trinity of salvation which we experience *is* the inmost Trinity. This means that the Trinity of God's relationship to us *is* the reality of God as he is *in* himself: a trinity of persons.[66]

Nature and Grace: God and the World Process

Mention has been made of the fact that in God's self-communication the causality which God exercises is best designated as quasi-formal; with respect ot God's self-communication, God's causality is not of the inner-worldly efficient kind.[67] I want to provide a more extensive discussion of this point because it is an essential element in Rahner's understanding of God's relationship to the world. Because God's communication of Godself *is* the most basic form of grace (uncreated grace), the only adequate way to discuss God's quasi-formal causality is to discuss Rahner's understanding of the relationship between nature and grace. It is, of course, beyond the scope of the present study to examine the whole of Rahner's position on this issue and for this reason the treatment here will be confined to an exploration of the supernatural existential as an instance of the operation of God's quasi-formal causality and a model for understanding it.

William Shepherd has argued convincingly that Rahner's entire theology may be understood as a theology of nature and grace even where these terms are translated into other categories.[68] This means that

Rahner's position on the question of how grace, as the order of divine action, is related to nature, as the order of human endeavor, actually determines the position he proposes on all other major doctrines in the theological *cursus*.[69]

For Shepherd, Rahner's view of the relationship between nature and grace is actually an attempt to discuss the relationship between God and the world. Therefore, Rahner's refusal to isolate grace from nature is indicative of his refusal to isolate God from the world process. Grace (and therefore God) is neither alien to the world nor an extension of its potentialities.

The problem of nature and grace is an old one with a complex history, a history that can not be discussed here.[70] It is possible, however, and necessary to situate Rahner's position within the context of positions he opposes. Without undue risk of oversimplification, it can be said that Rahner's position is developed in contradistinction to two views.[71] The first view is what Rahner calls the "average" concept of grace found in post-Tridentine and neo-scholastic theology. In this view, grace is added to nature which is itself understood as already complete, the result being that the relationship between nature and grace is conceived in such a way "that they appear as two layers so carefully placed that they penetrate each other as little as possible."[72]   This understanding of "pure nature" is helpful in that it calls attention to the absolute gratuity of grace--but grace appears here to have a completely extrinsic relationship to nature. This view also undstands the *potencia oboedientialis* for a supernatural end in terms of mere non-repugnance to grace, reinforcing the impression that grace is extrinsic to nature. Rahner (following Blondel) actually labels this view "extrinsicism" and in so doing gives an indication of the direction in which he does not wish to move.

The second view which Rahner rejects is that characteristic of the *nouvelle theologie* associated particularly with Rahner's fellow Jesuit Henri de Lubac.[73]   The position of the *nouvelle theologie* on the relationship between nature and grace was not unprecedented, especially in light of Aquinas's *desiderium natrualie visioni beatificae* which was stressed by Marechal. This view resisted extrinsicism by postulating a *desiderium natrualis* for grace in nature. For Rahner, the question is how this desire is to be interpreted. If the *desiderium naturalis* is thought of an *openness* to grace (which is probably what de Lubac originally advocated), the *nouvelle theologie* is correct. If, however, it is interpreted as a *positive desire* for grace, this view is incompatible, in Rahner's judgment, with the unexactedness of grace.[74] If there is a natural ordination to grace in nature, the problem of extrinsicism is overcome, but

> it follows that on the supposition of such an ordination...the actual granting of the end of this ordination can no longer be free and unexpected. Thus if the ordination cannot be detached from the nature, the fulfillment of the ordination, from God's point of view precisely, is exacted.[75]

While it is really open to question whether Rahner really understood de Lubac's position when he wrote these words, the point made is true nevertheless.[76] If the distinction between nature and grace is blurred too much, grace appears as something which God could not reasonably have withheld. Again, whether de Lubac actually held this view is, for our purposes, not important. What is important is Rahner's reaction to the possibility of such a view. In other words, while Rahner is critical of the idea of "pure nature" because it fosters extrinsicism, he is also critical of any move to completely abandon this concept. Nature and grace (the world process and God) should be neither completely separated nor collapsed into each other. This view fits in well with Rahner's dialectical understanding of God's relationship to the world.

Transposed into the terminology of God and the world process, the guiding principles of Rahner's treatment of the relationship between nature and grace can be stated thus: (1) The world must not be understood as being alien to God. (2) God's real relationship to the world must not be understood in such a way that God's freedom is compromised. Nature and grace must be understood *in relationship to each other*:

> The strictly theological concept "nature" therefore does not mean a state of reality, intelligible in itself and experienced by us separately (apart from grace inaccessible to experience) on top of which, according to revelation, an additional higher reality would be superimposed [as in the extrinsic view]. *Nature is rather that reality which the divine self-communication [uncreated grace] creatively posits for itself as its possible partner* in such a way that in relation to it that communication does or can remain what it is: a free and loving favor. *Nature in contradistinction to the supernatural is, therefore, understood as a necessary element in a higher whole*, which is experienced in grace and explicitly declared in revelation. The difference between nature and grace must be understood on the basis of the radical unity of God's free self-communication as love.[77]

Rahner's point is that if we are to really understand the relation between nature and grace we must grasp the fact that God created the world (nature) for the purpose of communicating Godself (uncreated grace) to it. Nature is intrinsically related to grace while being distinct from it. In other words, nature was created (and is being created) as ordered to grace, its creation being an inner moment in the larger process of God's self-communication.

Thus, the concept of nature occupies an unusual status in Rahner's theology. Because there is an ecology of nature and grace, because the two are intrinsically related, nature in the theological sense has the status of a *Restbegriff*, a "remainder concept". This is to say that "pure nature" is a concept to be employed for analytical purposes only and does not designate a reality which actually exists by itself. As a *Restbegriff*, nature is a useful concept which allows us to distinguish nature from grace and in so doing to see the absolute gratuity of grace as something upon which nature has no claim. Yet, as a *Restbegriff* nature does not designate an empirical reality because in our concrete experience we never have to do with nature in its "pure" state. By virtue of the supernatural existential, we encounter a nature which is *always already graced*. As Rahner puts it, we never encounter nature in a "chemically pure" state.[78] We can never speak of nature as a self-contained reality to which grace is added (almost as an afterthought) in an extrinsic way. It would be *possible*, as Rahner does in *Spirit in the World*, to think of the natural, self-transcending dynamism of the human being as a finite spiritual creature. This self-transcending dynamism, which is open to the infinite and grounds the possibility of objective knowledge, freedom, and love, could be considered apart from grace. Were we to do so we could say that this natural dynamism approaches God asymptotically. Such a "natural" relationship to God would, of course, be a spiritual life in *umbris et imaginibus* in comparison with God's self-communication in grace, but this possibility would suggest that grace is the *unexacted fulfillment* of human spiritual life and of creation as such.[79]

The supernatural existential is best understood not as a component of human being but as an aspect of the human condition, a condition fundamentally characterized by God's continual self-offer in grace to the human being. Thus, the supernatural existential should not be thought of as a "thing" in the human being but as *the continual action of God upon the human being*.[80] Rahner's concept of the supernatural existential rules out extrinsicism because it

> yields an understanding of grace as the conscious and pervasive environment of human life, not a new thing laid beside human nature, but the absolute fulfillment which is ever present as possibility, meaning, and invitation.[81]

If one sees the supernatural existential in its full significance, it is possible to claim, as Karl-Heinz Weger does, that it is the heart of Rahner's theology.[82] To see the supernatural existential in its full significance is to see it as being synonymous with general revelation and uncreated grace and, thus, concerning God's intimate and continuous relationship with the world.[83] The supernatural existential, as God's always already present offer of Godself to the human being as creature is an instance of God's intimacy with the created order, God's radical presence to creation. The supernatural existential is an instance of God's unique quasi-formal causality in that is represents the fact that

> God communicates himself in his own reality to what is not divine without ceasing to be infinite reality and absolute mystery, and without man ceasing to be a finite existent different from God.[84]

The supernatural existential is *supernatural* in that it is God in God's own proper reality but it is also an *existential* of human life in that it is "really an intrinsic, constitutive principle of man as existing in the situation of salvation and fulfillment."[85] It is at this "point" that God can be seen as an intrinsic movement in the world process, as the world's innermost dynamism. God, without ceasing to be God, becomes the innermost dynamism of human life without this life ceasing to be really human and without it being absorbed into God. God is not simply the fulfillment of human life, God is also the means of attaining this fulfillment. Thus,

> the essence and meaning of God's self-communication to a spiritual subject consists in the fact that God becomes immediate to the subject as spiritual, that is, in the fundamental unity of knowledge and love...But this very closeness to God in immediate knowledge and love, to God who remains absolute mystery, is not to be understood as a strange phenomenon which is added to another reality which is understood in a reified way. *It is rather the real essence of what constitutes the ontological relationship between God and creatures.*[86]

This intimate relationship between God and creation in which God becomes a constitutive principle of what is finite and the innermost dynamic of the finite towards its fulfillment is, as has been said, an instance of the relationship that pertains between God and created reality. The importance of this view for our topic can not be gainsaid. Rahner wishes to claim that God's relationship to the world is such that God is not merely the world's fulfillment (and certainly not its extrinsic fulfillment), but that God actually intrinsic to the world, without being pantheistically identified with it, as the innermost dynamism of its fulfillment. This means that creation, the material world, plays an *essential* role in the fulfillment of God's purposes. In considering the supernatural existential, we have been considering how this is the case for human beings. Yet, Rahner understands this to be true of the rest of creation as well. The intimate relationship implied by quasi-formal causality does not simply apply to human beings; it is an instance of God's relationship to the world process as a whole:

> this most general relation between God and the mutable world consists in the fact that God as most immanent--and yet precisely for that reason absolutely superior to the world--confers on finite beings themselves a true active self-transcendence in their change and becoming, and is himself ultimately the future, the final cause, which represents the true and really effective cause operating in all change...God in his relation of freedom to his [creatures] is, after all, not a finite cause side by side with others in the world, but *the living, permanent transcendent ground of the self-movement of the world itself.*[87]

Having attempted to discuss Rahner's understanding of God's relation to the world, it might be appropriate to return to the emphasis with which this discussion began, to remind us of the limitations of what has been said. Rahner notes that the history of revelation is not the history of our idea of God becoming increasingly clear, but the history of God's absolute mysteriousness becoming increasingly clear. Within this history,

> all the provisional realities are dismantled which can lead to the belief that we can only achieve a relationship to God through what we believe we know about him. But such knowledge only offers figures and images, either good or bad, which represent him and shape him to our needs. This process only lasts until we finally let go of everything in the assurance that God, the one who fundamentally can not be shaped to our needs, becomes through his self-gift the being who along is fitted to us. For through his own very being God has granted to us that the measure of our knowledge, desire and activity need not be ourselves but is the immeasurability of God himself.[88]

Notes

1. Karl Rahner, "Observations on the Doctrine of God in Catholic Dogmatics," *Theological Investigations*, vol. 9, 144.
2. See, for example, these works by Rahner: *Theological Investigations*, vol. 3, trans. Karl-Heinz and Boniface Kruger (New York: Crossroad, 1982), *Theological Investigations*, vol. 8, trans. David Bourke (New York: Seabury, 1977), and *The Practice of Faith: A Handbook of Contemporary Spirituality*, ed. Karl Lehman and Albert Raffelt (New York, Crossroad, 1984).
3. Rahner, "Observations on the Doctrine of God in Catholic Dogmatics," *Theological Investigations*, vol. 9, 138.
4. Ibid.
5. Rahner, "On Being Open to God as Ever Greater," *Theological Investigations*, vol. 7, 44, 45.
6. James J. Bacik, *Apologetics and the Eclipse of Mystery: Mystagogy According to Karl Rahner* (Notre Dame, IN: University of Notre Dame Press, 1980), 17.
7. Ibid.
8. "The transcendental orientation of man to the incomprehensible and ineffable Mystery which constitutes the enabling conditions for knowledge and freedom, and therefore for subjective life as such, in itself implies a real, albeit a non-thematic, experience of God." Rahner, "Experience of the Self and Experience of God," *Theological Investigations*, vol. 8, 123.
9. Ibid., 126.
10. "Listen to Christianity as the message which does not forbid anything except man's shutting himself off in his finite nature, except man's refusal to believe that he is endowed with the radical infinity of the absolute God and that the *finitum* is *capax infiniti*...Christianity, among all religion, says the least in

detail since it always says one thing...the absolute fullness itself, incomprehensible and nameless, infinite and unspeakable, has without diminution become the interior splendor of the creature, if only the creature will accept it." Rahner, "Thoughts on the Possibility of Belief Today," *Theological Investigations*, vol. 5, trans. Karl-Heinz Kruger (New York: Crossroad, 1983), 10.

11. Rahner, "Theology and Anthropology," *Theological Investigations*, vol. 9, 28.

12. Rahner, "The Experience of God Today," *Theological Investigations*, vol. 11, trans. David Bourke (New York: Crossroad, 1982), 154.

13. Rahner, "Theological Considerations on Secularization and Atheism," *Theological Investigations*, vol. 11, 183. "The experience of God which we are pointing to here is not some subsequent emotional reaction to doctrinal instruction about the existence and nature of God which we receive from without and at the theoretical level. Rather it is prior to any such teaching, underlies it, and has to be there already for it to be made intelligible at all. This experience of God is not the privilege of the individual 'mystic', but is present in every man even though the process of reflecting upon it varies greatly from one individual to another in terms of focus and clarity." Rahner, "The Experience of God Today," *Theological Investigations*, vol. 11, 153.

14. For a helpful discussion of the place of mystery in Rahner's philosophical theology, see John J. Mawhinney, "The Concept of Mystery in Karl Rahner's Philosophical Theology," *Union Seminary Quarterly Review* 24 (Fall, 1968). "The unlimited and transcendent nature of man, the openness to the mystery itself which is given radical depth by grace, does not turn man into the event of absolute spirit in the way envisaged by German idealism...it directs him rather to the incomprehensible mystery, in relation to which the openness of transcendence is experienced. Man as transcendent subject is not the shepherd of being but the one protected by the mystery...man comes to himself and here he does not does not experience himself as the dominant, absolute subject but as the one whose being is bestowed upon him by the mystery." Rahner, "The Hiddenness of God," *Theological Investigations*, vol. 16, trans. David Moreland (New York: Crossroad, 1983), 236.

15. Karl Rahner, "Mystery," in *Sacramentum Mundi*, vol. 4, ed. Karl Rahner, et. al., trans. W.J. O'Hara, et. al. (New York: Herder and Herder, 1969), 135.

16. Ibid. "What if it [mystery] be essential and constitutive of true knowledge, of its growth, self-awareness and lucidity, to include precisely the unknown, to know itself oriented from the start to the incomprehensible and inexpressible, to recognize more and more that only in this way can it truly be itself and not be halted at a regrettable limit? Mystery can not be regarded as a deficiency of truth." Rahner, "The Concept of Mystery in Catholic Theology," *Theological Investigations*, vol. 4, trans. Kevin Smyth (New York: Crossroad, 1982), 41. See also Rahner, "The Human Question of Meaning in the Face of the Absolute Mystery of God," *Theological Investigations*, vol 18, trans Edward Quinn (New York: Crossroad, 1983), 97-99.

17. Rahner, "The Concept of Mystery in Catholic Theology," *Theological Investigations*, vol. 4, 56.

18. Rahner, "Mystery," *Sacramentum Mundi*, vol. 4, 134. "...in the ultimate analysis the mystery of the direct vision of God does not cease to exist in heaven; rather this incomprehensibility is experienced as the reality which offers itself directly to human vision. For it is God in his simplicity *as a whole* who is perceived. His incomprehensibility can not be understood as a 'part' of God which remains beyond the visual field." In Rahner's interpretation, Aquinas held that God remains absolutely mysterious even in the beatific vision; what is experienced in the vision is precisely God in God's absolute incomprehensibility. See Rahner, "An Investigation of the Incomprehensibility of God in St. Thomas Aquinas," *Theological Investigations*, vol. 16, 247.

19. "One thing, however, has always remained clear to me--in spite of every temptation against the faith which I, too, believe I have had to undergo--one thing has supported me as I kept fast to it: the conviction that we must not allow what has been inherited and transmitted to be consumed by the emptiness of the ordinary, by a spiritual indifference or apathetic and somber skepticism...Inherited belief has certainly always also been faith tempted and liable to temptation. But I have always experienced it as the faith which asked me: 'Will you too go away?' and to which I could always merely reply, 'Lord, to whom shall I go?'..." Rahner, "Thoughts on the Possibility of Belief Today," *Theological Investigations*, vol. 5, 5.

20. Rahner, "The Concept of Mystery in Catholic Theology," *Theological Investigations*, vol. 4, 50. "...the *concept* of God in this [human] knowledge only avoids an idol by referring to the God who, without an image of himself, standing fundamentally over against man gives himself." Rahner, "Observations on the Doctrine of God in Catholic Dogmatics," *Theological Investigations*, vol. 4, 135. See also Rahner, "The Hiddenness of God," *Theological Investigations*, vol. 16, 228-234.

21. "For *that* God really does not exist who operates and functions as an individual existent alongside other existents, and who would thus as it were be a member of the larger household of reality. Anyone in search of such a God is searching for a false God. Both atheism and a more naive form of theism labor under the same false notion of God, only the former denies it while the latter believes that it can make sense out of it. Both are basically false: the latter, the notion that naive theism has, because this God no longer exists; and the former, atheism, because God is the most radical, the most original and in a certain sense the most self-evident reality." Rahner, *Foundations of Christian Faith*, 63.

22. Karl Rahner, "The Specific Character of the Christian Concept of God," *Theological Investigations*, vol. 21, trans. Hugh M. Riley (New York: Crossroad, 1988), 191.

23. Rahner, "The Experience of God Today," *Theological Investigations*, vol. 11, 163.

24. Rahner, "The Concept of Mystery in Catholic Theology," *Theological Investigations*, vol. 4, 56.

25. Ibid., 57.

26. Rahner, "The Specific Character of the Christian Concept of God," *Theological Investigations*, vol. 21, 191.

27. See Mark Lloyd Taylor, *God is Love: A Study in the Theology of Karl Rahner* (Atlanta: Scholar's Press, 1986), 154.

28. "After all, Christianity understands the world within the framework of salvation *history*; this means, however, that properly speaking and in the last analysis it is not a doctrine of the static existence of the world and of man which, remaining always the same, repeats itself in an of-itself-empty period of time, without actually progressing; rather, it is the proclamation of an absolute becoming which does not continue into emptiness but really attains the absolute future, which is indeed already moving *within* it; for, this becoming is so truly distinguished from its yet-to-come future and fulfillment (without implying pantheism, therefore) that the infinite reality of this future is nevertheless already active within it and supports it as an inner constitutive element of this becoming, even though it is independent of this becoming itself (and in this way every form of primitive deism and every merely external relationship of God and the world are eliminated from the very start, and the truth *in* pantheism preserved)." Karl Rahner, "Marxist Utopia and the Christian Future of Man," *Theological Investigations*, vol. 6, 60.

29. See Taylor, *God is Love*, 158.

30. Rahner, *Foundations of Christian Faith*, 77.

31. Ibid., 62-63. Emphasis mine. See also, Karl Rahner, "Natural Science and Reasonable Faith," *Theological Investigations*, vol. 21, 35-36.

32. Ibid., 63. Emphasis mine. "...God and the world are not identical; we must be clear about this once and for all. For the non-identity in itself, and our recognition of it, still do not make God one special, individual reality, *parallel* to the realities of the world. It means a difference of a completely different kind. Karl Rahner, "The Theological Dimension of the Question About Man," *Theological Investigations*, vol. 17, trans. Margaret Kohl (New York: Crossroad, 1981), 58.

33. Ibid., 197.

34. Rahner, "Philosophy and Theology," *Theological Investigations*, vol. 6, 76.

35. Ibid. "If and to the extent that we have understood that the created world is the subject to whom the divine self-bestowal is addressed, and is the condition and prior setting posited by this self-bestowal of God in itself, and enabling it to take place, if, in other words, the world emerges within the process of God's self-bestowal, then it naturally follows that there is an immanence of God in the world (though always, of course in a way that allows for the difference between it and that which belongs intrinsically to the world)." Karl Rahner, "Christianity in the Setting of Modern Man's Understanding of Himself and of His World," *Theological Investigations*, vol. 2, trans. Karl-Heinz Kruger (New York; Crossroad, 1990), 225.

36. See, for example, *Foundations of Christian Faith*, 71-75.

37. Karl Rahner, "*Theos* in the New Testament," *Theological Investigations*, vol. 1, 87.

38. Taylor, *God is Love*, 175.

39. Rahner, *Foundations of Christian Faith*, 78.

40. Ibid.

41. Karl Rahner, "Current Problems in Christology," *Theological Investigations*, vol. 1, 162. "God establishes the creature and its difference from himself. By the very fact that God establishes the creature and its difference from himself, the creature is a genuine reality different from God, and not a mere appearance behind which God and his own reality hide. The radical dependence and genuine reality of the existent coming from God vary in direct and not inverse proportion...In the realm of the categorial, the radical dependence of the effect on the cause and the independence and autonomy of the effect vary in inverse proportion. But when we reflect on the transcendental relationship between God and a creature, then it is clear that here genuine reality and radical dependence are simply two sides of one and the same reality..." Rahner, *Foundations of Christian Faith*, 78-79.

42. Rahner develops this idea in his essay "Some Implications of the Scholastic Concept of Uncreated Grace," *Theological Investigations*, vol. 1, 334-346.

43. Karl Rahner, "Reflections on Methodology in Theology," *Theological Investigations*, vol. 11, 107.

44. Rahner, "*Theos* in the New Testament," *Theological Investigations*, vol. 1, 111. See also Karl Rahner, "Dialogue With God?," *Theological Investigations*, vol. 18.

45. Hans Urs Von Balthasar, *Theo-Drama; Theological Dramatic Theory*, vol. 2, *Dramatis Personae: Man and God*, trans. Graham Harrison (San Francisco: Ignatius Press, 1990).

46. Rahner, "*Theos* in the New Testament," *Theological Investigations*, vol. 1, 111.

47. Rahner, "The Specific Character of the Christian Doctrine of God," *Theological Investigations*, vol. 21, 195. See also, Karl Rahner, "Christianity's Absolute Claim," *Theological Investigations*, vol. 21 and Taylor, *God is Love*, 122-123.

48. Taylor, *God is Love*, 104.

49. If this is an overstatement, it is not much of one: "If and to the extent that we have understood that the created world is the subject *to whom* this divine self-bestowal is addressed, and is the condition and prior setting *posited by* this self-bestowal of God in itself, and enabling it to take place, if, in other words, the world emerges *within* this process of God's self-bestowal, then it naturally follows that there is an immanence of God in the world (though always, of course, in a way that allows for the difference between it and that which belongs intrinsically to the world). This immanence is not merely that the Creator is the creature, but rather that the recognition of which comes to be developed in Christian theology in dealing with the question of the indwelling of God in a spiritual creature through grace...The proper *topos* for achieving an understanding of the immanence of God in the world in theology, therefore, is not a treatise on God worked out in abstract metaphysical terms, but rather the treatise on grace...teaching that the existence of God bears a *quasi-formal* relationship to the world such that the reality of God himself is imparted to it as its supreme

specification."   Rahner, "Christology in the Setting of Modern Man's Understanding of Himself and His World," *Theological Investigations*, vol. 11, 225. Emphasis mine.

50. Karl Rahner, "Some Implications of the Scholastic Concept of Uncreated Grace," *Theological Investigations*, vol. 1, 334.

51. Ibid., 336.

52. Taylor, *God is Love*, 116.

53. Rahner, *Foundations of Christian Faith*, 121.

54. Rahner, "Some Implications of the Scholastic Concept of Uncreated Grace," *Theological Investigations*, vol. 1, 330.

55. Rahner's concern is to avoid the idea that God is one object upon which others exercise influence even if this means, as in process theology, that God is the supremely relational one. He wishes to articulate what he understands to be the Christian (i.e. biblical and patristic) concept of God which, and this takes us back to what was said about mystagogy, "contrary to all theism, pantheism, panentheism, deism, and concealed polytheism...lets God really be God..." ("The Specific Character of the Christian Concept of God, *Theological Investigations*, vol. 21, 194.) On the same page of this essay, Rahner has a footnote which sheds light on his appropriation of Hegel. God's presence in history, he cautions, must not be understood in the sense of many "Protestant and Catholic theologies" because these "no longer really uphold the immutability and blessed sovereignty of God in himself beyond creaturely history. Instead they want to move beyond the statement that God himself really has a history in the world to an assertion of a history of God in his own most proper divinity in itself." Rahner seems to by saying that God does have a history in the world but that this is because the world has its history in God. God's being as such has no history because this would mean that God is one reality in a larger process, which is exactly the idea that he wishes to avoid.

56. Rahner, "*Theos* in the New Testament," *Theological Investigations* vol. 1, 92.

57. Ibid., 93.

58. Rahner, "Christology Within the Setting of Modern Man's Understanding of Himself and His World," *Theological Investigations*, vol. 11, 220. "...we shall have to show that basically such a creative, efficient causality of God must be understood only as a modality or as a deficient mode of that absolute and enormous possibility of God which consists in the fact that he who is *agape* in person, and who is by himself the absolutely blessed and fulfilled subject, can precisely for this reason communicate himself to another." Rahner, *Foundations of Christian Faith*, 122.

59. Rahner, "*Theos* in the New Testament," *Theological Investigations*, vol. 1, 124.

60. Rahner, "Christology Within the Setting of Modern Man's Understanding of Himself and His World," *Theological Investigations*, vol. 11, 220.

61. Karl Rahner, *The Trinity*, trans. Joseph Donceel (New York: Seabury, 1974), 14. The first chapter of this book is an expanded version of Rahner's earlier essay "Remarks on the Dogmatic Treatise 'De Trinitate'," *Theological*

Investigations, vol. 4.

62. Ibid., 18.

63. Ibid., 56.

64. Ibid., 72. Rahner is aware of the danger of tritheism, especially as this has been a perception of Christianity held by Islam and Judaism. For his attempt to overcome this perception, and thus to clarify the doctrine of the Trinity, see "Oneness and threefoldness of God in Discussion with Islam," *Theological Investigations*, vol. 18.

65. Ibid., 47.

66. Rahner, "The Concept of Mystery in Catholic Theology," *Theological Investigations*, vol. 4, 69. "If one supposes that this immediate vision of God can only be based on a quasi-formal self-communication of God in vision, and not (adequately) on a created quality in the spirit of man; and if one recalls the obvious truth, that each of the divine persons is the object of immediate intuition in his personal propriety: then the entitative (ontic) quasi-formal communication of God, which takes the place of a *species impressa* as the ontological foundation of man's possession of God in knowledge, must include a non-appropriated relationship of each of the persons to man. On this basis the relation of the 'immanent' to the 'redemptive' Trinity could be thought out anew...It could be seen that God is not only Trinitarian in himself, but also communicates himself in a Trinitarian way, in grace which means more than efficient causality on the part of God..." Karl Rahner, "Nature and Grace," *Theological Investigations*, vol. 4, 175.

67. "...God does not bestow merely a certain kind of saving love and intimacy, or a certain kind of saving presence (such as ontologically is necessarily implicit even by the abstract concept of a relation between Creator and still creature). God does not confer on man merely created gifts as a token of his love. God communicates *himself* by what is no longer efficient causality. He makes men share in the very nature of God...called therefore to receive God's own life." Karl Rahner, "Grace," *Sacramentum Mundi*, vol. 2, 415.

68. William C. Shepherd, *Man's Condition: God and the World Process* (New York: Herder and Herder, 1969), 98.

69. Ibid., 107.

70. For an orientation to the problem, see Eugene A. TeSelle, "The Problem of Nature and Grace," *Journal of Religion* 60 (July, 1965): 239-244 and Juan Alfaro, "Nature and Grace," *Sacramentum Mundi*, vol. 4.

71. For more on this, see L.H. Yearly, "Karl Rahner on the Relation of Nature and Grace," *Canadian Journal of Theology* 16 (1970): 221-224.

72. Rahner, "Nature and Grace," *Theological Investigations*, vol. 4, 167.

73. For historical background on the *nouvelle theologie*, see Henri Rondet, "*Nouvelle Theologie*," in *Sacramentum Mundi*, vol. 4. De Lubac was one of the casualties of Pius XII's *Humani Generis*, though not a permanent one since Paul VI later made him a cardinal. De Lubac was wrongly interpreted to have held that the human being had a right to grace in his *Le Surnaturel*. He later attempted to clarify his position in *The Mystery of the Supernatural*, trans. Rosemary Sheed (New York: Herder and Herder, 1967).

74. Karl Rahner, "Concerning the Relationship Between Nature and Grace," *Theological Investigations*, vol. 1, 309.

75. Ibid., 306.

76. De Lubac himself points out that when Rahner wrote these words he was not only disagreeing with an article not written by de Lubac and that Rahner had only read one of de Lubac's own articles. See de Lubac, *The Mystery of the Supernatural*, 139, note 36.

77. Rahner, "Grace," in *Sacramentum Mundi*, vol. 2, 417. "God wishes to communicate himself, to pour forth the love which he himself is. That is the first and last of his real plans and hence of his real world too. Everything else exists so that this one thing might be: the eternal miracle of infinite love. And so God makes a creature whom he can love: he creates man. He creates him in such a way that he *can* receive this Love which is God himself, and that he can and must at the same time accept it for what it is: the ever astounding wonder, the unexpected, unexacted gift." Rahner, "Concerning the Relationship Between Nature and Grace," *Theological Investigations*, vol. 1, 315.

78. Rahner, "Concerning the Relationship Between Nature and Grace," *Theological Investigations*, vol. 1, 315.

79. Ibid., 316.

80. See Shepherd, 98-99. Ann Carr comes to the same conclusion in her study of Rahner's theological method. She argues that "the only way to understand this distinction [between nature and grace] is to see the supernatural existential as God's grace in his self-giving action, as universally present in an abiding historical *situation*." Carr, *The Theological Method of Karl Rahner*, 201.

81. Carr, *The Theological Method of Karl Rahner*, 206.

82. Karl-Heinz Weger, *Karl Rahner: An Introduction to His Theology*, trans. David Smith (New York: Seabury, 1980), 87-109.

83. Shepherd, *Man's Condition*, 206.

84. Rahner, *Foundations of Christian Faith*, 119.

85. Ibid., 121.

86. Ibid., 122. Emphasis mine.

87. Karl Rahner and Joseph Ratzinger, *Revelation and Tradition*, *Questiones Disputate* 17, trans. W.J. O'Hara (New York: Herder and Herder, 1966), 12.

88. Rahner, "The Hiddenness of God," *Theological Investigations*, vol. 16, 239.

The Word made flesh is, then, the absolute symbol of God in the world, the expression in concrete reality of what God is and in his free and gratuitous grace wanted the world to be.[1]

Chapter 4

The Transfiguration of the World:
The Incarnation

The present chapter is something of a theological *intermezzo*, a shorter movement between two major movements in a theological symphony. It does not seek to answer any of the three questions posed at the outset of this study. Rather, it attempts to explore why Rahner's ecological theology, as I have called it, may legitimately be said to operate according to what has been designated as the Catholic incarnational, sacramental model. In this exploration I will attempt to elucidate Rahner's understanding of the *significance* of the Incarnation and to suggest that it is the source of the way in which he conceives God's relationship to the world (discussed in the preceding chapter) and the ground of his conception of the place of the material world in the *ordo salutis* (to be discussed in the following chapter). It is hoped that the results of this exploration will show that the Incarnation is the center of Rahner's ecological theology, a theology which proceeds according to the "incarnational principle," a principle which asserts that "God was made flesh and attached his grace to the concrete, historical here and now of human realties." In other words, Rahner's theology is ecological because he adopts as his guiding principle Tertullian's dictum that *caro cardo salutis*--the flesh is the hinge of salvation.[2]

Because of the limited scope of this exploration, a thorough analysis

of Rahner's christology can not be undertaken.[3] Yet, in attempting to
elucidate the significance of the Incarnation for Rahner, it will be
necessary to discuss the Incarnation as a dogma and as a unique historical
event as well as Rahner's understanding of the hypostatic union and the
cosmic significance of the Incarnation.

The Incarnation as Dogma

Without question, the word dogma is in need of rehabilitation and
much of Rahner's work is aimed at doing just this. To say that the
Incarnation is a dogma of the faith is to say something about its absolute
significance for Christian faith. The Incarnation is the central *mystery* of
Christianity because it is the key to understanding all else:

> Only in him [Jesus Christ], and in the union and distinction between God
> and the world found in him, is the God-world relationship and, as a
> consequence, God's very essence, made clear as self-communicating
> love.[4]

So important is the Incarnation that for Rahner the whole task of
christology is to elucidate its meaning, to expound the meaning of the fact
that the Logos *became flesh*.

Thus, the Incarnation is a dogma, Rahner argues, not in the sense of an
extrinsic proposition imposed by an external authority but in the sense that
without it Christianity would cease to be what it is. Showing that this is
the case is central to Rahner's rehabilitation of dogma. He is quite aware
that the very idea of dogma is discredited in many minds for a valid
reason:

> "Dogma" suggests the idea of a rigid doctrinal system, of constraint of
> conscience, of high-sounding statements containing venerable ideas which
> have nonetheless become so far-removed from the original gospel that
> they appear to conceal belief rather than reveal it.[5]

Because this is the case, dogma "must be related to that center of the
Christian mystery which the Church proclaims" or it will be in danger of
being seen as a "rigid and merely authoritative framework of formulas."[6]

To see the Incarnation as dogma is to accept the classical christology
of Nicea and Chalcedon as binding, as expressing something of *permanent*
validity, yet as also expressing a mystery which can never be adequately

communicated or expressed. What is binding about the Chalcedonian formula in particular is not the actual wording but the permanent truth which it seeks to convey. This means that the dogma must be *interpreted*. For Rahner, any orthodox christology will take the Incarnation as defined by Chalcedon as an operative assumption:

> The Church's teaching--to the extent and on the level and in the way it is put forth by the Church--is assuredly a binding norm for a Catholic theologian of today, yet as it always has been in the past...We have to involve ourselves in Christology and this Christology must be the Church's Christology and this Christology of the Church has found its expression in traditional Christology whose keystone--at least until now-- has been Chalcedon, and this Christology must also be ours.[7]

To see the Incarnation as a binding point of departure is to accept that it still has meaning for us today and is not simply a matter of antiquarian interest. We must, Rahner says, avoid the "cheap and hasty lamentations" that the traditional christology has become alien and that its presuppositions are no longer accepted, for to not avoid these lamentations would simply be an admission of "our own spiritual and mental laziness...and our bondage to a fashionable present."[8] Yet while the Incarnation is a binding point of departure it is not the case that our only approach to is must be "an ignorant and superficial parroting of these traditional christological formulations" for this does no service to Christianity.[9] Simple repetition of the dogma is insufficient because its formulation, Rahner holds, can stray, however unintentionally, into Monophysitism and Monothelitism which render it "mythological".[10] In addition to this, the dogma in its traditional formulation does not make a clear enough connection between christology and soteriology.[11]

The fact that the Incarnation is a dogma does not mean, therefore, that nothing further on this topic need be said beyond the Chalcedonian definition. Nor does Rahner maintain that the binding character of the dogma is incompatible with a plurality of christologies, since scripture itself reflects such a plurality. Christologies are to be judged not by how closely they repeat the Chalcedonian formula but by how well they express what is, in Rahner's judgment, its unchanging truth:

> Any christological formulation which on the one hand allows Jesus to be quite objectively man, in the most radical sense, and which on the other hand allows him to be, in his life and death, the unsurpassable God for us, could be enough; because it would then also be stating what is really meant by the classical christological formulations.[12]

Any christology which holds that Jesus in his radical and genuine humanity is God's final and definitive--which is to say eschatological-- self-communication, in however nascent a way, expresses the essential truth of the hypostatic union.

It would seem that, for Rahner, to speak of the Incarnation as dogma is to speak of a *construal* of its permanent validity, a validity open to a variety of expressions. Rahner's construal of the permanent validity of the hypostatic union can be expressed in two propositions. Negatively stated, this dogma is permanently valid in that it prevents Jesus from being reduced to one of many prophets or saviors. Positively stated, the dogma is permanently valid in that it expresses the central conviction of Christianity that in Jesus and precisely in his humanity, God has turned to us in a unique and unsurpassable way in loving self-communication, so that in Jesus God is not represented by something other than Godself.[13] Rahner's approach to the Incarnation as dogma involves neither the simple repetition of the ancient formula nor its simple abolition in favor of some more "contemporary" formulation, but rather a "certain broadening of horizons, of modes of expression and viewpoints for the statements of the ancient Christian dogma."[14] It is in this light that Rahner's "transcendental christology" should be understood.

The Incarnation as Unique Historical Event

Any interpretation of the Incarnation which draws upon Hegel, among other resources, has to deal with the question of the relationship between the *Vorstellung* and the *Begriff* of the Incarnation. What is the relationship between the incarnate Word (*Vorstellung*) and the conceptual truth of the Incarnation (*Begriff*)? In distinguishing between the official formulations of the dogma (and possible alternative formulations of it) and its *abiding validity*, Rahner seems at least implicitly to adopt Hegel's approach even if he modifies it. Of course, making the distinction raises the question, which Hegel attempted to answer, of whether the two are *essentially and necessarily* related. Is it possible--and necessary--to "elevate" the Incarnation from a theological doctrine to a philosophical truth? It was the answer to this question that divided the practitioners of the *Vermitlungstheologie* and the left wing Hegelians; the former answering affirmatively to the question of the essential and necessary relation between the two with the latter answering in the negative.[15] In speaking about the permanent validity of the Incarnation as dogma, is it possible to leave the historical figure of Jesus, in so far as we have access to him, behind?

In arguing that the Incarnation is a unique historical event, Rahner takes a path similar to that of the *Vermitlungstheologie*. The essential connection between *Vorstellung* and *Begriff* seems to be demanded by the kind of event which the Incarnation is: "The miracle of God's incarnation is an absolutely free act of God himself."[16] Because the Incarnation is a *free act of God* it is not possible to deduce it in advance of its actual occurrence. In other words, Rahner does not fully adopt Hegel's approach to the Incarnation which employs a "logical" demonstration of its possibility, actuality, and necessity.[17] For Rahner, it is possible to speak only about the possibility of the Incarnation in a transcendental way, and this only *after* the actual historical event. Transcendental christology is not possible prior to faith in the Incarnation of the Logos in Jesus, and even after the historical event transcendental christology can never replace the historical event but only provide a "framework of understanding" in which the Incarnation can be comprehended.[18] Because of the uniqueness and contingency of the Incarnation (as a free act of God), it is impossible to deduce it from a metaphysical system before the event or to subsume it into such a system after the event and then dispose of the event itself while maintaining its "truth". The Incarnation's status as mystery means that neither of these moves is a possibility. It is possible for a transcendental christology to sketch an "idea" of Christ which would be related to the human being's transcendental condition as being oriented to God and searching for God's self-communication in history as its absolute fulfillment. In other words, transcendental christology "asks about the *a priori* possibility in man which makes the coming of the message of Christ possible."[19] But such an "idea" could only tell us about the possibility of the Incarnation as something for which there is an unthematic hope, as an implicit expectation. Apart from the *fides ex auditu*, apart from the message (*kerygma*) about the Incarnation, transcendental christology not only imparts nothing of any saving significance but also in the final analysis is *not a possibility*. Transcendental christology owes its existence to an *a posteriori* object.[20] It is clear that Rahner does not regard his commitment to a kind of actualism and his commitment to a transcendental christology as being in conflict, even if interpreting their precise relationship is not a simple matter.

The Incarnation's status as a unique historical event does not simply rest on the fact that it is a free act of God. The Incarnation is also a unique historical event because it is an *eschatological event*. It is not possible to dispense with the historical event of the Incarnation for two reasons: (1) because the event is not simply the historical occasion of an already existent reality and (2) because the *event* of the Incarnation actually *brings about* what it represents. As an eschatological event, it can not be left behind:

> To the stature of this Event [the incarnation] all humanity can only asymptotically grow, in all its cosmic and moral dimensions, in the dimensions of grace and eschatology, whatever conceivable "evolution" it may undergo. It can never surpass this Event, because the summit of all "evolution", the irruption of God into the world and the radical opening of the world to the free infinity of God in Christ, has *already been realized for the whole world*, however true it may be that what has already taken place definitively in this Event must still reveal itself within the world...[it is] an eschatological climax.[21]

For Rahner, Incarnation and eschatology imply one another in that the world in its consummated state in proleptically present in the Incarnation and the Incarnation is the point towards which the process of eschatological consummation moves. More will be said about this in the next chapter. For now it can be said that in the event of Jesus Christ what we are confronted with is the "irrevocable Word of God's blessed promise of himself," a promise "in which God himself is involved" and this is precisely the consummation to which the world is directed in grace.[22]

Any attempt to speak of the Incarnation must deal with the historical Jesus. A theology of the Incarnation can not be uninterested in the historical Jesus because lack of such an interest could result in the creation of the idea of Christ on the occasion of Jesus (which is what Rahner accuses Bultmann of doing). While Rahner is aware of the difficulties involved in speaking about the historical Jesus, he insists that if the historical event is not to be merely the occasion of an idea there must be some continuity between Jesus's pre-resurrection self-understanding and the dogma of the Incarnation.[23] Rahner does not think that these two can or need to coincide in an unambiguous way. Minimally they must not contradict each other. But he rejects the approach that would *confine* christology to Jesus's pre-resurrection self-understanding, an approach taken by some reductive christologies which are based on Enlightenment presuppositions. In following a path that lies between the view that history is unimportant for christology and the view that would confine christology to a reconstruction of Jesus's pre-resurrection self-understanding, Rahner believes that he is taking seriously the claim of New Testament faith to be related to specific historical events.

There is, Rahner argues, genuine continuity between Jesus's pre-resurrection self-understanding and the Chalcedonian formula. To put the argument briefly, Jesus, it may be said, saw himself as

> the one who inaugurates the kingdom of God through what he says and
> what he does in a way that did not exist before...At least in this sense the
> pre-resurrection Jesus already knows himself to be the absolute and
> unsurpassable savior.[24]

Jesus did not understand himself to be one in a line of prophets but rather
saw himself as bearing a message that was final and definitive, a message
of God's eschatological presence in his words and deeds; Jesus saw his
message as being inseparable from himself. On the basis of this
interpretation of Jesus' self-understanding, it is completely possible to say
that Jesus is the "historical presence of the final and unsurpassable word
of God's self-disclosure."[25] Jesus, as he understood himself, brings not a
word from God that will be superseded at some future date, but an
eschatological word. This means that Jesus *is the Word of God*--not a
word from God but God's own word about Godself. The point to be made
here is that the dogma of the Incarnation is not simply the product of a
"christology from above" (even though it was officially formulated as
such), but also the legitimate product of a "christology from below". The
Incarnation is not (*contra* Harnack) simply the result of the imposition of
a foreign metaphysic on a simple gospel but is a legitimate interpretation
of the gospel which is grounded in Jesus's own self-understanding.

It should be noted that Rahner's view of the Incarnation as unique
historical event have been criticized. In a book examining the "identity of
the savior" in the christologies of Rahner and Barth, Bruce Marshall has
argued that Rahner's conviction that christology must be related to Jesus
as a specific, historical person and his transcendental christology are at
cross purposes. While this is not the place to provide a review of
Marshall's book or to recapitulate his entire argument, two points about
his position need to be made.

First, Marshall's argument can, without undue simplification, be stated
thus. While Rahner insists that christology can not proceed without
reference to Jesus as a particular person, "in his transcendental
christology, Rahner does in fact strive to define 'that which is significant
for salvation' [*heilsbedeutsam*] without any reference to Jesus Christ as a
particular person."[26] In other words, Marshall claims that Rahner does
exactly what he accuses Bultmann of doing--creating christology merely
on the occasion of Jesus. As we have seen, transcendental christology
asks after the transcendental and necessary conditions in the human
subject which make the acceptance of a savior possible. Marshall argues

that Rahner draws his understanding of salvation from an essential anthropology so that his understanding of the agent of salvation (Jesus Christ) is formulated with reference to this anthropology and not with reference to Jesus as a specific individual. Jesus is, then, not the savior *in his particularity* but simply an instance of a savior, an instance of a generic savior that might appear under other identities since the criteria for what constitutes a savior are drawn from a source other than Jesus's particular history. Marshall argues, then, that Rahner goes precisely in the direction which he disavows. On Marshall's reading, Jesus can not be (in Rahner's christology) the absolute savior as a particular person; he is the absolute savior "only with respect to the bare form of individuality in him, that is, only in so far as he is an indeterminate, independently existing human subject."[27] This is a serious charge indeed, for if Marshall is correct Rahner's christology actually veers in the direction of left wing Hegelianism.

The second point that needs to be made is that any attempt to evaluate Marshall's argument must focus on his *interpretation* of Rahner's transcendental christology. In my judgment, his argument that Rahner's christology is actually derived from an essential anthropology rather than Jesus's particularity is not completely convincing. More specifically, his view that Rahner thinks "that the reality of salvation can be adequately (if not completely) apprehended without reference to Jesus Christ" is open to question.[28] Marshall acknowledges that transcendental christology operates on the *assumption* that Jesus is the incarnate Word of God but does not appear to acknowledge the full significance of this fact. He seems to see transcendental christology as drawing its criteria of what constitutes a savior in a way that is almost completely independent of faith. In my judgment, this is not a fair interpretation of Rahner or, at least, not the only *possible* one. Transcendental christology does attempt to make christology intelligible by bringing it into contact with an account of certain essential features of human existence. But this is how Rahner seeks to make christology *intelligible*; his "conditions of possibility" are not necessarily the source from which he derives its content. One could plausibly say that Rahner's account of what can be "significant for salvation," an account drawn from an essential anthropology, is actually informed from the start by his theological convictions so that what he looks for as a point of contact between christology and anthropology is guided by what he has *already found* in the Christ event. This entire dispute hinges on Rahner's understanding of the relationship between categorial and transcendental experience. As should be clear from the second chapter, Rahner sees these two forms of experience as mutually conditioning each other. As has already been indicated, a transcendental christology would not be possible prior to the historical event of Jesus Christ. This fact seems to place Marshall's central thesis that Rahner thinks it possible to speak of the reality of salvation apart from the historical event of Jesus into question. It seems that he has made transcendental christology (or at least Rahner's version of it) out to be far more a prioristic than Rahner intends it to be.

While this is not a complete response to Marshall's critique, it is enough, I think, to suggest that this critique is open to question. It seems worth noting that Marshall does have an agenda. He is a proponent of the "Yale theology" and is not merely critical of Rahner's transcendental theology but of transcendental theology as such. This agenda is not irrelevant in evaluating his construal of Rahner's position.

The Incarnation as Hypostatic Union

What is the significance of the Incarnation for Rahner's ecological theology? We are now prepared to answer this question. To do so it will be necessary to explore Rahner's interpretation of the hypostatic union. It would be good to begin this exploration by noting Rahner's basic principle for understanding the Incarnation:

> every concept of the incarnation which views Jesus's humanity, either overtly or implicitly, merely as the guise God takes upon himself in order to symbolize his speaking presence, is and remains heresy.[29]

An understanding of God's relation to a concrete human being in the person of Jesus Christ is fundamental to Rahner's understanding of God's relationship to the world and to his understanding of salvation. Rahner rules out a number of approaches by excluding at the outset any view which sees Jesus's humanity, his flesh, as extrinsic to God's presence. The implication of this for our topic shall soon become clear. For now, it might be said that the full significance of the Incarnation could be summarized thus:

> The incarnation is not so much an event in space and time, simply requiring to be accepted in its factualness, but is rather the historical supreme point of a transcendental, albeit free, relationship of God to that which is not divine, in which God, himself positing the non-divine, enters into it in order himself to have his own personal history of love within it.[30]

Schleiermacher defined Christianity as being essentially a religion of redemption, redemption which was always and necessarily related to Jesus Christ. Rahner's own definition follows this closely though it uses different language. For Rahner, Christianity is essentially "the self-communication of God to the world which reaches its goal and its climax in Jesus Christ."[31] In the event of the Incarnation God's relationship to the world reaches its most intimate point and attains its most absolute depth and this event thereby becomes the eschatological destiny of the world. This most intimate point of contact between God and the world is described in the dogma of the hypostatic union. The attempt to expound this doctrine becomes an exercise in explaining what can not possibly be, if it is assumed that God and human nature are somehow closed to each other or that the world and God are mutually exclusive. For Rahner this is definitely not the case:

> We could still say of the creator, with the scripture of the Old Testament, that he is in heaven and we are on earth. But if God is the God whom we confess in Christ we must say that he is precisely where we are, and can only be found here. And although he still remains the infinite, this does not mean that he is "also" that and different elsewhere. It means that the finite itself has been given an infinite depth and is no longer a contrast to the infinite, but that which is the infinite himself has become, to open a passage into the infinite for all the finite...[32]

The hypostatic union is the supreme instance of what Rahner calls the "incarnational principle" which says, as noted earlier, that God's grace-- God's presence--is always attached to concrete, historical realities. In Rahner's interpretation, the hypostatic union means that God's self-communication in grace takes place *in and through the concrete, historical human reality of Jesus*. It is not that God's self-communication comes through this because no more "spiritual" means is available. Rather, the concrete human reality of Jesus *was the most fitting means through which God could become radically present in the world*. The assumption of a human nature by the Logos does not result in the abolition of that human nature but its radical fulfillment because human being as such has an unlimited openness to God; human being only comes to itself when it gives itself over to God. Human nature is not a static, closely circumscribed entity but a mystery which opens out to the absolute mystery of God. It is therefore possible to say that the "incarnation of God...is the unique, supreme case of the total actualization of human reality, which consists of the fact that man *is* in so far as he gives up himself."[33] There is in human being a *potentcia oboedientialis* for possible assumption by the Logos. Considered in its full radicality, the hypostatic union means nothing less than that

> in this human potentiality of Jesus the absolute salvific will of God, the absolute end of God's self-communication to us along with its acceptance as something effected by God himself, is a reality of God himself, unmixed but also inseparable and therefore irrevocable.[34]

Without Rahner's particular interpretation of the hypostatic union, without the event of the Incarnation, what was said about God in the preceding chapter would be unsupportable. For Rahner, God's relationship to the world (or the relationship between nature and grace) can not be fully comprehended without reference to the hypostatic union. In this union we see something of immense importance, something which goes to the heart of Christianity. We see that the finite, material world (represented in Jesus's concrete humanity) is not a barrier to God's presence in the world but is actually a medium of it:

> Objectively the affirmation of the one divine person in Jesus Christ can with certainty only mean that the (in the modern sense) personal, human reality of Jesus Christ has entered into such a unique God-given union with God that it becomes God's *real self-utterance* and a radical gift to God to us.[35]

It is therefore not possible to see Jesus's human reality

> solely as something intrinsically alien which the Logos merely "assumes"...Jesus himself is what comes to be if God wills to express and communicate himself "externally". *God's self-utterance* (as content) *is the man Jesus*, and this self-utterance (as process) is the hypostatic union.[36]

In the hypostatic union, Jesus's humanity is not simply something joined to the Logos in a merely formal way, resulting in a bare humanity joined to the Logos. Rather, Jesus's full and real humanity becomes the genuine other which is also the reality of the Logos. Jesus's human reality is not human and in addition to this *also* God's reality but is God's reality precisely as human reality.[37] The finite reality of Jesus's human nature can become God's own reality while remaining distinct from God. This is not the abolition of the Creator-creature relationship but its *perfection and fulfillment*:

> In Jesus matter is borne by the Logos exactly as the soul is, and this matter

is part of the reality of the history of the cosmos, a part which can never be understood as detached from the unity of the world. The Logos of God himself establishes this corporeal part of the world as his own reality, both creating and accepting it at the same time. Hence he establishes it as what is different from himself in such a way that this very materiality expresses *him*, the Logos himself, and allows him to be present in his world.[38]

This understanding of the hypostatic union not only grounds Rahner's approach to God's relationship to the world but also grounds his understanding of the place of the material world in the *ordo salutis*. If we want to understand salvation and the destiny of the world, we must turn to the Incarnation and when we do this we are confronted with a basic theological fact: the Incarnation

> constitutes the eschatological response of God primarily not in words but in the *deliverance of concrete reality*. And precisely if this is true, then the response of God is *ipso facto* an event *in the material world*, albeit one which *brings about eschatological transformation in it*.[39]

The Incarnation must be considered an eschatological saving event because in it the material world has been definitively accepted by God for salvation.[40] The material world can not be extrinsic to salvation just as Jesus's human nature can not be extrinsic to the hypostatic union. In other words, in the Incarnation God "makes most radically his own what he has created."[41] Since the Incarnation represents the perfection of the Creator-creature relationship, there can be no doubt that salvation can not mean the disappearance of the materiality of creation. For Rahner, the Incarnation not only makes it clear that God in God's own reality can be present in the world through a material reality (Jesus's humanity), but also realizes the radical openness of the material world to God. Without this openness the Incarnation as Rahner understands it would be inconceivable. It is only in the Incarnation that the fundamental truth about salvation is made known: *that God loves creation*. It is thus possible to say that

> when God becomes more and more truly God for us [in the Incarnation]-- the consuming fire, the simply incomparable, the one who in his grace becomes near after being most radically distant--then only a mature Christian relationship to God would be still capable of recognizing and realizing in this burning flame and blinding light that this makes the rest of reality loved by him even more real, even more true and valid, and that in this boundless sea of fire of infinite degree everything is not destroyed but that in it everything finds its real life.[42]

The Incarnation is the foundation of Rahner's understanding of the human being's relationship to the world. In the hypostatic union, Jesus's humanity becomes a means of God's self-communication, a reality of God. This takes place not in spite of but because of the fact that Jesus is fully human, having a real body, a real intellectual and spiritual life, and a real relationship to the world. The christological heresies of Monophysitism, Monothelitism, and Docetism all assume that closeness to God and closeness to the world are opposites. The Incarnation, in Rahner's interpretation, shows that this is a mistaken view. If God has accepted the world in accepting Jesus's humanity as God's own proper reality, an attempt to disregard human being's essential relationship with the world and any failure to see the infinite depths which the Incarnation has opened up in the material world would be a failure to understand what stands at the heart of Christianity. The resulting doctrine would be less than Christian.

For Rahner, we must avoid seeing God without the world and human being without the world, as if God and human being could be thought of as a-cosmic; the Incarnation stands as a bulwark against our doing so. In the second chapter an attempt was made to show why it is impossible on Rahner's account to love God without loving the world. The foundation of this conviction can now be made clear. The Incarnation is God's radical declaration of love for and acceptance of the world. To not love the world is to make God into something that God is not--a God without a world. Because of the Incarnation, we must love the world as "something valid in the sight of God, as something eternally justified and hence as something divinely and religiously significant before God."[43] We are not in the situation of having to choose between the numinous powers of nature and the one true God. This is not because of a pantheist world view or nature mysticism but because of the Incarnation; because the world is something loved and willed by God.

The Incarnation:
The Transfiguration of the World

The only way to do full justice, it seems, to Rahner's understanding of the Incarnation is to say that for him the Incarnation is a *cosmic event*. The Incarnation is not simply the central event of human history (a claim of great magnitude in itself) but the central event in the history of the cosmos. If the Incarnation is seen as paradigmatic for understanding

God's relationship to the created order and not just an isolated event in history (however significant), one comes to some perception of its full significance:

> the Christ event is not something which is enacted upon a sort of cosmic stage which is static and unaffected by what is taking place in him [Christ], but rather constitutes the point to which the becoming of the world in its history is from the outset striving to attain.[44]

To focus on the cosmic dimension of Rahner's understanding of the Incarnation is to see how his version of human being's relationship to the world, God's relationship to the world, and the place of the material world in the *ordo salutis* are inseparably linked. In order to deal satisfactorily with each issue, it is necessary to find a single basis upon which an approach to all three can be founded. This is precisely what Rahner does and the basis upon which his approach is built is the Incarnation. If one wanted to suggest how the Incarnation founds an approach to all three of these issues, perhaps the best thing to say would be that for Rahner the Incarnation results in the *transfiguration of the world*. The word transfiguration is helpfully imprecise and exactly what is called for here; a term that stimulates though without unduly restricting it. To say that something is transfigured is to indicate the radical presence of God in the thing without reducing God's presence to it. The transfigured reality remains what it is while at the same time becoming radically *more than it is*. Transfiguration implies not the abolition of a reality but its being given a radically new depth and meaning. If this is correct then we must say that for Rahner the cosmos is transfigured in the Incarnation. The fact that the cosmos is transfigured suggests a new approach to God and the created order:

> Leaving creatures is the first and, for us sinners, always a new phase of finding God. Yet it is merely a first stage. Service towards creatures, the mission away from God back into the world, may be the second phase. Yet there is still a third [underwritten by the Incarnation]: to find the very creature itself, in its dependence and autonomy, *in* God, in the midst of the jealously burning inexorableness of his being-all-in-all; to find the creature even in the very midst of this...the circumscribed in the boundless, the creature...in the Creator--this is only the third and highest phase of our relationship to God.[45]

The Incarnation is of cosmic significance because part of the cosmos (Jesus's humanity) is transfigured as it becomes an expression of God's immediate and real presence. This is the case for two reasons. First, Rahner holds, as has been seen, that human being is radically in-the-world and thus part of the world's movement towards its consummation. This is true to such a degree that Rahner is willing to say that human being is essentially that point in the development of the cosmos where it becomes self-conscious. What occurs in the human nature of Jesus occurs in the cosmos as a whole as its highest point of development. Second, in the Incarnation the cosmos at its highest point of development is brought into the immediate presence of God. It is thus possible to say that

> Jesus is true man; he is truly part of the earth, truly a moment in the biological evolution of this world, a movement of human natural history...he is a man who in his spiritual, human and finite subjectivity is just like us, a receiver of that self-communication of God by grace which we affirm of all men...as the climax of development in which the world comes absolutely into its own presence and into the direct presence of God.[46]

In the hypostatic union a finite human nature becomes an expression of God's own reality while remaining a finite reality and retaining its integrity as such. For Rahner, in the event of the Incarnation we see the destiny of the whole cosmos, not simply the destiny of human being. In the Incarnation we see the meaning of salvation which consists in finite reality being brought into the immediate presence of God while remaining what it is (finite, material) yet radically transcending itself. The essence of Rahner's soteriology is God's immediate self-communication to creatures in love and forgiveness. Through this self-communication, finite reality is "divinized" or transfigured. Soteriology is finally the whole of theology and can not be reduced to hamartiology. There is and should be a hamartiological soteriology but ultimately *cosmic soteriology* is more important as Rahner accepts the Scotist view that the world was made for the Incarnation or, as we saw in the preceding chapter, the world exists as that to which God communicates Godself.[47] The cosmos reaches its highest point of development, its highest point of self-transcendence, when it is transfigured,

> when the absolute ground itself [God] becomes directly interior to that which is grounded by it...this movement of the development of the cosmos is thus carried along both from the outset and in all its phases by the urge toward ever greater fullness and intimacy and towards a more conscious relationship to its ground...[48]

Perhaps the best way to indicate the cosmic significance of the Incarnation is to say that without it we would not know that the order of creation (nature) and the order of salvation (grace) constitute a dialectical unity. The order of creation is not abolished by the order of salvation; the material world is never dross to be consumed by the refining fire of salvation. Nor, as we have seen, is the order of salvation simply added to the order of creation as its extrinsic fulfillment, as if the relationship between nature and grace was that of subdued country to conquering army. In the Incarnation we see that the order of salvation graces the order of creation in all its dimensions giving to it a supernatural significance while confirming it in its naturalness and, thus, healing it. This idea will be further developed in the following chapter. The Incarnation reveals the radical importance of the order of creation or nature; it is a *factor in the order of salvation*. The order of salvation presupposes and affirms the eternal validity of the order of creation. The relationship between these two orders, between nature and grace, can only be properly understood as being analogous to the relationship between the persons of the Trinity, which is to say that they are related perichoretically:

> The redemptive order must develop within the created order as it all-informing, elevating and divinizing principle...The created order remains included with the redemptive order...in so far as it is a distinct, necessary factor within the redemptive order having its own task in it and attaining its own share in the salvation of the whole order of things.[49]

In the Incarnation it is possible to see that this is indeed the case. In this event, the order of creation and the order of salvation can be seen as constituting a dialectical unity and this means that God has definitively taken the cosmos as a whole, in its ontological unity, into God's own life and has thus transfigured it. It is this theological fact which founds a truly Christian view of the world, a view which must of necessity be dialectical. Living in such a transfigured world has immense consequences for the Christian life in that

> [the Christian] cannot...simply flee from the world as though it were merely unredeemed and doomed to destruction, able to contribute nothing to his salvation except as something to flee from, see through and renounce as non-being. But nor can he feel called upon to construct and control the world in such a way as would suppose that this construction would ever have..an absolute success.[50]

This theme will be further explored in the final chapter.

To accept the Incarnation as Rahner interprets it as a basis for understanding human being's relation to the world, God's relation to the world, and the place of the material world in the *ordo salutis*, is indeed to take seriously the idea that the flesh is the hinge of salvation. This seriousness leads inevitably to an ecological perspective because the human being "may not, for example, regard his *human* "biosphere" as something merely provisional which he must leave behind or could possibly reject when the perfect state dawns."[51]

Notes:

1. Donald L. Gelpi, *Life and Light: A Guide to the Theology of Karl Rahner* (New York, Sheed and Ward, 1966), 13.

2. Karl Rahner, "Membership of the Church According to the Teaching of Pius XII's Encyclical '*Mystici Corporis Christi*'," *Theological Investigations*, vol. 2, 34. One could say, as Rahner does on page 68 of this same essay, that the incarnational principle means that "each and every grace of God has, in a certain sense, an incarnational, sacramental and ecclesiological structure." Rahner consciously appropriates Tertullian's dictum in "The Body in the Order of Salvation," *Theological Investigations*, vol. 17, 77.

3. A general discussion of Rahner's christology can be found in Gelpi, *Life and Light*, 4-13, 40-56.

4. Karl Rahner, "Incarnation," in *Sacramentum Mundi*, vol. 3, ed. Karl Rahner, et. al., trans. W.J. O'Hara, et. al. (New York: Herder and Herder, 1969), 110. Another, equally valid way to make this point would be to say that the Incarnation "is the very center of the reality from which we Christians live...For the mystery of the divine Trinity is open to us only here; only here is the mystery of our participation in the divine nature accorded to us." Karl Rahner, "On the Theology of the Incarnation," *Theological Investigations*, vol. 4, 105.

5. Karl Rahner and Karl Lehmann, *Kerygma and Dogma*, ed. Thomas F. O'Meara, trans. William Glen-Doepel (New York: Herder and Herder, 1969), 27. See also Rahner's article "Dogma" in *Sacramentum Mundi*, vol. 2, 96 where he notes that "dogma is the *form* of the abiding reality of the tradition of the deposit of the faith in the Church which itself remains always the same. Dogma helps to constitute the unity of faith and makes it visible" and also that dogma is "God's absolute self-communication in the *form of human truth* ot the Church and through the Church..." Emphasis mine.

6. Ibid., 39-40. See Rahner's discussion of the elements of a dogmatic statement, 82-98.

7. Karl Rahner, "Brief Observations on Systematic Christology Today," *Theological Investigations*, vol. 21, 229.

8. Karl Rahner, "Christology Today?," *Theological Investigations*, vol. 17, 26.

9. Rahner, "Brief Observations on Systematic Christology Today," *Theological Investigations*, vol. 21, 238.

10. This is because, in Rahner's judgment, the traditional understanding of the hypostatic union has no intrinsic interest in Jesus's humanity and sees his human nature as an abstraction. It is thus easily overshadowed by the Logos. More will be said about this when the hypostatic union is discussed. See Rahner, "Current Problems in Christology," *Theological Investigations*, vol. 1, 191. "We must acknowledge classical Christology and yet see that it is not the only possible one, in the sense that there could be no other orthodox statements of a christological kind. For there are in fact statements which also lead to classical christology and which protect it better and more effectively from misunderstanding than it can protect itself..." Rahner, "Christology Today," *Theological Investigations*, vol. 17, 37.

11. "From the outset Christology must be soteriology. The simple implication of this is of course that we have every right in the light of the New Testament and other more speculative viewpoints to attempt a formulation of the nature and meaning of Jesus which is from the outset a soteriological statement and at the same time really expresses the 'nature' of Jesus Christ in a truly orthodox way." Rahner, "Brief Observations on Systematic Christology Today," *Theological Investigations*, vol. 21, 234.

12. Rahner, "Christology Today," *Theological Investigations*, vol. 17, 27. On the plurality of New Testament christologies, see Rahner's essay "Two Basic Types of Christology," *Theological Investigations*, vol. 13.

13. Rahner, *Foundations of Christian Faith*, 288-289.

14. Karl Rahner, "Jesus Christ," in *Sacramentum Mundi*, vol. 3, 197.

15. For a helpful account of this split in the Hegelian school, focusing particularly on Strauss and Bauer, see Alister E. McGrath, *The Making of Modern German Christology* (Oxford: Blackwell, 1986), 32-47.

16. Rahner, "Jesus Christ," in *Sacramentum Mundi*, vol. 3, 203.

17. See Peter C. Hodgson, "Georg Wilhelm Friedreich Hegel," in *Nineteenth Century Religious Thought in the West*, vol. 1, ed. Ninian Smart, et. al. (Cambridge: Cambridge University Press, 1985), 100-105.

18. Rahner, "Brief Observations on Systematic Christology Today," *Theological Investigations*, vol. 21, 236.

19. Rahner, *Foundations of Christian Faith*, 207.

20. Rahner, "Current Problems in Christology," *Theological Investigations*, vol. 1, 186. See also Rahner, "Jesus Christ," in *Sacramentum Mundi*, vol. 3, 197. Rahner reminds us that in constructing a transcendental christology "We are presupposing the situation of our Western Christian and ecclesial faith, and even real and absolute faith in Jesus as the Christ." Rahner, *Foundations of Christian Faith*, 230.

21. Rahner, "Current Problems in Christology," *Theological Investigations*, vol. 1, 198-199. Emphasis mine.

22. Rahner, "Christology Today?," *Theological Investigations*, vol. 17, 34.

23. Rahner has a positive view of the relationship between exegesis and theology. See, for example, "Exegesis and Dogmatic Theology," *Theological Investigations*, vol. 5. For Rahner, the uncertainty of our knowledge of the historical Jesus is not ultimately problematic: "If, therefore, in our case the historical knowledge of Jesus, of his self-interpretation and of the justification he gave for it is burdened with many problems, uncertainties, and ambiguities, this fact is to be readily admitted and it is no reason to abstain from an absolute commitment to him and to the salvific significance of his reality for us." Rahner, *Foundations of Christian Faith*, 235.

24. Rahner, *Foundations of Christian Faith*, 254.

25. Ibid., 280. See also "Two Basic Types of Christology," *Theological Investigations*, vol. 8, 215.

26. Bruce Marshall, *Christology in Conflict: The Identity of the Savior in Rahner and Barth* (Oxford: Blackwell, 1987), 79.

27. Ibid., 58.

28. Ibid., 25.

29. Rahner, "Christology Today?," *Theological Investigations*, vol. 17, 38. In understanding the term "hypostatic union," "we must repeatedly take our bearing from the simple insight of faith that precisely this concrete individual who acts and encounters us, is true God and true man, that these two predicates do not mean the same, yet both are the reality of one and the same being." Karl Rahner, "Incarnation," in *Sacramentum Mundi*, vol. 3, 113.

30. Rahner, "Two Basic Types of Christology," *Theological Investigations*, vol. 13, 219.

31. Rahner, *Foundations of Christian Faith*, 176.

32. Rahner, "On the Theology of the Incarnation," *Theological Investigations*, vol. 4, 117.

33. Ibid., 110. "Man is the radical question about God which, as created by God, can also have an answer, an answer which in its historical manifestation and radical tangibility is the God-man, and which is answered in all of us by God himself...When God wants to be what is not God, man comes to be." Rahner, *Foundations of Christian Faith*, 225. "...when God brings about man's self-transcendence into God through his absolute self-communication to all men in such a way that both events constitute a promise to all men which is irrevocable and which has already reached fulfillment in one man, then we have precisely what is signified by hypostatic union." Rahner, *Foundations of Christian Faith*, 201.

34. Rahner, *Foundations of Christian Faith*, 202.

35. Rahner, "Jesus Christ," *Sacramentum Mundi*, vol. 3, 207. Emphasis mine.

36. Ibid., 208. Emphasis mine. Because of the limited scope of the present inquiry, I do not propose to examine the ontology upon which Rahner's position is based. This is set forth in his essay "The Theology of the Symbol," *Theological Investigations*, vol. 4, 236-248.

37. Rahner, "Current Problems in Christology," *Theological Investigations*, vol. 1, 191-192.

38. Rahner, *Foundations of Christian Faith*, 196. "For it is only in the case of God that it is conceivable at all that he himself can constitute something in a state of distinction from himself. This is precisely an attribute of his divinity as such and his intrinsic creativity: to be able, by himself and through his *own* act *as such*, to constitute something in being which by the very fact of its being radically dependent (because *wholly* constituted in being), also acquires autonomy...with respect to the God who constitutes it in being." Rahner, "Current Problems in Christology," *Theological Investigations* , vol. 1, 162.

39. Rahner, "Two Basic Types of Christology," *Theological Investigations*, vol. 13, 220. Emphasis mine.

40. Rahner, "Incarnation," in *Sacramentum Mundi*, vol. 3, 110.

41. Rahner, "Current Problems in Christology," *Theological Investigations*, vol. 1, 165.

42. Karl Rahner, "The Eternal Significance of the Humanity of Jesus for Our Relationship to God," *Theological Investigations*, vol. 3, 42. On page 42 of this same essay Rahner makes the following statement: "One loves 'the absolute', but not God who is the creator of heaven and earth. Basically one hates created reality, since it is not the absolute itself; one calls it the relative, the contingent, that which--in relation to God--is determinable in a merely negative sense...and one forgets that precisely this conditional reality is what is loved unconditionally by the Unconditioned, that it therefore has a validity which makes it more than something merely provisional--something which dissolves in the face of God..."

43. Ibid., 41. "Christ is already at the heart and center of all the poor things of this earth, which we cannot do without because the earth is our mother. He is present in the blind hope of all creatures who, without knowing it, are striving to participate in the glorification of his body. He is present in the history of the earth, whose blind course he steers with unearthly accuracy through all victories and all defeats onwards to the day on which his glory will heal out of his own depths and transform all things...He is there as the inmost essence of all things, and the most secret law which still triumphs and imposes its authority even when every kind of authority is breaking up...he is there, the heart of this earthly world and the secret of its eternal validity." Karl Rahner, "Hidden Victory," *Theological Investigations*, vol. 7, 157-158.

44. Rahner, "Christology in the Setting of Modern Man's Understanding of Himself and His World," *Theological Investigations*, vol. 11, 227.

45. Rahner, "The Eternal Significance of the Humanity of Jesus for Our Relationship to God," *Theological Investigations*, vol. 3, 43.

46. Karl Rahner, "Christology Within an Evolutionary View of the World," *Theological Investigations*, vol. 5, 176. For Rahner it is axiomatic that Jesus must really be human and thus really part of the cosmos in order to be the absolute savior: "He cannot simply be God himself as acting in the world, but must be a part of the cosmos, a moment within its history, and indeed at its climax...In Jesus matter is borne by the Logos exactly as the soul is, and this matter is a part of the reality and of the history of the cosmos, a part which can never be understood as detached from the unity of the world. The Logos of God himself establishes this corporeal part of the world as his own reality...Jesus

is truly man with everything which this implies, with his finiteness, his materiality, his being in the world and his participation in the history of the cosmos in the dimension of spirit and freedom, in the history which leads through the narrow passage of death." Rahner, *Foundations of Christian Faith*, 195, 196, 197.

47. See Karl Rahner, "Salvation," in *Sacramentum Mundi*, vol. 5, ed. Karl Rahner, et. al., trans. W.J. O'Hara, et. al. (New York: Herder and Herder, 1970), 430-437.

48. Rahner, "Christology Within an Evolutionary View of the World," *Theological Investigations*, vol. 5, 172.

49. Karl Rahner, "The Order of Redemption Within the Order of Creation," in *Mission and Grace: Essays in Pastoral Theology*, trans. Cecily Hastings (London: Sheed and Ward, 1963), 81.

50. Ibid., 89.

51. Rahner, "The Secret of Life," *Theological Investigations*, vol. 6, 146.

...the absolute fullness of the divine reality is the ultimate reason, and since this very one who starts everything by giving himself as the end is the ultimate goal, any understanding of being and nature conforms to reality only if it seeks to understand in the light of that future...[1]

Chapter 5

Eschatology: God All In All

What is the place of the material world in the *ordo salutis*? This is the third of the three questions which I argued (in the first chapter) that an ecological theology must raise and attempt to answer. Rahner's answer to this question can be found, as might be expected, in his eschatology. If the preceding chapters have in any way accomplished what they were intended to, Rahner's answer to the question just posed should be before us in outline. Since eschatology aims at elucidating the "end" of the world in terms of the fulfillment of God's purposes, and so the fulfillment of the world itself, the central concern of the present chapter is with the precise place of the material world in this fulfillment. Eschatology is essential to a ecological theology since convictions about *God's* purposes for the material world ultimately shape (or should shape) human attitudes toward the world.

In the first chapter, I rejected the idea that the Bible presents a picture of God as unconcerned with the destiny of the material world. I want to repeat this rejection here.[2] The Bible has an eschatological imagination which means that its understanding of the "end" (the "last things"), the fulfillment of God's purposes, is imaginative and pictorial. One part of this picture may serve to illustrate its intentions:

But the day of the Lord will come like a thief, and then the heavens will pass away with a loud noise, and the elements will be dissolved with fire, and the earth and everything that is done on it will be disclosed. Since all these things are to be dissolved in this way, what sort of persons ought you to be in leading lives of holiness and godliness...But in accordance with his promise, we wait for new heavens and a new earth, where righteousness is at home.[3]

The picture presented here is not simply that of the world being incinerated like so much refuse but that of the emergence of a new world, a world, unlike the present one, *where righteousness is at home.* This picture is important because it links human life now with the world to come, suggesting that human destiny and the destiny of the world are closely linked (as in Romans 8:18-23) in God's intentions. It is also important because it expresses the idea that what differentiates the old world from the new, the unconsummated from the consummated, is not that the first is a material world while the second is a purely spiritual one. The new world is not new because its materiality has been purged away but because *righteousness is at home in it.* This is a good picture to keep in mind as we explore Rahner's "ecological" eschatology.

Rahner's Approach to Eschatology

Eschatology: Theology Conjugated in the Future Tense

Rahner's theology is essentially eschatological.[4] He is critical of all attempts to treat eschatology as if it were simply the caboose on the train of theology, something simply to the end having no organic relationship to what comes before and whose detachment from the train would not essentially alter it.[5] Rather, eschatology must be organically related to all branches of theology, to theology proper (the doctrine of God), christology, anthropology, soteriology, hamartiology, and ecclesiology.[6] There are a number of ways in which this thesis might be demonstrated.

That Rahner's theology is essentially eschatological can be seen in his attempt to devise brief formulations of Christian faith. He argues that while the traditional creed remains valid, it is necessary to devise short formulas of the faith which are accessible to most Christians. Such formulas would provide the contemporary Christian with a "point of access and departure" for the *whole content of the faith.*[7] Rahner devises three such formulas each of which has a different emphasis due to its focus on a different person of the Trinity.[8]

The third of these three formulas, which focuses on the Spirit, attempts to provide an eschatological point of departure for understanding the content of Christian faith. This formula makes it clear that Christianity is an essentially eschatological faith. While it is doubtful that this formula will ever be used in a liturgical context, it does make a point:

> Christianity consists in an attitude of open inquiry into the absolute future which wills to give itself as such...in an act of self-bestowal, and which in Jesus Christ has confirmed this will which it has with eschatological irrevocability. It is the absolute future in this sense that is called God.[9]

This brief (and dense!) formula is an example of Rahner's view that the whole of theology must be set in an eschatological context. The first person of the Trinity is not simply the creator of the world but also its absolute (consummating) future. The second person is the irreversible manifestation of this future in history and the third person is the agent which enables human beings to receive this future. Christianity is an eschatological faith because God's relation to the world is essentially dynamic (as we saw in the third chapter) and future oriented.

We would be justified in hypothesizing that Rahner's *theology* is essentially eschatological in that his doctrine of *God* is essentially eschatological. Eschatology is the doctrine of God in the future tense. This thesis seems to find support in Rahner's first brief formula which he labels "theological". Emphasizing God's essential and irreducible mysteriousness, Rahner notes that God is the point of reference towards which the human being's transcendence is oriented. But God is not just a mysterious X, because God actually imparts Godself to human beings in their historical existence in an act of forgiving love. The historical dimension of this self-communication is essential because the "supreme eschatological point of God's self-bestowal in history, in which this self-bestowal is revealed as irrevocably victorious, is called Jesus Christ."[10]

Unless we recognize the eschatological setting of Rahner's doctrine of God we will fail to fully understand this doctrine. We must not simply think of God as the creator of the world or even simply as intimately present in the world. We must not think that the present relationship between God and the world is either static or permanent. As self-communicating love, God intends to communicate God's own self to the world in a complete and final way and it is at this point that the doctrine of God and the "end" of the world coincide because the fate of the world is such that God will be, in St. Paul's helpfully imprecise words, "all in all" (I Corinthians 15:28). God *is* the future of the world.

From what was said about it in the third chapter, it should be clear that this view is a consequence of Rahner's doctrine of the Trinity which stands at the center of his theology. Rahner's doctrine of the Trinity reminds us that the creation of the material world and human history within that world are moments in the process of God's self-communication, a communication which shows itself to be absolute in the Incarnation and the foundation of its own acceptance in the Holy Spirit.[11] Because creation is the condition of possibility for this self-communication (in that it constitutes an addressee) and because human history is the context in which this self-communication is either accepted or rejected, both of them take on a radical significance. Simply put, eschatology is the realization of the *one* God's *threefold* relationship with the world:

> It [the doctrine of the Trinity] may very well mean that the threefold God *as* threefold possesses in his divine self-communication "one" relationship to creation, but precisely a relationship which refers him *as* threefold, each person in his own way, to the world...the threefold, free, and gratuitous relation to us *is* not merely a copy or an analogy of the inner Trinity, but the Trinity itself...[12]

Christianity is essentially eschatological in that it is concerned with the *completion* of God's self-communication to the world, a communication which will consummate the world. This is the foundation of Rahner's conviction that Christianity is the *absolute religion*; among all religions it is the most unambiguous instance of "God's self-communication to what is not God...the self-communication in grace of God forgiving and divinizing his creatures."[13] Another path, not essentially distinct from the one just mentioned, to seeing the essentially eschatological character of Rahner's theology is his theological anthropology. This path gives the clearest indication of the impact of Rahner's theological method on eschatology. The essential relationship between Rahner's anthropology and eschatology can be put thus:

> It is indisputably clear that for Rahner all Christian theology is in a very genuine sense eschatology, since for him Christian eschatology is nothing but Christian anthropology read in the future tense, and Christian anthropology in turn is necessarily Christian theology.[14]

For Rahner, eschatology is essential because it transposes Christian anthropology into the terms of its fulfillment rendering it always already eschatological. Attempting to discuss Christian anthropology in a non-eschatological way is like discussing rose bushes while passing over the fact that they bloom; such a discussion would undoubtedly be interesting but it would neglect the very reason for which rose bushes are planted (and assiduously cared for).

If Rahner's eschatology is his anthropology conjugated in the future tense, we should not understand this to mean that eschatology concerns only human beings, that Rahner has reduced eschatology to a subjective human state (Bultmann) or understands it only to refer to the religious destiny of human beings (Schleiermacher). Rahner's eschatology is certainly not another version of Bultmann's. We need to remember the first principle of Rahner's theological anthropology, that the Incarnation allows us to think of dogmatic theology as theological anthropology because it shows that God has chosen to fully communicate Godself to us in and through a human being. Before we begin to debate whether Rahner's eschatology is either theocentric or anthropocentric, we must realize that he refuses (as is the case at so many other points!) to choose between the two options:

> As soon as man is understood as the being who is absolutely transcendent in respect of God, "anthropocentricity" and "theocentricity" in theology are not opposites but strictly one and the same thing, seen from two sides. Neither of the two aspects can be comprehended at all without the other.[15]

Only when we realize, through a transcendental anthropology, that the human being is characterized essentially by the *potencia oboedientialis* for the hypostatic union, only when we see that the human being is essentially oriented toward the absolute mystery of God who communicates Godself absolutely to the human being, do we understand why theocentricity and anthropocentricity are not necessarily opposites but must be seen as dialectically related. And when this is understood, we have a firm grasp of why Christian anthropology is essentially eschatological. To say that the human being is essentially the *potencia oboedientialis* for the hypostatic union is to say simultaneously what the end or consummation of this being will be. For Rahner, the destiny of the human being--and of the whole cosmos--has been made known and actualized in the Incarnation. Thus, when we say that eschatology is anthropology in the future tense, anthropology in its consummated state, we mean that eschatology is the "revelation of the fulfillment promised by God's trinitarian self-disclosure and graceful self-communication" in Jesus Christ to creation."[16]

Having established that eschatology is an essential feature of Rahner's theology and having suggested two vantage points from which this point can be seen, we must advance to the question of what, specifically, is the content of eschatology and how eschatological statements are to be interpreted.

Eschatology: Its Possibility and Meaning

There is, it hardly need be said, a certain mistrust of eschatology on the part of many theologians because they see it as they see metaphysics, as "news from nowhere". This view is derived from the fact that scripture does not present us with a theory of eschatology, a coherent doctrine, but with a collage of eschatological pictures and images. To make matters even more difficult, even many theological discussions of eschatology have not, as Rahner notes, advanced beyond "a relatively superficial arrangement of the statements from scripture".[17] Given that this is the case, it is not surprising that much has been said on the theme of eschatology not fitting in with the "modern world view". One of the most notable writers on this theme is Rudolf Bultmann for whom New Testament eschatology is unintelligible. After a lapidary account of the New Testament's "mythological world view" he concludes that

> *mythological eschatology* is untenable for the simple reason that the parousia of Christ never took place as the New Testament expected. History did not come to an end, and, as every schoolboy knows, it will continue to run its course. Even if we believe that the world as we know it will come to an end in time, we expect the end to take the form of a natural catastrophe, not of a mythological event such as the New Testament expects.[18]

Bultmann says, correctly, that liberal Protestant theology ignored eschatology and thus reduced Christianity to a collection of timeless religious truths and ethics. Rather than ignore eschatology, Bultmann interprets it yet interprets it away. In Bultmann eschatology is anthropology in a reductionist sense. Eschatology becomes "eschatological existence" in which the

> believer has life here and now, and has passed already from death to life...*Outwardly everything remains as before*, but *inwardly* his relation to the world has been radically changed. The world has no further claim on him, for faith is the victory which overcomes the world (1 John 5:4).[19]

While Bultmann is to be commended for wanting to make sense of eschatology instead of ignoring it, and for his rejection of dualistic interpretations of New Testament eschatology, it must be said that the effects of Kantianism, which, as was noted in the first chapter, rendered Christian theology unable to think about the natural world, are to be seen here too. In Bultmann eschatology undergoes a double reduction. First, eschatology is divorced from the course of human history; it does not involve the consummation of human history but involves an ever renewed *existential (existentiel!)* orientation on the part of the individual. Second, the cosmic dimension of eschatology is completely eliminated, because of the Kantian view that we can not make statements about the cosmos as such since this would be falling into transcendental illusion. Eschatology has to do solely with invididual human self-understanding.

While this is not the place for a complete discussion of Bultmann's program, it may be noted that Rahner sees in this eschatology a mixture of insight and theological error.[20] While more about this will be said later, for the moment we can say that from Rahner's viewpoint Bultmann's anthropology renders human being a-cosmic; for all his good intentions, Bultmann can not speak of eschatology as the *consummation of the whole cosmos* in God. It is Rahner's conviction that it is possible to so understand eschatology without falling into "mythology".

While he does not so express it, Rahner criticizes Bultmann's hermeneutic of eschatological statements because it fails to realize an essential truth:

> The Catholic faith is the reconciliation [of mythology and philosophy] because it is the realization of both mythology and philosophy. It is a story and it that sense one of a hundred stories; only it is a true story. It is a philosophy and in that sense it is life itself. But above all, it is a reconciliation because it is something that can only be called a philosophy of stories. [21]

The point here is that Christianity is a true *story* and as such we do not have access to its truth apart from the story and its pictures, images, and imaginative content. While Bultmann criticizes liberal Protestant theology for reducing Christianity to timeless truths, his position does not go beyond this view; for him eschatology involves a set of timeless truths even if these must constantly be appropriated anew.

This is not a minor point. Unclarity about the nature of eschatological language results in unclarity about what such language means and about what we can reasonably expect to learn from it. It will be impossible to think about an eschatology which includes the cosmos if Bultmann's view of eschatological language is not overcome. We can not, Rahner insists, attribute the cosmic dimension of eschatology to the pictorial character of biblical language, as if all such language were simply a naive way of making statements about human existence. Human beings are essentially imaginative creatures and this means that for them all knowledge about any reality "no matter how supramundane the object or strict and abstract the notion, is knowledge in 'likenesses and parables'."[22] This is an essential anthropological fact which any analysis of human knowing must accept, a fact which Rahner makes much of in *Spirit in the World*. The *conversio ad phantasma* means that there is no human knowledge apart from sense experience which means that all "human knowledge is always bipolar--conceptual and intuitional at the same time."[23] It is not, as Bultmann seems to think, as if pictorial thinking is a sign of intellectual helplessness, something no longer necessary for mature, sophisticated moderns. The *conversio ad phantasma*, of which Bultmann's anthropology is insufficiently aware, means that

> a "myth" can only be replaced by another, but not by language utterly devoid of images. And here of course one will not be so naive as to think that the thing had once been thought of without images but that this lofty concept had then been clothed in "imagery" for the sake of the weaker brethren.[24]

Thus while Rahner agrees that something like "demythologization" (he does not particularly like the term) is necessary, since theology can not simply take eschatological statements at face value and attempt to arrange them in some coherent way, any attempt to understand eschatology must have a transcendental moment in which it is examined according to "the necessary conditions given by the possibility of knowledge and action on the part of the subject himself."[25] If eschatology treats of God's fulfillment of the human being and the world, we must be clear about the conditions of possibility which make such a fulfillment understandable, we must consider *transcendental eschatology*. Bultmann did this insufficiently. Even to think about eschatology we must understand, for example, that it concerns a spiritual being whose knowledge is essentially a mixture of concept and image and who, as we saw in the first chapter, has an essential relationship to the body and to the world. Transcendental eschatology makes it impossible for us to think that the cosmic dimension of eschatology is simply the result of a regrettably pictorial imagination and that it is possible to speak of human fulfillment apart from the fulfillment of the world. Transcendental eschatology attempts to make eschatology comprehensible by connecting it with a non-reductionist understanding of the human being and its relation to the world. Rahner is not so much interested in demythologization as he is in transmythologization.[26]

Eschatology had fundamentally to do with consummation, the consummation of God's self-communication to the world which is its highest fulfillment. In the third chapter we attempted to show that this means that the world participates in the mystery of the Trinity. Because of this, Rahner says that eschatology must be considered mysterious, something *forever* beyond our understanding. This deceptively simple idea implies at least three somewhat complex notions.

First, it means that eschatology does not simply concern the future because it concerns the self-communication of God which is now taking place. Eschatology has an intrinsic relationship to the present because the "end" is not added to history like a second story is added to an already complete house, having an essentially superfluous relationship to it. The present, as Bultmann realized, is an eschatological moment even though eschatology can not be reduced to the present but retains an element of futurity. The future of the cosmos is an intrinsic part of the present because the future of the cosmos is God who is, as we have seen, an intrinsic part of the world process, if this may be so stated. Eschatology does not involve idle speculation about the future. Thus, on this account, the "eschatological future remains uncontrollable and hidden and yet also present, something we really look forward to, something in the presence of which we hope, love, trust, and surrender ourselves.[27]

Second, because eschatology involves not simply the future of the world but also the future of the Triune God, eschatological statements are not to be seen as predictions; because eschatology deals with God's own self-communication, which remains essentially mysterious even in revelation, eschatology can not have the status of a cosmic weather forecast. Eschatological statements do not give us information about the future *before the fact*. Using the word "apocalyptic" in a way of which recent biblical scholarship would not approve, Rahner says that "to extrapolate from the present into the future is eschatology, to interpret from the future into the present is apocalyptic."[28] While his use of the term apocalyptic in this way is questionable, what Rahner is rejecting is the idea that eschatological statements are predictions of the future, predictions which come from glimpses of a future already realized in a supra-temporal realm and waiting to be actualized in the history of the world. Rahner rejects this view because it disregards the essential historicity of the human being; human history is reduced to a screen on which an already made movie is projected.

Third, eschatology must be seen as based on the *present situation of salvation viewed in terms of its fulfillment*. This is the opposite of "apocalyptic". Eschatology is not about the projecting of a future into the present but about a future already present in history seen in terms of its culmination. The future is the dynamism which moves the present into its fulfillment.[29] This is an essential point. The *possibility* of eschatology rests not on privileged glimpses of the future but on the present situation of salvation, which is an eschatological present. Eschatology "derives from the situation of the history of salvation brought about by the event of Christ" and, therefore, "Christian anthropology and Christian eschatology are ultimately Christology, in the unity...of the different phases of the beginning, the present, and the completed end."[30] In speaking about eschatology we are not speaking about a future which has yet to arrive but a future whose culminating point has been manifested in a historical event, the Incarnation. This event reveals and inaugurates the destiny of the cosmos for it is the culmination of God's self-communication--the point at which God irrevocably commits Godself to the world--and this self-communication is the proper consummation of the cosmos.

Eschatology as the Fulfillment of the Human Being's Relation to the World

Transcendental Eschatology

Rahner's eschatology is shaped by his theological anthropology. This much has been alluded to already. What needs to be made clear now is why eschatology *must* be thought of in part as the fulfillment of the human being's relationship to the world, not the dissolution of this relationship or the eternal prolongation of it in its present condition. In order to do this we shall have to enter into a brief discussion of transcendental eschatology, a concept which has been mentioned already.

For our purposes, transcendental eschatology focuses on three essential features of the human being as presuppositions which must condition eschatological thinking. In the case of each feature, we must begin by asking this question: Given that this is an essential feature of human being, how must we then understand eschatology as the situation of the consummation of this being in the world?

(1) *The human being is a material/spiritual unity.* The human being, as we learned in the second chapter, is a worldly spirit in that this being is spiritual (self-transcending) and realizes this spirituality precisely in matter

(the body and the world). Because of this, the relationship between body and soul can not be thought of in a dualistic way but must be conceived, as argued in *Spirit in the World*, dialectically. The human being is not simply a spirit but a spirit-in-the-world whose relation to the body and the world is not fortuitous but essential. Because eschatology deals in part with the consummation of a "corporeal person...an absolute and ultimately irresolvable unity of matter and spirit," it can not understand the destiny of the soul apart from that of the world.[31] A false eschatology would speak of an abstract soul for which the destiny of the world is of no importance. Salvation has often been understood as a drama in which the world is merely a stage on which the action is carried out but which is irrelevant to the drama itself. If the human being is an essentially material/spiritual unity, then this way of thinking about salvation must be radically revised and we may say that the

> *whole* is a drama, and the stage itself is also part of it. It is a dialogue
> between spiritual and divinized creatures and God, a dialogue and a drama
> which has already reached its irreversible climax in Christ. The world,
> then, is not merely a stopping-off place which is always there and which
> gives an individual the opportunity to make further progress in the course
> of his own individual history.[32]

In taking this view, Rahner lays the foundation for understanding the place of the material world in the *ordo salutis*. Whether eschatology is concerned with the consummation of the human being's relation to the world or the consummation of the world itself, both of which fall into its purview, it must realize that matter is not a provisional element which will be abolished at the consummation but a permanent factor in the human being's relationship to God.[33]

(2) *The human being is temporal and free.* The rudiments of both these essential features were discussed in the second chapter. As was noted there, temporality is not simply something that the human being happens to be "in" but is an essential determination of the human being as kinetic, as a being who *becomes* and who is in the process of self-realization. Temporality is essentially related to freedom in that freedom, for Rahner, is the human capacity for self-realization; in as much as the human being is a *finite and free* being, this being is temporal. For Rahner temporality fundamentally indicates incompleteness, moving toward completion; temporality is not simply a mere succession of moments but also a movement toward the attainment of fullness of being.

Because this is the case, human existence is fundamentally (transcendentally) future oriented; the human being *is* a movement toward a future self-realization.   In this way human existence is essentially eschatological.   Eschatology does not concern the abolition (or circumvention) of human freedom but rather its essential fulfillment. For Rahner "man experiences himself as a historical being endowed with responsibility and freedom in such a way that he exists in a time the meaning of which involves a clear and irreversible forward orientation".[34] Knowing this, it is possible to better understand Rahner's critique of Bultmann's eschatology.   Rahner holds the view that Bultmann has insufficiently understood human temporality (and this is interesting because both have been influenced by Heidegger). In seeing eschatology as having to do simply with the moment in which a genuine self-understanding is realized, Bultmann has eliminated futurity from temporality; he focuses on the "eternal now" of individual decision while Rahner emphasizes the movement toward definitive fulfillment.   Of course, ultimately behind these two concepts of temporality there are two different views of God's relation to the world. Bultmann's view does not go beyond verbalism while Rahner's involves God's real ontological self-communication to the world:

> Time is a unique process posited in its beginning by God's free timeless act of creation and dependent, throughout its course, on that creative act; it moves in a definitive way, though one hidden from temporal beings, towards a perfectly determined, final and irrevocable end, in which the whole of reality, each creature according to its kind, will, in a way that we cannot more precisely conceive, *participate in a created way in the eternity of God.*[35]

Rahner opposes the view which contrasts human freedom to the material world as if they were opposites; for him such a contrast is gnostic. Because of the human constitution, human freedom must be thought of as a freedom which is realized in the world. As finite freedom it must always be so.   This understanding of freedom emphasizes the essential relationship between the human being and the world. It is not the case, as the gnostic view would have it, that human freedom will be fulfilled when it is removed from the context (constraint) of the body and the world. Rather, the world is precisely the environment in which human freedom is realized so that the world is essential to human self-realization. Since this is the case, the world can not be a static entity for a static world could not be the proper context of a dynamic freedom. The idea of a dynamic human freedom which is opposed to a static, lifeless world rests on a philosophical mistake because the human being can not "conceive that this history as a free being, considered as something that takes place in the material world as subject to time, is something enacted, as it were, on a static stage".[36] Human freedom is realized in a world which is itself, because God has become its innermost dynamism, becoming and moving toward a definitive realization.

(3) *The human being is individual and social.* Any eschatology which ignores the corporate dimension of salvation makes a fundamental mistake. This is because one of the transcendental features of the human being, as Rahner argues in *Hearers of the Word*, is sociality. The human being is fundamentally an interpersonal being situated in a cosmos and therefore eschatology must be conceived as the consummation not only of the human being's relation to the world but also as the consummation of the human being's relation to other human beings. It is interesting, as Phan notes, that even after abandoning monogenism as a theological theory, Rahner continues to insist on the fundamental unity of humankind. For him, there is among human beings an indissoluble solidarity in guilt and salvation.[37] There is no good reason for thinking that the consummation of the world involves the abrogation of this solidarity.

Yet, just as it would be a fundamental mistake to develop an eschatology which concerned only individuals (especially individual souls), so it would be equally mistaken to develop an eschatology which failed to see the genuinely individual dimension of human existence. This view is the logical consequence of Rahner's understanding of human freedom. Eschatology must take seriously the fact that human beings become what they are through choices and decisions which they themselves make. Eschatology must consider the consummation of what human beings have become through freedom in history as either salvation or damnation. To neglect individual eschatology would be, for Rahner, to fail to take human history seriously.

This ultimately means that eschatology must be viewed stereoscopically; the two different dimensions of eschatology must be viewed simultaneously:

> Man as corporeal, historical reality and man as transcendental spirit; man as an individual and man as a member of the human race, or a member of a collective reality; man as a spiritual person and man as a reality to whom there necessarily belongs a world as the milieu and envornoment in which he actualizes his existence: all of these phrases in their plurality are the presupposition for eschatological statements...the fulfillment of this concrete person cannot be expressed in any other way except by his being regarded *both* as an element in the world *and also* as an ever unique and incalculable person who cannot be reduced to the world and to society.[38]

This means that eschatology will have to be dialectical, considering both the individual and corporate dimensions of salvation, dimensions which include not only human beings as a whole but the cosmos as well. These two dimensions will have to be dialectically related without the expectation that they can be harmonized because, as *Spirit in the World* makes clear, the human being itself can only be understood dialectically.[39]

Transcendental eschatology is inevitably ecological eschatology because of its presuppositions. It presupposes that the human being is a spiritual/material unity and that the two dimensions of this unity (soul and body) must be dialectically related rather than separated. It also presupposes that since human existence is fundamentally corporeal existence, we can not think of this existence atomistically because being corporeal it is essentially related to, as Rahner put it in the passage cited above, the "milieu and environment" in which human existence is actualized.

The Pancosmicity of the Soul and the Resurrection of the Body

In order to get a clearer idea of Rahner's understanding of the place of the material world in the *ordo salutis*, I propose to look briefly at two aspects of his eschatology, the relationship of the soul to the world after death and the meaning of the phrase "resurrection of the body". In each case we will be looking at the fruit of Rahner's transcendental eschatology and in each case we will be asking whether the material world plays an intrinsic or extrinsic role in the two dimensions of eschatological fulfillment.

Rahner's theology of death is an important aspect of his eschatology (and of his christology as well), yet it will only be possible here to comment on it as it is relevant to the limited aims of the present inquiry.[40]

The basic principle of Rahner's theology of death stems directly from his transcendental anthropology. In this context, "body" and "soul" are not "substances" but two dimensions of one existence. Because the human being is essentially spirit-in-the-world, a spiritual/corporeal unity, death can not simply be something which affects the body alone. For Rahner, the view that death is simply the liberation of the soul from the body is gnostic and not Christian. He also rejects as mythological the view that eternal life involves the eternal continuation (after death) of life as we now experience it. It is not true that, in Feuerbach's phrase, at death we simply change horses and ride on. It is not surprising that Rahner rejects both these views as not being sufficiently dialectical and, therefore, as not treating the full reality of death.

Death must be seen as both the separation of the soul from the body and the definitive end of the pilgrimage of life. It will be helpful to explore both these ideas though our primary interest is in the former.

Death is the definitive end of the human pilgrimage. The idea that life after death is essentially a continuation of the present life fails to see that death is the radical end of life as we know it. This view sees death simply as the point at which we change horses and ride on. What it fails to see is the fact that death is the point of "final and definitive completion" and as such is the goal toward which all temporal life is directed.[41] Rahner shares Heidegger's sense, though it means something different for him, that human life is a being-towards-death. While it is possible to speak of death as the consequence of sin, this does not get at the full reality (mystery) of death. This is so for Rahner because it is death as the radical end of temporal life that gives meaning to human freedom. As has been noted already, for Rahner freedom is the capacity to attain a definitive realization of one's existence in history. If historical, temporal human life extended on for eternity, freedom as Rahner conceives it would be rendered meaningless because if there is no definitive point of self-realization, then "the self-disposal of the subject could at any time be revised, so that each particular decision would become irrelevant since it could always be revised and replaced by another."[42] In other words, it is the fact that the human pilgrimage come to an *end* that gives consequence to free human acts because the time for attaining a definitive self-realization is *limited*; we are not free, because of the fact of death, to continually revise our lives and this makes each moment and each act radically important. To see death as the end of the human pilgrimage is to see that death

> as the end of man as a spiritual person must be an active consummation from within brought about by the person himself, a maturing self-realization which embodies the result of what man has made of himself during life, the achievement of total self-possession, a real effectuation of self...[43]

Death is also the separation of the soul from the body. We might regard the way in which Rahner treats this subject as a test of his seriousness about the necessary place of the material world in the *ordo salutis*. We have already noted that Rahner rejects the view that in being separated from the body the soul becomes a-cosmic, that it ceases to have any relationship with the world, and the associated view that salvation is to be understood as the liberation of the soul from the body and the world.

In the second chapter it was argued that Rahner's metaphysical vision is essentially non-dualistic and an exposition of *Spirit in the World* showed that soul and body are dialectically related to one another in that the soul needs the body for its own fulfillment. How, then, is the separation of the soul from the body in death to be understood? In order to answer this question, it needs to be remembered that in generating the body as its own self-realization, the soul "must also have some relationship to the whole of which the body is a part, that is, to the totality which constitutes the unity of the material universe."[44] It is through the body that the soul is related to the world *as a totality*. This is to say that the soul's relationship to the material world through the body is not accidental or extrinsic but is necessary and intrinsic because the world is a unity. The soul has a necessary and intrinsic relationship to the body because the soul's informing of the body is a substantial rather than an accidental act. This act of the soul is "built into the material reality, as an act which is not really distinct from the soul.[45]

This means, Rahner concludes, that at death the soul *can not become a-cosmic*. If the soul can not become a-cosmic when it is separated from the body only one logical possibility remains which is that the soul's relationship to the totality of the material world (its pancosmicity) *is more fully realized*. In Rahner's view, this is demanded by Thomistic metaphysics. When separated from the body at death the soul becomes not *a-cosmic* (removed from the world) but more fully *pancosmic*, which means that what is attained is a "deeper and more comprehensive openness" in which the soul's comprehensive relation to the universe is more fully realized.[46] This new relationship is comprehensible in light of the fact that the soul is never to be understood as a closed monad but is always already open in principle to the whole of reality. In this way, Rahner shows that the material world remains essential in the *ordo salutis*. Rather than being "released" from the world at death, the soul's transcendental relationship to the world is fulfilled; what is realized is a more intimate relationship to that ground of the unity "of the universe which is hard to conceive yet very real and in which all things in the world are interrelated."[47] This is the pancosmicity of the soul. It may well be understood as the logical consequence of Rahner's view that as a worldly spirit the human being's destiny is always bound up with that of the earth. (How this is to be imagined or experienced is not the question, for Rahner is concerned with the structure of human existence and experience.)

The pancosmicity of the soul does not exhaust the consummation of the human being's relation to the world; eschatology is not complete without a consideration of the resurrection of the body. One of the problems posed by the view that salvation involves the liberation of the soul from the world is that it renders the resurrection of the body problematic, if not superfluous. If this view is correct and the soul is given the ontological promotion of being free of the world, then the resurrection of the body can only appear to be a demotion. In this view, the symbol "eternal life" has wrongly eclipsed the symbol "resurrection of the body" as in much popular thinking about eschatology. While Rahner does not wish to totally abandon the immortality of the soul, he does think that resurrection of the body should be used to describe the eschatological state of human fulfillment in relation to the world. According to the doctrinal tradition, the soul remains pancosmic after death until the eschaton, at which point it receives a glorified spiritual body (I Corinthians 15). In order to enter into its final fulfillment, the soul must receive a body which is appropriate to it; the glorified body possesses a "corporeality which is the actual expression of spirit."[48] This body becomes the "perfect expression of the enduring relation of the glorified person to the cosmos as a whole."[49]

In speaking of the resurrection of the body, Rahner wishes to speak of the eschatological fulfillment of the human being whose unity is composed of matter and spirit. Resurrection of the body should be taken to mean "the termination and perfection of the *whole* man before God, which gives him eternal life."[50] It is not that resurrection of the body and eternal life are incompatible concepts (the Creed sets them side by side without any apparent difficulty), yet one gets the impression that Rahner chooses to speak of resurrection because he sees the concept of eternal life as having lost much of its usefulness through its association with "gnostic" types of thinking. For Rahner, using the phrase resurrection of the body to describe the human being's eschatological fulfillment is a way of emphasizing that the material world is not a provisional reality but also has a permanent place, with the soul, in the *ordo salutis*:

> When we say "bodily" resurrection, we are simply saying that we are thinking of the whole man as brought into perfect fulfillment and that in accordance with our own experience of human reality we cannot divide him into an ever-valid "spirit" and a merely provisional "body".[51]

To affirm the resurrection of the body is to affirm that even in its state of final eschatological fulfillment the human being's destiny is bound to that of the earth and that the human being "is not merely a strange guest in the world remaining untouched by it."[52] To speak of the resurrection of the body is not necessarily to lapse into mythology; it is not necessarily a naively pictorial way of speaking of authentic existence or some "spiritual" reality. The eschatological symbols of resurrection of the body and of new heaven and new earth (Revelation 21:1) express the important truth that, as transcendental anthropology and eschatology make clear, it is *impossible* to think of the human being's eschatological fulfillment in abstraction from the material world. An eschatology which overlooks this is not an eschatology which deals with the human nature which Christian faith knows:

> Anyone who despises this earthly world and dismisses the perfected man from this earth for good, spiritualistically or existentially or in whatever way, directing him into a beatitude of (supposedly) pure spirits, stultifies and betrays the true reality of man, the child of the earth.[53]

As we saw in the third chapter, the fulfillment of the human being consists in receiving God's complete self-communication which results in an immediate relationship with God. What is communicated, as was noted, is God's own self and the result of this self-communication is divinization--not that human beings become absorbed into God but that they enter the intimate life of God. There is no contradiction between this idea and the resurrection of the body; indeed, the resurrection of the body is part of the process of divinization. The point to be made here is that neither the body nor the world is to be understood as an obstacle standing between human beings and God:

> We must simply try to realize clearly and soberly that a spiritual union with God cannot be regarded as something which grows in inverse proportion to the belonging to the *material* world...Remoteness-from-the-world and nearness-to-God are not interchangeable notions, however much we are accustomed to think in such a framework.[54]

It would be a mistake to see the resurrection, as Rahner understands it, simply as the fulfillment of the human being; the resurrection of the body has cosmic significance. The resurrection of Jesus, like the Incarnation (as we saw in the previous chapter), has significance for all created reality, not simply human beings. This is so because Jesus's glorified body represents the effects (in a mode similar to sacramental causality, in which a finite reality mediates the immediate presence of God) the complete fulfillment of God's saving purpose for the world and for human beings.[55] God irrevocably communicates Godself to Jesus whom "the resurrection definitively identifies and acknowledges, and so admits the world to salvation with eschatological finality."[56]

The resurrection of the body is not a symbol of a destiny which applies only to human beings but is a symbol of the destiny of *the whole cosmos*. In the glorified body of Jesus there is the "beginning of the transfiguration of the world as an ontologically interconnected occurrence," a beginning in which "the destiny of the world is already in principle decided and has already begun."[57] In other words, "the world as a whole flows into his Resurrection and into the transfiguration of his body."[58]

Rahner's interpretation of the resurrection takes seriously the intrinsic relationship between the human body and the cosmos. As was noted in the second chapter, while the human being is the culmination of created reality in the sense of being closest to God, Rahner does not see this preeminence as meaning that the human is somehow abstracted from the world or manages to get beyond it. The human being is a creature of the earth and shares its destiny even if the destiny of the earth is revealed in a human being as it is in Jesus Christ. In terms of our question as to whether Rahner preserves the necessary and essential place of the material world in the *ordo salutis*, I think that it is clear that his non-dualistic metaphysic comes to its fruition in his eschatology. Rahner's position on the place of the material world in the *ordo salutis* can, I think, be summed up thus: Because the human being is an incarnate, inter-mundane spirit, the world must participate in the fulfillment of this being by ontological necessity. The material world is and remains the "connatural surrounding" of the eschatologically fulfilled human being even as it attains a realized intimacy with God.[59] In other words, the fulfillment of the human being in God and the fulfillment of the world in God *coincide*. Thus:

> I believe, that we will one day be the living, the complete and achieved ones, in the whole expanse and in all the dimensions of our existence; I believe that... the material in us and in the world surrounding us...is not simply identical with what is unreal and mere appearance, with what has been cast off once and for all and which passes away before the final state of man.[60]

Eschatology as the Consummation of The World's Relationship to God

Immanent and Transcendent Consummation of the World

In speaking of the resurrection of the body we have already touched upon the subject of the consummation of the world, the fulfillment of the cosmos. Strictly speaking, the consummation of the world is, as we have seen, God. The world attains its fulfillment in a definitive immediacy to God through God's self-communication in grace. God is the world's absolute future. As the absolute future, God is "not the object among others with which one is concerned as an individual object" but rather as the "ground of this whole projection toward the future."[61] If God is the absolute future of the world in this way, we must be reticent about describing the world's consummation because it is, strictly speaking, a mystery. God as the absolute future of the world

> does not constitute any specific event within the world, representing one particular element in it such as can be defined in "this worldly" categories. Rather it is the specification of the world as a whole, comprehending the whole of reality and determining where its consummation is to be achieved.[62]

This future has a mysterious character and should not be identified with any particular hope for a planned future state of affairs.

Nevertheless, for Rahner there are two ways of speaking about this consummation. It can be spoken of both as immanent and as transcendent provided that these are related dialectically and that their common origin-- God--is kept clearly in mind. Immanent consummation of the world means, of course, that consummation which comes from within the world and its history. What Rahner means by this is indicated in a comment he makes about the eschatological imagery of the new heaven and new earth and the resurrection of the body. What these images indicate is

> the all-powerfulness of God over the dead, who even when dead can not escape him; indeed, we may conjecture that God in his omnipotence, just because he is all-powerful and never in danger of being rivaled, *will give even the created forces of the world a share in the work of consummation* of the dead into the life beyond all death.[63]

The absolute future is of necessity something which can only be brought about by God.   Yet because of his understanding of God's relation to the world, Rahner thinks that the processes immanent within the world have a role in its consummation.   In other words, God's omnipotence, as Rahner understands it, does not mean that God must exercise all power and that the world is passive before God.

In speaking of the immanent consummation of the world, in according the world a role in its own consummation, Rahner is making the point that it would be wrong to think of the absolute future as simply involving the abolition of the present world.   The world, as we have seen, is not simply a training ground for souls in the making, which, having served its purpose, can be dispensed with.   The world is not merely a boot camp for heaven.   It is precisely *this world* which is consummated.[64]   It is this world and its history, which constitute the connatural setting of human fulfillment, which is "the dimension in which the final consummation and the absolute future are made real."[65]

If the world and its history are participants in their own consummation, not only does the material world have an essential place in the *ordo salutis* but human activity does so as well.   For Rahner, as we saw in the second chapter, this world is not simply the world that God created; it is also a world which is shaped by what human beings *do*.   Human Beings, in the language of *Gaudium et spes*, "project further the work creation".[66]   The human being participates in the continuing creativity of God and what this being achieves (in terms of who he or she becomes) and what this being does with the world will pass into the consummation of the world.   This means that what human beings do in history with themselves and to the world has eschatological significance.   Eschatology, as we have seen, does not dissolve human responsibility but rather radicalizes it.   Human beings have the capacity, Rahner seems to be saying, and the awful responsibility of making the world more open to its absolute future.   This is because

> history itself constructs its own final and definitive state. That which endures is the work of love as expressed in the concrete in human history. It [human effort] remains itself as something achieved by man, and not merely a moral distillation of this, something which history becomes behind it as though it were the "grapes" from which the wine had been pressed.[67]

The exact way in which the immanent consummation contributes to the eschatological state of the world is something which Rahner says is beyond our knowing, because this touches upon the mystery of God. We can, however, say that the task of completing the creation and the fulfilling of it appear as an intrinsic element in the one total redemptive and divinizing will of God for the world in which his self-bestowal is achieved, and this task and the fulfilling of it derive from this totality their ultimate meaning and a concrete form.[68]

There is also a transcendent consummation of the world. As we saw in the third chapter, immanence and transcendence are not opposites but two dimensions of the one reality of God. We should not, then, see immanent consummation and transcendent consummation as being in competition or opposition; both have their origin in God. This is what the passage just cited affirms. The eschatological consummation of the world, as a transcendent consummation, is God, yet, in an important sense, God is immanent within the world as its innermost dynamic. Because of this, Christian eschatology is not a "doctrine of a static existence of the world and of man which...repeats itself" but rather a doctrine of an "absolute becoming which does not continue into emptiness but really attains the absolute future" which future is indeed "already moving *within* it."[69] In other words,

> God is not only the Creator of a world different from himself. Of his own initiative, and in that act of immediate self-bestowal which we call grace, he has made himself the intrinsic principle of the world...[70]

Ultimately, this is the reason why the material world has an essential place in the *ordo salutis*--because God as creator is not only the *telos* of the world but also the immanent principle of the world which moves it toward this *telos*. The material world is the connatural environment of the human being's fulfillment because God is the connatural principle of the world's fulfillment. The world as a totality is essentially oriented in all its dimensions toward the absolute, uncontrollable, incalculable, and inconceivable mystery of God. This is, as we have seen, the definitive truth of the Incarnation. Because of this orientation, Rahner believes that no description of its fulfillment is possible. It is possible, however, to say two things about this state, a state which all the colors of the Christian palette can not paint. It is possible to say that the world undergoes or achieves (depending upon one's vantage point) a self-transcendence. This does not mean that the world is abolished or absorbed into God; it simply means that--and this is all we can say about it--it attains a relation of deepest intimacy with God. The Incarnation is the model here. The Incarnation of the Logos in the man Jesus does not, as we have seen, destroy his humanity or result in his absorption into God but rather fulfills his transcendence which is precisely a *self-transcendence toward God*. God is the fulfillment of human self-transcendence just as God is the source of it in the supernatural existential. The same is true, *mutatis mutandis*, of the cosmos as a whole.

It is also possible to say that this self-transcendence is a transcendence into the absolute mystery of God. After the achievement of such self-transcendence it would be impossible to regard God and the world, spirit and matter as disparate realities because their true relationship would have become apparent. Whatever might be said about this culminating self-transcendence, it must be said that its source is to be found in God's love and that it is a self-transcendence (as all love really is) into God's love. It would be possible to summarize this exposition by saying that God

is the "transcendent" consummation, and therefore can and will, precisely *as* God, himself be "immanent" consummation and the "immanent principle" of the movement toward this single real and uniquely fulfilling consummation that is the fullness of finality: God--all in all.[71]

Self-Transcendence: A Model

To say that the world as a whole attains its consummation as a self-transcendence into God is to say at the same time a great deal and not very much. On one hand it is to say a great deal because this unique self-transcendence and the means through which it is achieved is of tremendous significance. On the other hand it is to leave much that needs to be explained and illuminated. I think that it is possible to better understand what Rahner means by the self-transcendence of the world into the mystery of God if we take his understanding of evolution as a model for what he intends.

In terms of understanding the place of the material world in the *ordo salutis*, this model is significant because it is based upon a process within the material world. To see the cosmos as a dynamic and changing whole of which the Incarnation is the highest point is to avoid seeing matter as essentially static and dead, as mere dross to be burned away by the consuming fire that is God. The evolutionary process does bring about the new without creating the impression that the material world can at some point be left behind. As we have seen, the material world will itself be taken up into a final perfection, a perfection which is God, and this is because in Rahner's understanding of self-transcendence the world can not be seen "as a mere launching pad which is left, as the first stage of a movement which is simply cast off."[72]

We have already seen that for Rahner God is not one influence among many in the world but the world's innermost dynamism. This means that the world, which must always be thought of as a unity, must be seen as always being open to God, as possessing "in the physical and biological realm the characteristic of the possibility of self-transcendence" which means that each thing "in its own stage can become something else, can change and become 'more'."[73] As the immanent dynamism of the world and its creative and sustaining ground, God must be the "dynamic ground and bearer of all evolution."[74] Rahner understands evolution to be the actualization of the openness of all reality to God, to self-transcendence. Thus, God as the world's innermost dynamism must be seen as the "enduring, active support of cosmic reality" and must be thought of as "actively enabling finite things themselves by their own activity to transcend themselves."[75] The result of this process, considered ontologically, is an increase in being, the attainment of finite reality to a "more"--an ontological elevation.

The mechanism for accomplishing this becoming is, of course, God's quasi-formal causality. As we have seen, this causality is unique to God. Such a causality results in a development which can legitimately be said to have come from the creature; quasi-formal causality is not an interventionist causality. God becomes an intrinsic feature of the creature while transcending it and remaining distinct from it. Because of the intrinsic nature of this causality, the creature's becoming must be seen as a product of its own agency:

> The agent's rising beyond and above itself in action and becoming takes place because the absolute being [God] is the cause and ground of this self-movement, in such a way that the latter has this fundamental ground immanent within it as a factor intrinsically related to this movement. It is, therefore, true self-transcendence, not merely a passive being lifted beyond self. Yet it is not on that account a movement within absolute being, because the latter, though a factor immanent in the self-movement of the subject of change which is advancing beyond itself, at the same time remains free and unaffected above it, unmoved by giving movement...[76]

This brief discussion should make the process of the world's consummation at least somewhat more comprehensible. The point to be kept in mind when speaking about the eschatological consummation is that the world as such is open to it by its very constitution. The process of evolution represents many points of self-transcendence while eschatological consummation represents the radicalization and the fulfillment of all self-transcendence. To say that the outcome of this radicalization is, in St. Paul's words, "God all in all" is not just to be pious. To say this is to communicate the truth that the world has God as its source and *telos* and that God is the means for moving from the one to the other. This truth is grasped by the Apocalypse (Revelation 21:6) which understands God as *alpha* and *omega*, *genesis* and *telos*. Ultimately, Rahner insists, God is the world's *way*, *truth*, and *light* (John 14:6).

Notes

1. Karl Rahner, "Marxist Utopia and the Christian Future of Man," *Theological Investigations*, vol, 6, 60-61.
2. Helpful in this regard is John W. Cooper, *Body, Soul, and Life Everlasting: Biblical Anthropology and the Monism-Dualism Debate* (Grand Rapids, MI: Wm. B. Eerdmans, 1989).
3. II Peter 3:10-11, 13.
4. In light of this fact it is surprising that in her thorough study of Rahner's theological method Anne Carr does not discuss the impact of his method on eschatology in any extensive way, but only discusses Rahner's distinction between the absolute future and the intramundane future. In doing this, she fails to present Rahner's theology as the *eschatological theology* that it surely is. See Carr, *The Theological Method of Karl Rahner*, 225-237. "It is true that in Christian theology eschatology is treated as a special branch falling at the end of dogmatic theology. But...eschatology also constitutes the whole of Christian theology as at least a formal structural principle for all theological statements...we only know what is meant by God when we recognize our own status as being oriented towards an absolute future. We only understand what saving history and revelation history mean if we live through them and recognize then as the history of the promise of salvation extending more and more to the very roots of our being. We only understand what it means to say that Jesus Christ is the incarnate world of God if we believe in him as the one who will 'come again', in other words as he belongs to the future and *as such* constitutes the Word of God's absolute promise of himself to the world. We only understand what faith is if we recognize clearly the edifice of hope that is built upon it, in which it accepts God's revelation as promise. We only value the Christian sacraments at their true and intrinsic worth if we understand them as *signa prognostica*, to adopt the parlance of Thomas Aquinas." Karl Rahner, "The Question of the Future," *Theological Investigations*, vol. 12, 183.
5. See Karl Rahner, "Eschatology," in *Sacramentum Mundi*, vol. 2, 244.

6. Rahner's position is formally similar to Moltmann's view that all Christian doctrine must be thought of in light of eschatology. See particularly his *Theology of Hope*, trans. James W. Leitch (New York: Harper and Row, 1967).

7. Karl Rahner, "Reflections on the Problem of Devising a Short Formula of the Faith," *Theological Investigations*, vol. 11, 236.

8. The English and German texts of these three formulas may be found in *Foundations of Christian Faith*, 454-460.

9. Rahner, "Reflections on the Problem of Devising a Short Formula of the Faith," *Theological Investigations*, vol. 11, 241.

10. Ibid., 238.

11. Rahner, *The Trinity*, 89.

12. Ibid., 28, 35.

13. Karl Rahner, "Christianity," in *Sacramentum Mundi*, vol. 1, 304. This could legitimately be held to be Rahner's definition of the essence of Christianity which, more fully expressed, could also read (as Rahner puts it in this same article): "...the occurrence of God's free communication of himself to what is created and distinct..from himself, revealing itself as such and effecting its own acceptance on the part of man. The occurrence has in Jesus Christ its ultimate ground, its highest realization and unsurpassable historical manifestation...the event in which man by faith in Christ accepts the sacred mystery, called God, as absolutely and intimately present and freely pardoning him..." Rahner, "Christianity," 305. It is possible to see Rahner's *Foundations of Christian Faith* as an elaboration and justification of this statement. For Rahner's own remarks on this work, see his essay "Foundations of Christian Faith," *Theological Investigations*, vol. 19, trans. Edward Quinn (New York: Crossroad, 1983).

14. Peter C. Phan, *Eternity in Time: A Study of Karl Rahner's Eschatology* (Selingsgrove, PA: Susquehana University Press, 1988), 23. Phan expresses the essential connection between Rahner's anthropology and eschatology epigrammatically when he notes, on p. 43, that "Rahner's eschatology is his anthropology conjugated in the future tense." He is undoubtedly thinking about the way in which Rahner opens his discussion of eschatology in *Foundations of Christian Faith*, p. 431: "We are going to see that this Christian eschatology is nothing else but a repetition of everything we have said so far about man insofar as he is a free and created spirit who has been given God's self-communication in grace. *Eschatology is not really an addition*, but rather it *gives expression once again to man as Christianity understands him*: as a being who exists from out of his present 'now' towards his future." Emphasis mine.

15. Karl Rahner, "Theology and Anthropology," *Theological Investigations*, vol. 9, 28.

16. William M. Thompson, "The Hope for Humanity: Rahner's Eschatology," in *A World of Grace: An Introduction to the Themes and Foundations of Karl Rahner's Theology*, ed. Leo J. O'Donovan (New York: Crossroad, 1989), 158.

17. Rahner, "Eschatology," in *Sacramentum Mundi*, vol. 2, 243.

18. Rudolf Bultmann, "The New Testament and Mythology," in *Kerygma and Myth: A Theological Debate*, ed. Hans Werner Bartsch, trans. Reginald H. Fuller (New York: Harper and Row, 1961), 5.

19. Ibid., 20. Emphasis mine.

20. For a helpful analysis of Bultmann's enterprise, see Giovanni Miegge, *Gospel and Myth in the Thought of Rudolf Bultmann*, trans. Stephen Niell (Richmond, VA: John Knox, 1960).   For Rahner's evaluation of "demythologization" see Rahner and Vorgrimler, *Dictionary of Theology*, 118-119.

21. G.K. Chesterton, *The Everlasting Man* (Garden City, NJ: Doubleday, 1955), 251.

22. Karl Rahner, "The Resurrection of the Body," *Theological Investigations*, vol. 2, 209.

23. Ibid., 208. Rahner's definition of myth makes this clear: "It is an assertion about something (which may also be an event of the past or future) in which a set of concepts and imaginative elements are used, which cannot simply be derived from the thing in question, and are still necessary for the *conversio ad phantasma...*"   Rahner, "The Hermeneutics of Eschatological Assertions," *Theological Investigations*, vol. 4, 344.

24. Rahner, "The Hermeneutics of Eschatological Assertions," *Theological Investigations*, vol. 4, 344. On the same page of this essay Rahner notes that "It is never then a matter of aiming at a language devoid of imagery and hence when dealing with eschatological assertions of trying to rid oneself of the picturesque diction to reach a sphere where the thing itself appears as it is in itself in its pure objectivity: there is no way of discarding the imagery..." Thus, Rahner's shorthand evaluation (expressed imgistically!) of Bultmann: He has on "one hand--rightly--emptied out the bath water and--unjustifiably--the child with it." Rahner, "The Resurrection of the Body," *Theological Investigations*, vol. 2, 209.

25. Rahner, "Theology and Anthropology," *Theological Investigations*, vol. 9, 29.

26. See Phan, *Eternity in Time*, 74.

27. Thompson, "The Hope for Humanity," 158.

28. Rahner, "The Hermeneutics of Eschatological Assertions," *Theological Investigations*, vol. 4, 337. See also Phan, *Eternity in Time*, 71.

29. Rahner, *Foundations of Christian Faith*, 432.

30. Rahner, "The Hermeneutics of Eschatological Assertions," *Theological Investigations*, vol. 4, 334-335. This point, of course, is ultimately related to the first (and is made on page 332 of this same essay): "Knowledge of the future will be knowledge of the futurity of the present. An eschatological assertion is not an additional, supplementary atatement appended to an assertion about the present and past of man but an inner moment of the self-understanding of man. Because man is, by and in being toward the future, he must know about his future. But in such a way, that this knowledge of the future can be a moment in his knowledge of the present."

31. Rahner, *Foundations of Christian Faith*, 434.

32. Ibid., 446.

33. Phan, *Eternity in Time*, 47.

34. Karl Rahner, "Theological Considerations on the Concept of Time," *Theological Investigations*, vol. 11, 299.

35. Karl Rahner, *On the Theology of Death*, Quaestiones Disputatae 2, trans. C.H. Henkey (New York: Herder and Herder, 1972), 28. Emphasis mine.

36. Rahner, "Theological Considerations on the Concept of Time," *Theological Investigations*, vol. 11, 300.

37. Phan, *Eternity in Time*, 49.

38. Rahner, *Foundations of Christian Faith*, 444.

39. Rahner, "Eschatology," in *Sacramentum Mundi*, vol. 2, 246. Here Rahner says that "man in body and soul is united to one reality which forms the ontological basis of the dialectical and irreducible unity in duality of the mutually related statements which always concern the totality of this being."

40. In addition to the primary sources to be noted, the following secondary sources are helpful in understanding Rahner's theology of death: Roberts Ochs, *The Death in Every Now* (New York: Sheed and Ward, 1969) and Bartholomew J. Callopy, "Theology and the Darkness of Death," *Theological Studies* 39 (March, 1978).

41. Karl Rahner, "Ideas for a Theology of Death," *Theological Investigations*, vol. 13, 174. In this same essay, on p. 175, Rahner says that " 'Life after death', on the contrary, is something radically withdrawn from the former temporal dimension and the former spatially conceived time, and a state of final and definitive completion and immediacy to God which is absolutely disparate from space and time...the endpoint of that personal history which is brought to its completion in itself." This means that eternal life should not be thought of as the "other side" because it is "the radical interiority, now liberated and brought to full self-realization, of that personal history of freedom of ours which we are living through even now and which, once it has been fully brought to birth in death, can no longer be lost. The only further development which it can still achieve then is to loose itself in a loving immediacy to the ultimate Mystery of existence called God..."

42. Karl Rahner, "Christian Dying," *Theological Investigations*, vol. 18, 242. See also Phan, *Eternity in Time*, 82-83.

43. Rahner, *On the Theology of Death*, 31. See also Karl Rahner, "Death," in *Sacramentum Mundi*, vol. 2, 60.

44. Ibid., 18.

45. Ibid., 20. See also Rahner, "Death," in *Sacramentum Mundi*, vol. 2, 54.

46. Rahner, "Death," in *Sacramentum Mundi*, vol. 2, 59. See also Phan, *Eternity in Time, 84-86*.

47. Rahner, *On The Theology of Death*, 19. For a fuller discussion of the pancosmicity of the soul, see Marie Murphy, *New Images of Last Things: Karl Rahner and Life After Death* (New York: Paulist, 1988), 13-17.

48. Ibid., 26.

49. Ibid.

50. Rahner, "The Resurrection of the Body," *Theological Investigations*, vol. 2, 211. See also Karl Rahner "Jesus' Resurrection," in *Theological Investigations*, vol. 17, 17.

51. Karl Rahner, "Resurrection," in *Sacramentum Mundi*, vol. 5, 331.

52. Rahner, "The Resurrection of the Body," *Theological Investigations*, vol. 2, 213.

53. Ibid., 215.

54. Ibid., 211.

55. With respect to sacramental causality, it may be said that "the sacrament is precisely the 'cause' of grace, *in so far as* it is a 'sign' and...grace--seen as coming from God--is the cause of the sign, bringing it about and also making it present." The sacrament brings about what it signifies. See Karl Rahner, "The Theology of the Symbol," *Theological Investigations*, vol. 4, 242.

56. Rahner, "Resurrection," in *Sacramentum Mundi*, vol. 5, 331. See also Rahner, "Jesus' Resurrection," *Theological Investigations*, vol. 17, 22.

57. Ibid., 333.

58. Rahner, "The Resurrection of the Body," *Theological Investigations*, vol. 2, 213.

59. Ibid.

60. Ibid., 214.

61. Rahner, "Marxist Utopia and the Christian Future of Man," *Theological Investigations*, vol. 16, 62.

62. Karl Rahner, "The Question of the Future," *Theological Investigations*, vol. 12, trans. David Bourke (New York: Seabury, 1974), 185.

63. Rahner, "The Resurrection of the Body," *Theological Investigations*, vol. 2, 210. Emphasis mine.

64. "The physical world is not merely the outward stage upon which the history of the spirit, to which matter is basically alien, is played out, such that it tends as its outcome to quit this stage as swiftly as possible in order really to achieve full and complete spirituality in a world beyond that of matter." Karl Rahner, "Immanent and Transcendent Consummation of the World," *Theological Investigations*, vol. 10, trans. David Bourke (New York: Seabury, 1977), 285.

65. Karl Rahner, "The Theological Problem Entailed in the Idea of the New Earth," *Theological Investigations*, vol. 10, 268.

66. Ibid., 265. Eschatology does not necessarily lead to inactivity. See Rahner's essay "The Church's Commission to Bring Salvation and Humanization to the World," *Theological Investigations*, vol. 14, trans. David Bourke (New York: Seabury, 1976).

67. Ibid., 270.

68. Ibid., 271.

69. Rahner, "Marxist Utopia and the Christian Future of Man," *Theological Investigations*, vol. 6, 60.

70. Rahner, "Immanent and Transcendent Consummation of the World," *Theological Investigations*, vol. 10, 280.

71. Ibid., 283.

72. Karl Rahner, "Natural Science and Reasonable Faith," *Theological Investigations*, vol. 21, 54.

73. Ibid., 38.

74. Ibid., 45.

75. Rahner, *Hominization*, 69.

76. Ibid., 88. "This 'more' must not be imagined, however, as something simply added to what was there before, but on the one hand, must be the inner increase of being proper to the previously existing reality. This means, however, that if it is really to be taken seriously, 'becoming' must be understood as a real self-transcendence, a surpassing of self as active filling up of the empty...this self-transcendence cannot be thought of in any other way than an event which takes place by the power of the absolute fullness of being. On the other hand, this absolute fullness of being must be thought of as something so *interior* to the finite being moving towards its fulfillment that the finite being is empowered by it to receive a really *active* self-transcendence and does not merely receive this new reality passively as something effected by God. On the other hand, this power of self-transcendence must at the same time be thought of as so distinct from finite, acting being that it is *not* possible to conceive it as a constitutive principle of the *essence* of this finite being achieving itself." Rahner, "Christology Within an Evolutionary View of the World," *Theological Investigations*, vol. 5, 164-165.

For the obstinate reminder continued to occur: only the supernatural has taken a sane view of Nature. The essence of all pantheism, evolutionism, and modern cosmic religion is really this proposition: that Nature is our mother...The main point of Christianity was this: that Nature is not our mother: Nature is our sister. We can be proud of her beauty, since we have the same father...This gives to the typically Christian pleasure in the earth a strange touch of lightness that is almost frivolity.[1]

Chapter 6

Conclusion: The Eternal Revolution

The preceding chapters have attempted to show that Rahner's theology is profoundly ecological even thought it was not formulated to specifically address the ecological crisis. There is an important message in this fact. The ecological character of Rahner's theology is due to its grounding in an interpretation of the Incarnation which refuses to see the flesh and the world as an impediment to reaching God but rather sees the world and the flesh as things through which God has chosen to manifest Godself. In other words, the ecological character of Rahner's theology--especially his theological anthropology, doctrine of God, and eschatology--is not due to a conscious effort to respond to the ecological crisis but to his commitment to the centrality of the Incarnation and a metaphysical vision rooted in Thomism. Rahner's theology is ecological because of his attempt to remain true to the Christian faith.

This thesis is in no way intended to detract from the significance of the ecological theologies discussed in the first chapter. If nothing else, it only indicates that Rahner's ecological vision of theology, while not completely developed, might be a resource upon which other ecological theologies might draw. It will be the concern of the present chapter to suggest ways in which this could be done.

"Ecological Theology"

To say that a theology is "ecological" could mean that it takes the interconnectedness of all life seriously. It could also mean that a theology works toward an integrative vision in which God, human beings, and the world are seen in their interconnectedness. In one way or another, this is what characterizes the theologies which we examined in the first chapter. The basis upon which the integration of God, human being, and world is achieved differs in the case of each of the four models discussed yet the intention of each is the same.

One way to test whether or not Rahner's theology is truly and adequately ecological is to see if it addresses some of the major concerns raised by these four models. In what follows, I propose to focus on what in my judgment are the chief concerns of each model and then to see whether Rahner's theology is able to address them.

The central concern of the feminist model is the overcoming of dualism which this model sees as being, at least implicitly, a dimension of the Christian tradition. It is this concern which guides this model's doctrine of God and anthropology. The idea of the world as God's body and the emphasis on what Söelle calls the "dust factor" must both be understood as stemming from the feminist critique of dualism. Rahner deals with this concern in an impressive and comprehensive way as, I hope, this entire study has shown. His nondualistic emphasis is a thread which is woven through the fabric of his entire theology.

The process model is also concerned about dualism. For it, dualism has arisen in Western thinking because value has been identified with subjectivity and subjectivity has been seen as a uniquely human attribute. Thus, nonhuman life has been seen as having no *intrinsic* value, but only instrumental value--value only in relation to human purposes and needs. The process model deals with this issue by arguing that *all life* has subjectivity of some kind and that all subjectivity contributes something to God's own life (God's consequent nature). Thus, the process model attempts to overcome dualism (and anthropocentrism) by arguing that all life has *intrinsic value.* While Rahner does not address this issue in the same way, he is aware of the issue and provides resources for dealing with it. While Rahner does not deal with the subjectivity of nonhuman life, his doctrine of creation certainly gives it value independent of human life. Also, while Rahner does wish to distinguish human life from nature, he does not want to separate it from nature. The cosmos does come to fruition in human being but in this being the whole of the cosmos is *recapitulated* so that distinction does not mean separation.

The Catholic incarnational, sacramental model is chiefly concerned to articulate an integrative vision based upon the theological fact of the Incarnation. This model attempts to come to a theological evaluation of the material world guided by the knowledge that God took part of this world upon Godself to effect God's own self-expression. For this model, the material world must at least be seen as quasi-sacramental in that it is capable of being the medium of God's direct self-expression. Because of this, this model insists that creation must be understood in light of the Incarnation. As I argued in the fourth chapter, Rahner's theology can best be understood as an example of this model. Here an understanding of the Incarnation leads to a rejection of dualism and an assertion of the intrinsic place of the material world in the process of salvation. God, this model insists, did not become incarnate in the world so that we might escape from it.

The Hegelian, *creator spiritus* model's central concern is the formulation of a doctrine of creation; the doctrine of creation is this model's way into ecological theology. The way in which the doctrine of creation of formulated is complex because it is linked to eschatology and this is linked to the a doctrine of the Trinity. In my judgment, the central theme here is essentially that of Rahner's work on the Trinity--that in order to really understand creation we must understand God's relation to the world and this relation is essentially *open* and *threefold*. Seen in this light, the world is radically pervaded by God's presence. The world is not just the "world" but that which God has created (as Father), that in which God became incarnate (as Son), and that which God pervades and consummates (as Spirit). More will be said on this subject in a moment.

That Rahner's theology contains, to one degree or another, all of these emphases and addresses all of these concerns is a tribute to the richness of his thinking. What needs to be done now is to suggest a few ways in which these emphases might be creatively appropriated and used.

The Eternal Revolution

In his book *Orthodoxy*, G.K. Chesterton presents a kind of "informal fundamental theology" (though he certainly would not have called it this). In the process of arguing for the revolutionary character of orthodoxy, he makes the following observation:

Thus we may say that a permanent ideal is as necessary to the innovator as to the conservative; it is necessary whether we wish the king's order to be promptly executed or whether we only wish the king to be promptly executed...for all intelligible human purposes, for altering things or for keeping things as they are, for founding a system for ever, as in China, or for altering it every month as in the early French Revolution, it is equally necessary that the vision should be a fixed vision.[2]

Chesterton's point is that a firm view of the world is essential to those who wish to create a revolution as well as those who wish to resist it. A relativist, he notes, is of no use at all either for maintaining an order or for remaking that order. Chesterton goes on to make the further point that in Christianity the conservative tendency to assert a fixed truth against attempts at change and the revolutionary tendency to want to remake the world in light of an ideal coincide. For him, then, Christianity constitutes an "eternal revolution" in that if we take seriously the truth it asserts against present circumstances we shall always be involved in the business of remaking our circumstances.[3]

This is a helpful point to keep in mind when thinking about the relationship between ecology and theology. It may well be that any truly ecological theology must lead to an eternal revolution in our perception of the world and our place in it. If Rahner is to be taken as a reliable guide, it would seem that a meditation on the Incarnation could only revolutionize our perception of material reality. To assert the radical truth of the Incarnation, as Rahner perceives it, against our present circumstances could only lead to a radical reappraisal of our relationship with nature, God's relationship with the world, and the meaning of salvation. Perhaps the question raised by stating matters in this way is that of whether we are willing to live with this eternal revolution.

It may be that the best way to see ecological theology (or some forms of it) is to see it not as an attempt to be fashionable (always a temptation in academic theology) but as an attempt to be *catholic*--an attempt to understand and express the *fullness* of that Truth which results in an eternal revolution. Ecological theologies (like liberation theologies) pursue their agendas with the conviction that something has been left out of the articulation of Christian truth which makes it somewhat less than true and not very revolutionary, and that this "something" now needs to be shouted from the housetops (Matthew 10:27). Chesterton probably expressed the worry of those developing ecological theologies when he noted that it would be darkly ironical indeed if Christians came to be like relativists with respect to defending the integrity of creation--useless for the purposes of asserting the truth and remaking the world in light of that truth.

The question, then, is what in the Christian vision needs to be put forward so that Christianity can constitute an eternal revolution which continually challenges our understanding of the world. While what follows is not a complete answer to this question, it is at least a beginning.

The Human Being as Steward

The view that the human being is essentially different from nature and that nature is simply the stolid stage on which the drama of human history (where the things of real theological importance take place) unfolds is now the object of both theological and scientific criticism.[4] Perhaps the basic premise of all the types of ecological theology discussed in the first chapter is the view that this should be the case.

As we have seen, Rahner shares this view. He begins with the affirmation that the body and the world are essential to the human being's self-realization and proceeds to argue that human being and the world have a common origin and a common destiny. For Rahner, there is no point at which human being's relationship to the world is abrogated; even at the eschaton this relationship will not be dissolved but *radicalized*. This is an important theological affirmation and one which, if taken seriously, can not do other than challenge theological presentations of the world as something that is finally dispensable and whose destiny radically diverges from that of human being. If Rahner is correct in his view that our destiny and the destiny of the world actually converge, that they are finally inseparable, then the point at which we begin to destroy nature is, in Barth's words,

> the very point where we refuse and fail, offending and provoking God, making ourselves impossible before Him and in that way missing our destiny, treading under foot our dignity, forfeiting our right losing our salvation and hopelessly compromising our creaturely being...[5]

Rahner would agree, I think, that in destroying nature we really are "losing our salvation" and "compromising our creaturely being". But to say only this is not to say enough.

Rahner's concern to demonstrate the relevance to and the importance for the Christian life of theological affirmations would lead him to the position, I think, that all theological statements about human being's relationship to the world will remain just statements if they are not integrated into an understanding of the Christian vocation. It takes no more than some degree of enlightened self-interest to realize that some degree of responsibility must be introduced into our dealings with nature. But it takes something far greater to realize that the care of nature is *part of our vocation*. This requires what we might call "covenant faithfulness".

In this respect, two points of Rahner's theology might profitably be remembered. First, we might recall his insistence that human being is related to the world in the mode of *responsibility*, that this being's responsibility for the world is part of its relationship to God. As God's covenant partner, human being is not simply part of nature. But neither is it nature's master. Second, we might recall Rahner's view that human activity contributes to the world's eschatological consummation in a way that is real though difficult to express precisely. Both these points suggest that any theological treatment of human being's relation to the world must deal with the human vocation with respect to the world. We need to grasp the truth that our salvation does not consist in escaping or ignoring the world, but in an understanding of our *vocation as stewards*, an understanding that will lead us to remake the world in light of that vocation.

To draw upon the concept of stewardship is to have to take the good with the bad. The good here is the fact that stewardship already has an established place in Christian reflection upon the human vocation and is firmly grounded in biblical thought. Yet, there are difficulties with the concept. At present in much of Christian thinking, stewardship is but a shadow of its former self. While in its full, biblical sense stewardship is a term that properly characterizes the whole Christian vocation (see 1 Corinthians 4:1 for example), in its present etiolated usage is refers only to a part of the Christian vocation. Thus, stewardship is taken to refer to the acquisition and management of ecclesiastical property--it refers to the material means to the real (spiritual) end of Christianity. The concept of stewardship can not, then be employed without some rehabilitation because far

> from standing for a basic orientation to the world or even a major image of the life and work of the church, stewardship is regarded as a kind of optional ethic for the enthusiastic churchman or woman. People consider good stewardship something private and vaguely ascetic--the second mile gone by some zealous church members. Tithing![6]

Our present concept of stewardship needs to be broadened so that it can serve as a characterization of the whole Christian vocation. If this is effected and Christians so conceive their vocation, our present understanding of our relationship to the world will be challenged in at least three ways:

(1) *If the Christian vocation is a vocation to stewardship, we must rethink the meaning of having "dominion" over the earth (Genesis 1:28).*

Any interpretation of dominion must begin with a fundamental fact: a steward does not own that over which he or she has responsibility, but holds this in trust for another. The dominion exercised by human being is supposed to reflect the dominion of God, not the dominion of Pharaoh or Caesar; the God of Exodus and the God of the crucified Christ shows what real dominion is as opposed to distorted dominion. Understanding this fact helps to place human uniqueness in the proper context. If human being is to be a steward, we must understand our unique attributes not as justifying a hubristic superiority over nature (which is then seen as "subhuman"), but as equipping us to perform our servant role:

> We are different, then, from the beasts of the field and the birds of the air. Let us not be naive and imagine that we can just melt into nature. We have a reflective side that other creatures do not have...But the purpose of all this, that we should "have dominion": that is, that we should be servants, keepers, and priests in relation to the other [nature]. That we should represent them [other creatures] before their Maker, and represent to them their Maker's tender care.[7]

As a steward, human being can not look upon nature as a "standing reserve" (Heidegger) or mere raw material awaiting transformation into something "useful". It seems that the element in the Christian tradition which understands nature as given by God to sustain human being, while valid, has been given far too much emphasis. The human responsibility to husband nature, to till the garden and to look after it (Genesis 2:15), needs to be equally emphasized.

Any attempt to understand the Christian vocation as stewardship will have to develop a truly Christian understanding of dominion and the image of God in human being. Effort must be made to challenge culturally distorted interpretations of dominion which hold that nature has no intrinsic value and that this grants human beings an unrestricted mandate and right, to use James Nash's phrase, to "plunder, pollute, and prey upon the earth." This kind of anthropocentric oppression of nature rather than mirroring God's sovereignty is actually a distortion and usurpation of it. Any attempt to rehabilitate the concept of dominion must draw upon Israel's overwhelming sense that *everything* belongs to God: "The land shall not be held in perpetuity, for the land is mine; with me you are but aliens and tenants (Leviticus 25:23).[8] The plundering of nature to satisfy human greed, far from being a reflection of God's sovereignty is a negation and denial of it.

It may be that the distorted interpretation of dominion rests on a failure to understand the true meaning of the image of God in human being. The idea that the *imago dei* grants human being alone an intrinsic worth rests on a profound theological mistake. It assumes that human being *as it is now* bears the full image of God. This view is neither biblical nor Christian; the *imago dei* is present in full clarity and plenitude only in Christ who is the "image of the invisible God, the firstborn of all creation" and the one in whom "the fullness of God was pleased to dwell" and the one through whom "God was pleased to reconcile to himself all things" (Colossians 1:15, 19, 20).

As long as the *imago dei* is taken to indicate a present fact it will be of little use to ecological theology--or to any theology. It must be seen as the Christian tradition intends it to be seen, not as a present reality but as an *eschatological* one. Human being does not now manifest the fullness of the image of God; it can not claim a uniqueness that radically separates it from all creation. But even when human being does bear the full *imago dei*, it will not look at all like a domineering, exploitative ruler over nature. This is so because God intends not that we should be conformed to our own sinful image but that we should be "conformed to the image of his Son, in order that he might be the firstborn within a large family" (Romans 8:29), the same Son who "though he was in the form of God, did not regard equality with God as something to be exploited, but emptied himself, taking the form of a slave" (Philippians 2:6). Seen in an eschatological light, therefore, dominion can not mean exploitation but can only mean self-sacrificing service. If *imago dei* is an eschatological concept, dominion over the earth can only imply that human being has a preservative and restorative responsibility to creation and that only when this responsibility is fulfilled can it truly bear the image of God.[9]

(2) *If the Christian vocation is a vocation to stewardship, we must question quasi-heretical attitudes toward the material world.*

As long as the material world is viewed negatively, stewardship can never apply to creation. For theologies which, implicitly or explicitly, see the world as at best an impediment to be overcome, stewardship in its full sense can never characterize the Christian vocation because finally the world is something to be left behind. If Rahner's interpretation of Christianity is not completely erroneous, it must be said that we are not faced with a choice between God and the world. Rather, our vocation with respect to God essentially involves responsibility for the world. It is not necessary to embrace an interpretation of Christianity which hopes (and works for) a worldly utopia planned and realized by human beings to accept the idea that the world has an intrinsic significance for the Christian vocation.

It seems that Moltmann is justified in arguing that the term "nature" be removed from theological discourse and be replaced by "creation". Understood as nature, it is easy to think of the world as radically different from human being and having little or nothing to do with human salvation. To understand the world as *creation*, however, is to see the truth of Rahner's claim that the *world itself* participates in salvation. Even if we continue to use the word nature, we must understand it in the context of creation; it can only mean "a single act in the great drama of the creation of the world as the way to the kingdom of glory."[10] The order of *creation*, as Rahner insists, is intrinsically related to the order of *salvation*. Christian stewardship of creation is the test of whether we really regard the material world as a creation of God:

> If this world and its "fate"...are not the "ultimate concern" of the Christian, then stewardship in and of this world is no logical consequence of Christian faith but just an addendum; and we can expect it to be treated as such, as something tacked on. But if the world matters--really matters!--and if the secret for its mattering is felt in the very depths and center of the community of the crucified one, the stewardship of this beloved earth is of the very essence of our belief...[11]

(3) *If the Christian vocation is a vocation to stewardship, we must adopt a sane attitude toward nature.*

In the epigraph above Chesterton suggests that only when we see nature from the perspective of the supernatural can we have a sane view of nature. What he means, I think, is that our true relationship to nature can only be discerned in light of a God who really transcends nature. Seen in such a light, nature is neither our "mother" (a direct manifestation of God) nor our slave (something in which God has no real interest). Nature is our "sister"--something with which we share an origin and because of this a bond of affection as well. This is perhaps a shorthand way of expressing a crucial truth.

There seems to be no questioning the observation (or accusation) that Christianity has long neglected nature and that even when it has not, nature was not accorded the status due it as creation. But it seems to be a mistake of a similar kind to correct this by attempting, in various ways, to identify God and nature as much as possible; both moves involve an erroneous interpretation of God's relationship to the world. Both the view that the world is a "standing reserve" for human beings and the view that the world is somehow a direct expression of God (God's body) are equally mistaken.

Creation is distinct from God and not God's direct self-expression. Creation is different from God but this does not render it an object of indifference, either to God or to human beings. For us, creation is important because it is a *gift*, that which God has entrusted *to our care* and not given over to our complete possession. Our vocation is inseparably bound to the stewardship of the gift. For God, creation is important precisely because it is the genuine *other* which God loves and to which God has committed Godself irrevocably in the Incarnation.

Adopting a sane attitude toward nature means following a path that passes between the *contemptus mundi* tradition and the tendency to romanticize nature as a direct expression of God and thus to worship the creature rather than the creator (Romans 1:25). In short, nature must be seen as *creation*. It is neither something to be escaped or left behind on the way to God nor is it something to be sacralized (in however subtle a way) in an animistic or pantheistic sense. As creation, nature is that which has been brought about by God as that in and through which God accomplishes God's purposes. Nature is different from God yet in its deepest depth is open to God.

A sane attitude toward nature will involve an ecological understanding of sin. Sin is essentially a denial of relationship. In this sense Cain is the archetypal sinner in that when asked by God about the location of his (murdered) brother, Cain responds "I do not know; am I my brother's keeper?"[12] As we have seen, sin for Rahner is the refusal to entrust oneself absolutely to God; it is the human being's denial of its essential relatedness to God and to other human beings under God. This denial involves an implicit denial of relatedness to nature as well. Because human being is essentially related to others, sin must be thought of in relation to these others, to God, other human beings, and creation. An ecological understanding of sin would acknowledge that the debilitation and exploitation of creation constitutes not only a denial of human being's essential relatedness to creation (a relatedness intended by God) but also a refusal to accept the human vocation of stewardship. Understanding sin in an ecological sense would not be breaking completely new ground. Such an understanding was certainly present in Reinhold Niebuhr's mind when he wrote that

> Man's sense of dependence upon nature and his reverent gratitude toward the miracle of nature's perennial abundance is destroyed by his arrogant sense of independence and his greedy effort to overcome the insecurity of

nature rhythms and seasons by garnering her stores with excessive zeal
and beyond natural requirements. Greed is in short the expression of
man's inordinate ambition to hide his insecurity in nature.[13]

Creation is a reality not to be overcome but to be lived within. This is
certainly the emphasis of the first three chapters of Genesis (contrary to
Lynn White's interpretation). Sin consists in the human refusal to live
within the order of creation and the consequent subversion of that order
through decisions based upon a distorted understanding of the place of the
human being in the order of creation.

God and the World:
Reclaiming the Doctrine of Creation

In the first chapter it was argued that one of the contributing factors to
the ecological crisis was the etiolation of the doctrine of creation. Under
the pressure of anthropocentric philosophies, the doctrine underwent a
severe constriction, the result of which was that the world of nature was
deprived of most (if not all) of its *theological significance*. As has been
suggested, one of the primary objectives of ecological theology should be
the restoration of this significance; this is why an understanding of God's
relationship to the world is a central theme of this type of theology. But
the phrase "God's relationship to the world" does not reveal anything of
great significance. Is "God" to be understood in a merely deistic sense?
What significance could the world have for God? In order to discuss this
issue properly within the Christian tradition, it is necessary to reclaim the
doctrine of creation. God is not merely "God" but the Creator of heaven
and earth, and the world is not merely "the world" but the Creator's
creation. If nothing else, the doctrine of creation makes it clear that God
and the world can only be really understood in relation to each other. As
Creator, God's relationship to the world goes far beyond simply bringing
about the world; it also includes the sustenance of the world and its
consummation.

The biblical materials from which the Christian doctrine of creation
was derived suggest at least one important thing about God's relation to
the world: as a creation of God, the world *as a whole* is embraced by
God's purposes. Claus Westermann notes that the

simple fact that the first page of the Bible speaks about heaven and earth,
the sun, moon, and stars, about birds, fish, and animals, is a certain sign

that the God whom we acknowledge in the Creed as the Father of Jesus
Christ is concerned with all these creations, and not merely with humans.
A God who is understood only as the god of humankind is no longer the
God of the Bible.[14]

The idea of creation suggests an *essential* relationship between Creator
and creature; this relationship helps to define who God is (the One who
creates and is concerned with creation) and what the world is (that good
work which God has brought about and over which God is sovereign).
This relationship is thematized more explicitly in the universal covenant
of Genesis 9:8-17.   Here God makes a self-binding commitment to
preserve all life; unlike the covenant with Abraham which follows it, this
covenant is between the Creator God and "all flesh that is on the earth,"
the biblical shorthand for "all living creatures" (Genesis 9:17). This is an
"ecological covenant" which signifies God's intention to be faithful to all
creatures.[15] If the biblical materials are taken seriously, to speak of God
as Creator is to have already said a great deal about God's relation to the
world.

The attempt to reclaim the doctrine of creation and to develop it in an
ecological direction is central to Moltmann's work . For our purposes, his
work presents two essential and related insights. First, an ecological
doctrine of creation will not simply focus on the distinction between God
and the world but will recognize the presence of *God in the world* and the
presence of *the world in God*.[16] Second, such a doctrine will emphasize
that creation is part of the "kingdom of God," that this kingdom is not
simply a moral order but is a cosmic order as well.[17] These two insights
express the single truth which must be at the heart of any ecological
theology: that God and the world are essentially related.   God's
transcendence is the transcendence of the *Creator God*, not that of some
deistic, metaphysical construct, and God's immanence is that of the
Creator God, not that of an impersonal, pantheistic force. Likewise, the
world is genuinely distinct from God, but this distinction is that of a
creation; the world is finite and material, but this finitude and materiality
are created and sustained by God's *love*.

In my judgment, Rahner's theology contributes five elements toward
the formulation of an ecological doctrine of creation which merit attention.

(1) Rahner insists that the order of creation and the order of salvation
(*ordo salutis*) must be considered as a dialectical unity. Creation must not
be viewed in isolation, as something which salvation simply annuls.
Rahner holds that creation must be seen as the presupposition for salvation
and this means that the two orders are essentially related and find their

unity in God. The order of creation is precisely that which passes into the order of creation and the order of salvation is the consummation of the order of creation. This view affirms that God's saving purpose embraces the whole created order and denies the claim that nonhuman life is of negligible significance because it lies outside the realm of salvation. The scope of God's concern is universal (as Genesis 9:8-17 implies) rather than confined to human beings or human souls.

(2) Rahner's theology does much to set creation within its proper context--the life of the Triune God. The order of creation and the order of salvation constitute a dialectical unity because both orders are present in the life of God. Rahner's view that the economic Trinity and the essential Trinity are synonymous is the foundation of his doctrines of grace, salvation, and God. This affirmation leads to the idea that the relationship between creation and Creator can not be thought of as being parallel to the categorial relationship between maker and thing made. It is not completely correct to speak of creation simply as a work of God because the Triune God is also present in the "work" and communicates Godself to the world. At the heart of the mystery of the Trinity is the perichoretic love of the three persons for each other; creation is an expression of this love and exists within it while being distinct from God, just as the three persons remain distinct yet are joined in love. Love does not wish to swallow or dominate the beloved but wishes, rather, to be present to the beloved and to give itself away. This is precisely why the relationship between the Triune God and creation is best seen as one of love, a relationship which exists within the context of God's own threefold life. Rahner would undoubtedly agree with Moltmann's view that the world as creation must be seen as an open self-transcending system because the

> world in its different parts and as a whole is a system open to God. God is its extra-worldly and encompassing *milieu*, from which, and in which, it lives. God is its extra-worldly *forecourt*, into which it is evolving and out of which its realities are won.[18]

To set the doctrine of creation within the context of the Trinity as Rahner comprehends it is to see God as the origin, context and goal of creation.

(3) Rahner provides a satisfactory way of approaching the question of God's immanence and transcendence. This approach is, of course, bound to his doctrine of the Trinity. Rahner wishes to avoid understanding the relationship between God and the world in categorial terms; for our purposes this is the most important consequence of his mystagogy. It is

for this reason, it will be remembered, that he rejects what he calls traditional theism and pantheism. Both essentially understand God's relationship to the world as analogous to the relationship between two categorial objects, the former emphasizing their distinction and the latter emphasizing their unity. The former understands the relationship to be that of two separate objects, while the latter envisions two objects which have become one. For Rahner both contain an element of truth but are finally erroneous because they rest on categorial thinking.

In dealing with the question of God's immanence and transcendence, Rahner is in search of a transcendence that does not exclude immanence and an immanence that does not abolish transcendence. He actually has two ways of formulating his response to this problem. One formulation holds that the difference between God and the world is a *real* difference but a difference not to be seen as existing outside of God. Rather, the difference between God and the world is a difference which *God constitutes*. This is the meaning of creation. It is within the context of this idea that Rahner develops the concept of quasi-formal causality in which God actualizes and fulfills the world while remaining distinct from it. This is the meaning of grace. This quasi-formal causality is exercised through grace or, better, grace is God's quasi-formal causality. Creation and grace are two moments of God's one quasi-formal causality; creation is the presupposition of grace and grace is the fulfillment of creation. The two can not be seen in isolation or separation.

The other formulation holds that God's transcendence should be seen, to use a spatial metaphor, not in terms of height but in terms of depth. With this formulation, Rahner wishes to indicate that God's transcendence does not mean *distance from* but *closeness to*, as grounding origin and innermost reality. The Incarnation shows that the whole cosmos has in infinite depth, a depth that is open to God. Rahner's insistence that in the Incarnation a finite human reality becomes the reality of God only makes sense in light of this formulation of transcendence. A finite reality can become God's own proper reality because all reality has God as its ground, origin, and depth. The Incarnation is conceivable because (and for Rahner only because) God, while remaining distinct from the world, is the world's innermost reality. God can not be identified with the world process (to use Shepherd's language) but God is immanently present in it. Because this is the case, Rahner can say that nearness to God and a thing being truly what it is are not opposites but actually coincide. This is because of God's unique quasi-formal causality. The world is really the world in its materiality and finitude, not as God is removed from it (presumably to let it alone) but precisely as God is its deepest depth, as

God is present to it in God's transcendence.

While these two formulations of transcendence require clarification and elaboration, it may be that their real value consists not so much in what they assert but in what they deny and prevent. The formulation of God's causality as being quasi-formal is intended to deny that God's relationship with the world is mechanistic. God's transcendence understood as depth is intended to deny that God's presence in the world involves a disruption or displacement of the finite. Taken together, both ideas express Rahner's conviction that God's relationship to the world is *unique* and must be understood on its own terms. The degree to which we wish to understand it as being analogous to relationships with which we are familiar is the degree to which we will misunderstand it.

On this point Rahner is in disagreement with the process and feminist models, both of which wish to understand God's relationship to the world as closely analogous as possible to relationships with which we are familiar (categorial relationships). In doing so they tend to obscure God's real difference from the world. Moltmann's objection to process theology is certainly relevant to this point:

> God and nature are fused into a unified world process, so that the theology of nature becomes a divinization of nature. God is turned into the comprehensive ordering factor in the flux of happening.[19]

Moltmann believes that his claim that process theology compromises God's transcendence is further substantiated by the fact that in process doctrines of creation the world ceases to be a finite creation and is thought to be everlasting, that is temporal but without beginning or end. Of course, Moltmann's criticism needs to be balanced with the insistence of some process theologians (like Jay McDaniel) that they are advocating a relational rather than an emanational *panentheism*; the world is not a direct expression of God but is immanent in God and God is immanent in the world. Understood in this way, it might be said that Rahner's position could legitimately be seen as a form of relational panentheism. Rahner, however, insists, as McDaniel does not, that the world is not everlasting but is a *temporal creation*.

A similar sort of criticism might be made of the feminist model (at least as it is presented in the first chapter). The metaphor of the world as God's body runs counter to Rahner's basic intentions. He sees the world as a genuine other, a partner to whom God commits Godself and with whom God is present, but a genuine *other* nevertheless. To understand the world as God's body would seem to compromise this genuine otherness.

It would also present God's love for creation in a somewhat strange light. If the world is an other distinct from God, then God's love is, as Rahner sees it, an act of self-giving. If the world is God's body (even if this is understood metaphorically), God's love for the world inevitably seems like a kind of narcissism. The insistence that God must be seen as embodied seems to lead back to categorial thinking and its attendant difficulties.

To deny that God must be understood as embodied, as Rahner position does, is not to "spiritualize God and thus dispel the divine presence from the world and create a cosmic dualism. It is to say that to frame the issue of God's relation to the world in such a way that it is a matter of choosing between embodiment and disembodiment is to distort the issue from the beginning. The Triune Creator God is neither embodied nor disembodied. The attribute of embodiment does not apply to God. The presence of God must be understood *sacramentally*. God is the world's creator and it is through the world that we have fellowship with God. This is so not because the world is God's body but because God is present in the world in the power of the Spirit. God was present in a finite human reality in the Incarnation through the power of the Spirit. God is eucharistically present in the gifts of bread and wine not as embodied in them but present through the power of the Spirit. This theological fact is affirmed liturgically by the traditional *epiclesis:*

> We pray you gracious God, to send your Holy Spirit upon these gifts that they may be the Sacrament of the Body of Christ and the Blood of the New Covenant. Unite us to your Son in his sacrifice, that we may be acceptable through him, being sanctified by the Holy Spirit.[20]

The point here is that the Spirit is the principle of sacramentality and the source of God's sacramental presence.

What the feminist model hopes to accomplish with the metaphor of the world as God's body is accomplished just as well or even better by speaking of God's sacramental presence in the Spirit, without creating some of the difficulties of this metaphor. In my judgment, Nash is correct in remarking that sacramentality

> is not pantheism. Perhaps it can instead be described as pan-en-theism in the sense that God is all and all is somehow *in God* without being part of God. The metaphysical problem is how to insure that nothing exists apart from God and still assert that creatures are distinctive entities. The idea of the world as God's "body," however, suggests a merger of Creator and creation...The "body" metaphor seems to compromise divine

independence, and deny the distinctive integrity of creation and its creatures...*It certainly adds nothing to the value and holiness of nature that is not already accomplished through the traditional affirmation of the sacramental presence of the Spirit.*[21]

Rather than saying that creation is the body of God, it would be far better to say that creation os the sacramental expression of the Creator's presence.

(4) Rahner offers a non-dualistic metaphysic in which spirit and matter are seen not as opposites but as existing in fundamental continuity. It is this metaphysic which enables him to see creation as being fundamentally open to God and to see a fundamental kinship between human being and creation. Spirit and matter retain their integrity without being confused or separated as if they were opposites. This metaphysic enables Rahner to present a fairly coherent vision of God's relation to the world as one of both immanence and transcendence, the Incarnation as God's presence in a finite, material reality, and the world as having a fundamental unity which will not be abolished but confirmed in its eschatological consummation.

(5) Rahner places the doctrine of creation in an eschatological context. To many, this will not appear to be an obviously beneficial contribution to a renewed doctrine of creation. But an eschatological doctrine of creation does provide resources for addressing at least two important questions. First, such a doctrine of creation reminds us that creation can not be isolated but must be set within the full scope of God's redemptive purpose. Creation is not simply the stage on which the drama of redemption is played out but is actually *part of the drama*. Creation is the *theatrum gloria dei* in that it is destined to share in God's glory. Creation is not simply creation but creation-which-is-to-be-consummated in God.

Second, an eschatological doctrine of creation is one way of addressing the question of the appropriateness of thinking that both Creator and creation are good even when seen in light of creation's real need of reconciliation and redemption. Moltmann, for one, has expended considerable intellectual energy in arguing the point that without an eschatological expectation of fulfillment the goodness of Creator and creation is virtually indefensible. To place creation in an eschatological context is to see it as an unfinished work, as the theater in which God's final glory and justice have yet to be fully manifested. It is also to live in the hope that they will be fully manifested.

We have seen that eschatology plays an important role in Rahner's theology. His is an "ecological eschatology" in that it envisions the consummation of all creation, a consummation which is the forward projection of the Incarnation. So important is this theme that the final section of this chapter will be devoted to a consideration of it.

The Place of the Material World in the *Ordo Salutis:* The Labor Pains of Creation

It may be that Christianity can bring about an eternal revolution in our perception of the natural world precisely because of its eschatological vision. As we have seen in Rahner's eschatology, this vision is not a glimpse of the future before its actual realization but a hope. Understood in this way, Christian eschatology does not involve knowledge of the details of the future, the when and the where, but is an inference drawn from the experience of God's love; it knows nothing about the future but it does know about the God of the future. In speaking about eschatology it is good to remember Paul's dictum (admonition?) that we walk by faith and not by sight (2 Corinthians 5:7). If the Christian eschatological vision is anything, it is the hope for the universal realization of God's justice and the final manifestation of God's salvation. Eschatology is primarily a matter of God's faithfulness. Rahner is surely right: Christian eschatology is nothing else that faith's attempt to work out the implications of the Incarnation for all creation. And the Incarnation is God's ultimate pledge of faithfulness to creation.

Having said this, it might be helpful to mention a text that we have had occasion to consider at several points in the course of this inquiry. In my judgment, the substance of Rahner's eschatology is already found in Romans:

> For the creation was subjected to futility, not of its own will but by the will of the one who subjected it, in hope that the creation itself will be set free from its bondage to decay and will obtain the freedom of the glory of the children of God. We know that the whole creation has been groaning in labor pains until now, and not only the creation, but we ourselves, who have the first fruits of the Spirit, groan inwardly while we wait for our adoption, the redemption of our bodies.[22]

Of course, there can be no thought here of proof texting, as if the citation of this text, significant as it is, could justify Rahner's eschatology or the conclusions I have sought to draw from it. Such a move would violate all of Rahner's intentions. The importance of this text is that it says a definite "No!" to the ultimate dualism--the dualism which states or implies that nonhuman life has no place in he *ordo salutis*. For this dualism

> Heaven was exclusively for humans, who alone have "rational, immortal souls," and generally only for a few of them, who believe the appropriate doctrines and who believe in the appropriate manner. For most, even the resurrection of the body became the immortality of the soul. The "saved" will sing perpetual praise to their Redeemer in this scene of damnation-like dullness [!], but not "all God's children go a place in the choir." In this ultimate dualism, redemption is release from nature (including the body), and oblivion is the fate of nature.[23]

Romans 8:19-23 does not prove the Christian eschatological expectation to be true; it is an expression of faith's anticipation. It does, however, suggest that the case for such a dualism can not be made on biblical grounds. This text is neither a proof text nor a mere snippet from Paul thought. It expresses what can be regarded as the center of his theology, that is that there is no fulfillment without the world (God's creation), without Israel (Romans 9:4), without the resurrection (I Corinthians 15:13-17), and without God's faithfulness (Romans 8:31-39). Contrary to traditional Protestant interpretations, the crux of Romans is not justification by faith but the *faithfulness of God*.[24] This is the proper context in which to place Paul's eschatology. God acts in covenant faithfulness not only to humans (Jews and Gentiles) but also to *all creation*. God's covenant faithfulness is shown not only in the fact that Gentiles can be part of the covenant community of Israel but also in the fact that creation will be set free from its bondage and will share in the "freedom of the glory of the children of God." The ground of this hope is God's loving faithfulness which is preeminently manifested in Jesus's resurrection (Romans 5:1-11). For Paul, and for Rahner, the resurrection is intimately connected to a vision of *cosmic fulfillment and salvation*. J. Christiaan Beker has made this clear in his important study of Paul's thought:

> Resurrection language properly belongs to the domain of the new age to come and is an inherent part of the *transformation and the recreation of all reality* in the apocalyptic age. Thus, the resurrection of Christ, the coming reign of God, and the future resurrection of the dead belong together. The new creation in Christ...is an anticipation of the final resurrection of the dead and a *new act of creation* by the God who "raises the dead and who calls into existence the things that do not exist" (Romans 4:17). "Resurrection," then has not just ideational significance,

as it marks a new perception of things [as in Bultmann]...it has a clear *historical and ontological reference because it addresses itself to the transformation of the created order.* Therefore, the resurrection of Jesus is not simply synonymous with a heavenly "translation,"...Paul does not think of Jesus's ascension in terms of a removal scene, as if a Gnostic savior leaves the scene of corrupted matter by shedding his body...Neither is Jesus's resurrection a "historical reunion scene," as if Jesus returns to companionship with his disciples...It signifies the exaltation of the crucified Christ, that is, it is a proleptic event that foreshadows the apocalyptic general resurrection of the dead and thus *the transformation of the created order* and the gift of new corporeal life to dead bodies. Resurrection is a historical-ontological category, manifesting *in this world* the dawning of the *new age of transformation.*[25]

Beker's point is a crucial one. For Paul, without the resurrection, without eschatology, it becomes impossible to speak about the faithfulness of God to human beings and to creation. The resurrection becomes the foundation of our trust in God's faithfulness. God, of course, could be faithful in a Marcionite way by freeing us from Israel or in a Gnostic way by freeing us from the world; but God does not offer us salvation in either of these ways. There is no salvation apart from God's creation and God's covenant with creation.

In thinking about the significance of eschatology for an ecological theology, we at least need to be aware that eschatology can either hinder or greatly enhance and ecological vision. Construed along certain lines (lines which are only too familiar), eschatology can be the ultimate justification for seeing the natural world as being devoid of final significance. Yet, eschatology can serve to underwrite a very different view as does Rahner's and Paul's. In both visions eschatology provides a hope for the liberation of humans and creation itself from bondage. Our bondage to sin has led to creation being subjected to bondage. The pressing question is that of how we can possibly speak of God's being faithful to both in the breaking of these bondages.

Eschatological expectations, of course, need to be treated carefully. One reason for this, of which Rahner is well aware, is that these expectations are expressed in an essentially symbolic and pictorial way. While Bultmann's interpretation of such expectations as simply referring to *existentiel* realities is rejected (rightly) by Rahner, significant questions as to the content of eschatological statements remain. One real danger is that these expectations could be developed in the direction of a cosmological mythology in which a finite universe is gathered into a consummated state localized on this planet. It is such a mythology that

Bultmann was rightly intent on avoiding and this is certainly not the direction in which Rahner wants to move. He does not see the fulfillment of the cosmos as centered on this planet; while the Incarnation, which is the foundation of Rahner's eschatology, is an event in the history of this world, Rahner sees it as God's promise of final salvation to the universe as such. What this means beyond the fact that God's relationship to the created universe undergoes a radical change is not entirely clear and, perhaps, can not finally be clarified.

Despite the difficulties inherent in eschatological thinking, however, it remains important in the sense that it allows us to think about and express, in however an incomplete way, God's *absolute* faithfulness to all created reality. Eschatology does not ultimately give us the "answers" that we desire but rather leads us back to the mystery of God.

There is no questioning the fact that the whole creation is groaning. What can be questioned is whether the groans are the labor pains of a new creation emerging (as Paul insists) or whether they are simply the death agony of an old creation expiring. The way in which we answer this question makes all the difference in the world. There is no unambiguous evidence to suggest that a new creation is being born; in order to accept this we must trust in God's faithfulness as demonstrated in the resurrection. Creation should matter to God's people because it matters deeply to the incomprehensible, all-comprehending Creator God. As we think about God's faithfulness we would do well to remember Rahner's point (discussed in the fifth chapter) that the immanent and transcendent consummations of the world are dialectically related. What we do does contribute to or detract from, however mysteriously, the world's consummation. This should be accepted as both gift and task. Like the five wise bride's maids in Jesus's parable (Matthew 25:1-13), our hope for the future does not lead us to idleness or disinterestedness. Rather, as with them, it heightens our steadfastness and impresses upon us a sense of urgency. We know that "creation itself will be set free from its bondage to decay" and that it will "obtain the freedom of the glory of the children of God." To take seriously our role in the consummation of the world is to show that we do not regard this hope as, to use Newman's phrase, "unreal words" but rather that we take it in earnest, trusting that God will indeed one day be "all in all" (I Corinthians 15:28).

Notes

1. G.K. Chesterton, *Orthodoxy*, in *The Collected Works of G.K. Chesterton*, vol. 1, ed. David Dooley (San Francisco: Ignatius Press, 1986), 317.

2. Ibid., 314.

3. Thus his famous remark: "Christianity even when watered down is hot enough to boil all modern society to rags. The mere minimum of the Church would be a deadly ultimatum to the world." See *Orthodoxy*, 123.

4. See particularly Charles Birch and John B. Cobb *The Liberation of Life: From the Cell to the Community* (Cambridge: Cambridge University Press, 1981), 97-109.

5. Karl Barth, *Church Dogmatics*, 4/1, ed. G.W. Bromily and T.F. Torrance, trans. G.W. Bromily (Edinburgh: T and T Clark, 1956), 12.

6. Douglas John Hall, *The Steward: A Biblical Symbol Come of Age* (Grand Rapids, MI: Eerdman's, 1990), 15.

7. Ibid., 210.

8. Psalm 24:1-2 reflects this same theological presupposition. If this is not understood as a basic assumption, the instructions concerning the sabbatical year (Deuteronomy 15:1-23) and the jubilee year (Leviticus 25:8-55) will not be fully comprehended.

9. James A. Nash, *Loving Nature: Ecological Integrity and Christian Responsibility* (Nashville, TN: Abingdon Press, 1991), 106.

10. Moltmann, *God in Creation*, 39.

11. Hall, *The Steward*, 121.

12. Genesis 4:9.

13. Reinhold Niebuhr, *The Nature and Destiny of Man*, vol. 1 (New York: Scribner's, 1949), 190-191.

14. Claus Westermann, *Genesis 1-11: A Commentary*, trans. John Scullion (Minneapolis, MN: Augsburg Press, 1984), 176.

15. Nash, *Loving Nature*, 101.

16. Moltmann, *God in Creation*, 13.

17. Ibid., 63.

18. Ibid., 205-206.

19. Ibid., 78.

20. *The Book of Common Prayer* (1979), Holy Eucharist, Rite 2, Eucharistic Prayer B. Though this is a contemporary Anglican epiclesis, it faithfully reflects the one found in Hippolytus's *Apostolic Tradition*: "And we pray Thee that [Thou wouldest send Thy Holy Spirit upon the Oblation of the holy Church] Thou wouldest grant to all [Thy saints] who partake to be united [to Thee] that they may be filled with the Holy Spirit for the confirmation of [their] faith in truth." See Bard Thompson, ed. *Liturgies of the Western Church* (New York: Collins, 1961), 21.

21. Nash, *Loving Nature*, 115. Emphasis mine.

22. Romans 8:19-23.

23. Nash, *Loving Nature*, 124.

24. This is one of the fruits of recent Pauline scholarship which has provided a corrective to the "Lutheran Paul" by setting him not within the context of late medieval piety's search for certainty but within the context of Jewish apocalyptic expectations. For a helpful account of the complex developments in this area of research, see Stephen Neil and Tom Wright, *The Interpretation of the New Testament 1861-1986*, second edition (Oxford:Oxford University Press, 1988), 403-430. An example of this new type of scholarship is E.P. Sanders, *Paul and Palestinian Judaism: A Comparison of Patterns of Religion* (Philadelphia: Fortress Press, 1977).

25. J. Christiaan Beker, *Paul the Apostle: The Triumph of God in Life and Thought* (Philadelphia: Fortress Press, 1980), 152-153.